D0793491

Organization and Systems Design

Also by Nandish V. Patel

ADAPTIVE EVOLUTIONARY INFORMATION SYSTEMS (*editor*)
CRITICAL SYSTEMS ANALYSIS AND DESIGN

Organization and Systems Design

Theory of Deferred Action

Nandish V. Patel

First published 2006 by
PALGRAVE MACMILLAN
Houndmills, Basingstoke, Hampshire RG21 6XS and
175 Fifth Avenue, New York, N.Y. 10010
Companies and representatives throughout the world

PALGRAVE MACMILLAN is the global academic imprint of the Palgrave Macmillan division of St. Martin's Press, LLC and of Palgrave Macmillan Ltd. Macmillan® is a registered trademark in the United States, United Kingdom and other countries. Palgrave is a registered trademark in the European Union and other countries.

ISBN 13: 978–1–4039–9164–5   hardback
ISBN 13: 1–4039–9164–2   hardback

This book is printed on paper suitable for recycling and made from fully managed and sustained forest sources.

A catalogue record for this book is available from the British Library.

Library of Congress Cataloging-in-Publication Data

Patel, Nandish V., 1959–
    Organization and systems design : theory of deferred action /
by Nandish V. Patel.
        p. cm.
    Includes bibliographical references and index.
    ISBN 1–4039–9164–2
        1. Management information systems. 2. System design. I. Title.
HD30.213.P385 2006
658.4'038011–dc22

2005057505

10   9   8   7   6   5   4   3   2   1
15   14   13   12   11   10   09   08   07   06

Printed and bound in Great Britain by
Antony Rowe Ltd, Chippenham and Eastbourne

Risha who is blissfully brave

Contents

List of Tables

List of Figures

List of Abbreviations

AI	Artificial Intelligence
API	Application Program Interface
ARPANET	Advanced Research Project Agency
ASD	Autonomous Systems Design
BPR	Business Process Reengineering
CAO	Condition, Action and Output model of organized activity
CcTLD	Country Code Top-Level Domain Name
CMM	Capability Maturity Model for software development
COTS	Commercial-Off-The-shelf-Software
CRM	Customer Relationship Management
CSCW	Computer Supported Cooperative Work
CSS	Cascading Style Sheets
DD	Design Decisions
DDD	Deferred Design Decisions
DDFA	Deferred Data Flow Analysis
DFD	Data Flow Diagrams
DNS	Domain Name System
DPC	Deferred Procedure Calls
DSD	Deferred Systems Design
DSS	Decision Support System
DTD	Document Type Definition
eCRM	electronic Customer Relationship Management
EDI	Electronic Data Interchange
EIS	Executive Information System
EPS	E-Problem Solving
ER modelling	Entity Relationship modelling
ERP	Enterprise Resource Planning
gDRASS Matrix	Generalized Deferred, Real, Autonomous and Specified Systems Matrix
gTLD	Generic Top-Level Domain Name
HCI	Human-computer Interaction
HOT	Humans, Organization and Technology
HRM	Human Resource Management
HTML	Hypertext Markup Language

HTTP	Hypertext Transfer Protocol
IANA	Internet Assigned Numbers Authority
ICANN	Internet Corporation for Assigned Names and Numbers
ICT	Information and Communication Technology
IDEF	Integrated Definition
IDP	Individual Deferment Points
IEEE	Institute of Electrical and Electronics Engineers
IP	Internet Protocol
IS	Information Systems
ISDM	Information Systems Development Methodologies
ISP	Internet Service Provider
IT	Information Technology
JISC	Joint Information Systems Committee
KMS	Knowledge Management Systems
LDS	Learning Design Specification
LOM	Learning Object Metadata
MAPI	Messaging Application Programming Interface
MDA	Model Driven Architecture
MIME	Multipurpose Internet Mail Extensions
NIS	Non-information Systems
ODPs	Organizational deferment points
OLAP	On-line Analytical Processing
OSI	Open Source Initiative
PEE	Performance, effectiveness and efficiency
RAD	Role Activity Diagrams
RDD	Real design decisions
RDF	Resource Description Framework
RENISYS	Research Network Information System
RSD	Real Systems Design
RSS	Rich Site Summary
SAP	Service Access Points
SDD	Specified Design Decisions
SDLC	Systems Development Life Cycle
SDML	Strictly Declarative Modelling Language
SDO	Systemic Deferred Objects
SDP	Systemic Deferment Points
SDPAT	System Deferment Points Analysis Technique
SEST	Structure, emergence, space and time
SGML	Standard Generalized Markup Language
SPS	S-Problem Solving

SSD	Specified Systems Design
S-SEI	Systems-Systems Environment Interface
SSI	System-system Interface
TCP	Transfer Control Protocol
TDP	Technological Deferment Points
TSA	Tailorable Systems Architecture
TSO	Tailorable Organization Structure
Ttools	Tailoring Tools, also deferment mechanisms
UML	Unified Modelling Language
URI	Uniform Resource Identifier
XHTML	Extensible HyperText Markup Language
XML	Extensible Markup Language
XP	eXtreme Programming
W3C	World Wide Web Consortium

Preface

We make organization and systems complex by design. Real and actual is substituted by symbols in design in one-to-one correspondence by inadvertently following Newtonian formal systems. I seek to avoid this type of one-to-one correspondence of object and its representation by introducing the notion of *deferred action* as constitutive of rational design. It is interrelation design that makes design and designing simple.

> It is simple to make something complex, but complex to make something simple. (Anon. Jazz Musician)

I invoke this to develop understanding of design. Opposing complicating and complex views will meet it akin to Gauguin's synthetism in art. He reacted to impressionists and realists by producing brightly coloured abstractions of inner experiences. A notion of knowledge views the ontology of things as complex as we acquire theoretical knowledge we learn things are not simple. Herbert Simon disagrees:

> The central task of a natural science is to make the wonderful commonplace: to show that complexity, correctly viewed, is only a mask for simplicity; to find pattern hidden in apparent chaos. (1996: 1)

Profound contributions are simple formulations. Only their creators experience intellectual rigour required to realize it. They take empirical observations through the mind's complicating and distorting influence and render seemingly obvious knowledge. Isaac Newton's laws of physics, Albert Einstein's theory of relativity, Adam Smith's conception of economies, and democracy are simple formulations. Einstein wanted by design to express his idea in short mathematical formulae. Supply and demand governs all economic activity. Democracy's one vote for eligible citizens is a simple method. It works because it renders citizens' multifarious political needs to the exercise of power they want.

What does it mean to make something simple and why is it important not make it complex? The mind interprets empirical observations colourfully and independently of the nature of observed things. Is complexification a confusing function of the mind? Is the mind a complicating medium? Does it make things seem complex when they are simple? Our attempts to explain phenomena and make accurate predictions result in making them seem complex. The mind makes reality seem complex. Tim Berners-Lee designer of the Web states simplicity as one design principle of the Web:

> A (computer) language which uses fewer basic elements to achieve the same power is simpler.

Organization and systems are real, complex entities but the science of designing them should be simple possible with finite set of symbols and rules for abstraction and composition. All known mathematics can be expressed in elementary predicates, logical connectives and quantifiers of set theory. Albert Einstein stated:

> The real goal of my research has always been the simplification and unification of the system of theoretical physics.

Though he did not achieve the goal of unification, his formulae are the most simplest yet most relevant. Organized action can be represented with simple design objects. If only we could obtain them directly with no distortions of the colourful mind. Our task is to devise research instruments to see these objects as they exist to describe and explain them, or whatever theoretical or empirical quest, in simple form they exist.

> What is hard comes simple. What is natural comes hard. (Anon. Jazz Musician).

This captures the essence of the epistemological task. Harnessing a *natural* talent is hard. Again the mind raises a barrier. We can meet hard challenges. Our material goals are achieved with technological prowess. The knowledge we seek of design occurs naturally as natural design. That is what we find hard to develop in ways that are useful for rational design.

Organized action is natural but to harness it as rational organization is hard. It occurs in business, government, healthcare, military, voluntary and charitable organizations. Our ability to organize rests on conceptions of social action, of the formal and on empirical evidence. Knowledge of systems is no different. Notions of social and formal can be simple formulations for design. They are fundamental to understanding organized action, organized activity and design of organization and systems.

Organizations used printing technology to disseminate information, codify knowledge and manage both. Information and knowledge are now critical organizational resources. Organizations do not want to depend on its *natural* occurrence. They seek to exploit it by *design* with the power of ICT. They want information assets and commercially valuable knowledge by design.

Such design can be fulfilled with deferred action. Design is by definition prescriptive. Its science ought to prescribe an artefact as well as explain design as a phenomenon. A report on IS research in the UK stated it led in 'methodological areas related to systems design....There is little or no strong work that links into developments in computing....' (RAE, 2001). The Theory of Deferred Action redresses this gap by proposing a radically different research programme for designing cohered organization and systems. Deferred action is a simple formulation it combines rational organization set up to achieve formal objectives with limited resources and richness of social action that such organization engenders in pursuit of its objectives.

Deferred action synthesizes Cartesian rationality with naturalness of social action intrinsic to being human. This requisite analytical synthesis is necessary to understand and develop knowledge of formal design for purposeful action. It is proposed for cohered design of organization and systems. Being in control of something by rational design and being natural in action can coexist. Individually they seem inadequate to achieve formal purpose. Combined they provide intellectual tools to enable design theorists to develop deeper understanding and designers to create better design.

To understand the design trinity of organization, systems and management is a new challenge for discipline theorists in organization, systems and management. Discipline knowledge is necessary but the challenge is to develop interdisciplinary knowledge of the trinity as a composite entity, a third order concept.

Management relies on planning. The problem of 'aligning' systems with organizational business needs concerns strategic planners. Observations reveal that planning and plans are needed but actuality is not plan-friendly. Reliance on planning to produce *the* desired future often disappoints. Total planning stifles creative instinct and delivers dull results. The Soviet communist system of central planning is a clear example of its futility.

Design is no exception. Designers should not create a 'single point of complete failure' by design. They should determine what kind and level of prescriptive rational design is possible and how much scope to give to actuality. Deferred action is framing of this problem and its resolution. Design research needs to produce theories, frameworks and models that have practical relevance. Surveys reveal under even non-use of IS development methodology in practice. Systems analysis and design techniques and tools pose execution problems for practitioners. It all results from parochial planning perspective on design that does create 'a single point of failure'.

Deferred action should appeal to anyone interested in explaining and practising design of organizations and systems, two important entities in our lives. Researchers should glean radically different epistemological and ontological perspectives.

Designers should acquire radically different intellectual tools, principles and mechanisms of design. Managers should learn to think of organization and systems differently and possibly change their management approach.

Having read Herbert Simon's work on rational design I asked myself what my monograph contributes. He addresses problem-solving based on similar empirical observations using Peirce's 'retroduction' term to describe it. The difference is that Simon's means-ends analysis is rational design of 'state space', whereas the theory of deferred action addresses design for the space of natural design or actuality. Deferred action is a synthesis of rational design and natural design or actuality. State space design is necessary but it is not sufficient. Sufficiency is to be found in actuality. This can only be achieved by inventing deferment formalism to represent space of natural design in state space. Since deferred action is concerned with enabling actual action within formal design I felt justified in completing this monograph. Organization and systems design is abbreviated to 'design' throughout otherwise specifically stated. Organization is used in the singular and system in the plural because there are multiple systems in an organization.

Nandish V. Patel
London, August 2005

1
Design, Designing and Theory

Design

Purpose, function, emergence, manipulation, interrelation and aesthetic are some properties of design. What is rational design and how it interrelates with other naturally and socially occurring things is of theoretical and practical concern. In set theoretic terms if N is the set of natural design decisions the Theory of Deferred Action explains the set of design decision D such that:

$$D = \{ x \in N \mid x \text{ is a rational design decision with y properties} \}$$

Rational design of which deferred action design is a subset needs to relate well with natural design. Rational design decisions should interrelate well with natural design decisions. Designing is definition of internal interrelations between things in design itself and external interrelations between it and naturally and socially occurring things. Interrelation design is critical for successful rational design.

Interrelation of organization and systems has changed. Systems used to serve organization as managers determined what systems to develop to improve performance resultant systems automated clerical work. An inversed relationship now exists ICT drives organization design resulting in fused 'networked organization' of digital networks and computerized information architecture. Whether standalone automated system or networked organization designers' problem is to represent intentions, purpose, and activities in actual organized action meaningfully in design.

Organized action requires design by specification to sustain it to make it successful else it dissipates and ceases to exist. Design is formalization by specification of purposeful organized activity for success. Herbert Simon notes: 'Everyone designs who devises courses of action aimed at changing existing activities into preferred ones.' (1996: 111) Paradoxically, specification design hinders organized action by constraining actual action and can endanger sustainment of organization. This is because the set S of specified design decisions is finite S = {x} and the resultant design has to function in a space of a set D of infinite D = {x}∞ other off-design decisions. A stifling consequence of design by specification is over design and extreme prior specification. It is not flexible to enable organization to exploit actualities for success. Specification design is necessary but not sufficient.

Designers can *place* designed organization and systems *in* and *for* actuality (social and organizational contexts) so as to enable responses to richness of sociality and actuality. Formal design can be sustained in actuality by synthesizing specification design and deferment design. It requires invention of deferment formalism capable of reflecting actuality in placed design.

Deferred action accounts for emergence not recognized in specification design. Artefact designers are aware of emergent factors or 'shape emergence' in creative design process. Theoretical knowledge of shape emergence in organization and systems design is lacking and remains unappreciated. Knowledge workers in industrial innovation recognize shape emergence but KMS designers do not consider it. Shape of systems need to be so emergent.

Design is practice. Design and practice, work for which design is done, cannot be separated. They become incongruent when separated by time and space the result of specification design. Design is practice in actuality when the separation is absent the result of deferment design. Intention manifested as planned action is paramount in practice but practice caters to contingency manifested as deferred action. Design based on deferred action is a synthesis of this planned action and deferred action.

Technology and organizations

Comparative performance of service sector organizations with manufacturing organizations is poor. Whilst manufacturing sector productivity improved by 330 per cent between 1954 and 2003 productivity of the service sector has only increased by 47 per cent (Bureau of Labour Statistics and Bureau of Economic Analysis, USA). It would appear that the value added by systems to the service sector is poor.

Figures may only reflect the extent to which available IT at the time was suited to manufacturing. Measurement of productivity attributable to IT in service sectors though is difficult.

Technology has historically been the reason for setting up organiza-tion and the means to enable and sustain it. The British Empire was enabled by shipping and steam engine technologies that also sustained it aided with the brutal force of weapons technology. Giant car manu-facturing organizations were made possible by the combustion engine. Large oil producing organizations are possible because of oil explora-tion and drilling technologies. Telephony produced large organizations too. NASA is an impressive example of an organization enabled by science and rocket and space technologies. Recently, digital technology gave rise to global computer manufacturing organizations and latterly digital mobile telephony organizations.

Examples of organizations not enabled by or based on technology are based on and enabled by ideas, beliefs and faith. The Christian Roman Catholic Church and the Protestant Church are examples of faith organizations. Political parties are examples of powerful organiza-tions enabled by ideas and beliefs. The institution of university is an example of organization enabled by knowledge. It is the oldest institu-tion in Europe and even older in India. It alone has been the most sus-tainable among non-technological organizations. It has endured while others have lost vigour or ceased to exist. Its sustainability is attribut-able to knowledge and explains why commercial organizations are now keen to manage their knowledge *by design.*

The steam engine, combustion engine and telephony gave rise to organization and to some extent defined possible organization. Digital technology though not only defines possible organization but also creates new organization design by processing information and know-ledge. Information is a prerequisite of organization. It is a truism now that ICT can be used to design organization. Study of affect of IT on communication in organization, its use for organization design and its impact on organizational effectiveness is traceable to the early 1960s. Its influence on organization design stems from formal 'organizational engineering models' in the 1970s to 're-engineering organization' in the 1990s. Any medium for information generation and communica-tion has a significant impact on organization design especially if it extends human capabilities as digital technology does.

Formalism for design and particularly systems design should begin from the base of actuality. Much cost is incurred in devising rigorous formal methods and specification formalism focused on technical systems design, only to discover later that 'vision', 'high-level policy', 'people-oriented' and 'organization' are <u>necessary</u> 'issues'. These issues even when recognized tend to be put mistakenly in the category of better 'training', 'fielding' and 'end-user participation'.

Design failure

The importance of organization to achieve private and governmental objectives warrants more research on organization failure. Organizations fail to be innovative by lack of design. The microprocessor was carried into production by one vote and CERN did not fund the original World Wide Web design. Design fails because it ignores a crucial principle:

> A general philosophical principle of design (after Bob Scheifler and others) *is that*: The technology should define mechanisms wherever possible without defining policy. (Personal note by Tim Berners-Lee, W3C)

It is applicable to organization design too. Analyses of organization and systems design failures reveal inadequacy of designed policy in actuality. Failure is inherent in improper design. In Perrow's analysis of 'normal accidents' he attributes failure to organization design (read 'organizations' for 'systems'):

> ...certain kinds of systems those that had many nonlinear interactions (interactive complexity) and those that were also tightly coupled were bound to fail eventually. (Perrow, 2004: 2)

Strategy as design to achieve purpose fails too. The UK Health and Safety Executive records that strategy may fail because it is not the appropriate strategy, failure to implement it, failure to deliver caused by environmental elements and failure to demonstrate that benefits result.

Design failure occurs because designing for organized action is not well understood. Human failure is normally associated with organizations that make use of systems and it is termed 'operator failure'. Aviation authorities analysis of air crashes reveals that between 80 per cent and 85 per cent of jet crashes involve human error. There is no formal method to analyse failure. Fault trees using circuit diagram notations, normally used in systems engineering, have been applied to reason about organization failure. Organization failure is thought to

'…create the necessary preconditions for human failure' is tautological. Whether the cause of organization failure is design failure is not clear, but designers should strive to eliminate the 'risky shift' by design by careful considerations of social action theories.

Research into systems failure is hardly better. There is no analysis of design of failed systems seeking one-to-one correspondence. In IS failure is attributed to the process of systems development, focusing on systems, stakeholders, methodologies and project management. There is no research into adequacy of design as a cause of failure. There are few theories of systems design to enable critical analysis.

Organization theorists and designers' focus on structures of peoples' relationships or power relationships has had to give way to systems. Organization design is now intertwined, and even dependent, on systems design. Organizational information and knowledge supposes 'non-linear interactions' that need to be enabled in design as actual action rather than stifled by planned action. Networked organization is the default design for organization requiring systems integration and integration of systems with organized action. The work of e-Commerce, e-Business, ERP and KMS designers needs to be based on valid theory of organized action, and conceptions of systems and frameworks capable of preventing inherently flawed designs.

Deferred action accounts for Perrow's 'non-linear interactions' and 'interactive complexity' and 'discretionary mechanisms' (Garlikove, 2004) are suggested in other literature. It proposes design types suitable for actual conditions. It separates definition and design of 'mechanisms' and that of 'policy'. It is theoretic to explain organized action, systems developers and organization designers' design activity and informs design. Designs of exemplar systems cited in Chapter 9 do not draw on deferred action they adequately attest to the theory's validity and practical relevance. Such independently designed organizations and systems strengthen its veracity and evidence base.

Researching design

Organization design and systems design lack design research, design theory, design principles and workable practical techniques and tools based on theory. Herbert Simon defines the science of design as: 'a body of intellectually tough, analytic, partly formalizable, partly empirical, teachable doctrine about the design process.' (1996: 113). Here design research is divided into design research and organization and systems design research. These distinct research themes are ultimately combined for design.

Research topics include combination of abduction, deduction and actual implementation of design. The makers of the artefact and the people for whom it is made are subjects of research. Studies of usage of systems based on deferred action and studies of design of such systems are possible as industrial cases or prototypes. Presently, study of the design of deferred systems is only possible as a prototype built to study the systems and the design process.

Design research

Design research covers rational design, artefact (and organization as thing), design process, logics, formal methods, diagramming and verbal formalisms, axiomatic systems of specification, modelling, design, implementation and evaluation. In deferred action it extends to natural design, organized action, planned action, deferred action, emergence, diffusion management, deferment formalism, design types and active modelling.

Design research is understanding and explaining how artefacts and things are created and proposing how to design them. In deferred action it concerns theoretical understanding and invention of deferment formalism to enable interrelation design between formal design and actual action. Specification formalism only permits predetermined actions so assessment of its capability and limits is necessary. The aim is to invent deferment formalism inclusive of specification formalism to represent formal objectives and enable actual organized action to be a component of formal design.

Organization theory is mature to be the basis of organization design. Verbal organization theories are used for organization design and mathematical theories to create mathematical models to inform organization design. Similar theoretical work is lacking for systems design. In IS, KMS and other types of systems there are no theories of design with direct relevance for design. Design is based on poor and even misunderstood reference to General Systems Theory and engineering principles and approaches. There is lack of design research in systems generally and lack of design research of organization *and* systems as a composite third order phenomenon.

Formalism is based on logical reasoning. Herbert Simon defines the science of design as: '...concerned with how things ought to be, with devising artefacts to attain goals.' (1996: 114) He examines the logic required to design by assessing the adequacy of declarative logic for design given that his definition of design introduces the verb 'should', and whether, therefore, there is a need to develop imperative logic. He concludes that with some adaptation declarative logic is sufficient.

Three issues concern invention of formalism for design. Formalism needs to be conducive to natural design or actual action. The relationship between formal design, whether organization or systems design, and actuality requires 'discretionary mechanisms' capable of accounting for actual action. Second is the capability of formalism to produce sustainable design to determine design appropriate for sustainable organization. It should permit actual action that contributes to sustainment in relation to formal design. Where actuality is displaced by prescribed planned action problems arise. It results in litigation where consultants have designed systems causing organization to become bankrupt because directors claimed they followed formal design. The third issue is the capability of formalism to scale up. It should lead to non-trivial design capable of supporting organization and even society.

Formalism for organized action design is problematical more so when combined with systems design. It should represent purpose and rich social action from which organized activity draws for success and include varied facets: purpose, intention and meaning, social interaction and mutuality, ways of determining certainty, and catering for change and uncertainty organizationally. It should not constrain organized activity or individual action in organized activity. Specification formalism inhibits actual actions of individuals and organization by binding it to prescribed planned action, with a few notable exceptions, particularly context-free formalisms similar to context-free grammars.

Deferment formalism to enable deferred action should not lead to action contrary to the design itself or the ethos of formalism. Deferment formalism and consequent design that facilitates deferred action is relevant and workable. This is not subversive design since deferred action seeks to achieve organizational objectives as it encounters actuality. Actual action often needs to be contrary to rules whose value for guiding actual action is philosophically dubious as Wittgenstein observed:

> This was our paradox: no course of action could be determined by the rule, because every course of action can be made out to accord with the rule. (Wittgenstein, 1953: 201)

The thesis of deferred action results in deferment formalism that is necessary to enable organized activity by accounting for such social action within formal design.

Organization and systems

Deferred action design research is on how to design for and in actuality. Problematically, formal design of social action results in losing its *natural* momentum. A design problem is how to improve adequacy of formal organized action design or organization and systems for actuality. Design should be capable of representing organized purpose that may change and not result in losing social richness and flexibility that is so valuable to organized activity. Whereas extreme specification results in killing natural momentum off completely, in a bureaucracy for example, weak design results in unattained objectives and lack of sustainability. Naturalness of social (organized) action and its interrelation with formal design is central in deferred action.

Organization

Organization is social action where participants pursue predetermined objectives as a corporate identity, individuals have intentions and beliefs, people work in groups or collaborate with other groups and partners, and where there are power relationships to ensure that action is directed to achieve objectives. Actual organization is composed of rational and other non-rational modes of behaviour like belief and emotion. Though designers are concerned with enabling co-operative work in this diversity it is not reflected in organization design.

Designers consider organizational structure, internal processes, partner relationships and processes, environment and the affect of design on performance. Uses of computational and mathematical models as inputs to organization design have been limited by lack of scalability. Structural theory is concerned with adaptation of organization to its environment and the affect of design on organizational performance. Contingency theory opposes the premises of structural theory. It asserts that design guidelines cannot be prescribed because organization design is contextual or specific to situations.

Organization is space for expression of human intention and where action happens by design and off-design in actuality. It is off-design action that separates formal organization design from actuality. Questions addressed in the deferred action thesis concern the nature of off-design action or actuality and how its expression can be characterized to cohere with rational design. Organization design cannot be solely determined by rational design. Organizational action is either by design or off-design. Structure is designable by (specification) design. Off-design is the universal set of natural design. It is the emergent, spatial and temporal aspects of organized action that are nonspecifiable. Some structural properties of action cannot be specified either because they emerge.

Systems

System is artefactual representation of human and organized data, information and knowledge for organized work. Systems design is integral to organization design. Systems designers approach design in terms of inherent structure of IT rather than interrelate systems design to organized action. Systems design is poorer at representing meaning attribution and social action.

Techno-centric interpretation of IS and KMS imposes conceptual and practical limitations on organization design. Yet formal system is a crucial design concept. It affords formalism to structure technology, organizational information and knowledge by design. It is a formal basis to create, process, share and manage information. Whether it will have similar organizing and design impact on creating and managing organizational knowledge presently remains undetermined.

Formal systems basis of systems design is vital for responsive and sustainable design but presently it is failing to reflect social action adequately. Instead data is highly structured by specification and subjected to intensive formal modelling. It is problematical to devise modelling notation for information and knowledge that is responsive to social action. IS design is rigidly formalistic, ahistoric, and stripped of vital references to organization, persons, issues or other entities involved in social relationships and organizational work tasks or processes. KMS design too is abstract and highly formulaic.

Systems designers work by determining formal specification similar to organization structural theorists. Their work depends on inputs from requirements determination, systems analysis, modelling and project management. IS methodologists prescribe highly structured plans of action for systems developers. Software researchers propose engineering techniques or agility for software development. All overtly or inadvertently conceptualize design as specification design.

IS researchers have focused on scientific knowledge rather than design knowledge. Published research in leading US journals generates empirical scientific knowledge, statistically validated. Researchers in Europe are open to qualitative methods and interpretive methodology as reflected in leading European journals. Few researchers though have ventured into design research to describe what an IS 'ought to be'. Systems analysis and design and IS methodologies are more concerned with the rigour of specification design and applying diagrammatic formalisms in practice.

Analytical entities

Specification design by reflective designers is necessary but not sufficient for organized action design. It is incapable of representing actual action that has a tendency to waver from specified design to achieve formal objectives. Deferred action is this wavering. Design formalism and design needs to enable deferred action.

Limitation of specification design is determined in the theory of deferred action as is the veracity of extending design process to action designers. It contributes descriptions, analyses and explanations by developing constructs and defining relationships between them. It is theoretical understanding of natural design and rational design for organized action design. It describes design types, enables analysis of design domains in terms of design constructs, and explains interrelations in design and between designed artefact and other persons and objects. It informs improved techniques and tools to design. It is applied empirically to identify design domains and applications in organized activity of the design types proposed by the theory.

Its theoretical core aims are to invent deferment formalism, synthesize specification and deferment formalisms and synthesize it with organizational emergence, deferred action, and diffusion management. Deferred action examines these theoretical constructs individually and as synthesized entities. The expected result is design that encompasses social action and being capable of responding to actuality in which rational design takes place.

Presuppositions of deferred action, their interrelationships and implications are philosophical because they concern development of theoretical constructs relevant to design by rational argument. They are based on sense experience or empirical so can be ordered. The theory's pertinent philosophical argument is constructed on rationality, emergence, and deferred action. Their philosophical meaning and organizational and sociological relevance is important for the act of design, the process of design and the design itself.

Deferred action is interrelation design of organized action based on synthesis of prior rational objectification of intended action and its interpretation in actuality. This synthesis is of three aspects of organized action. Rationality concerning prior objectification of intention and purpose, emergence of events in actuality and deferred action required to cope with emergence. It is conducive for designing cohered organization and systems and caters for off-design actuality that cannot be bound as prior objectification by reflective designers.

Rationality

Rationality is an espoused norm in pursuing purpose in organization. Purpose and action pursed by objectified rational methods can be explained. When called to account for how purpose was set or how it was achieved it is possible to explain action because it is rationally explicable. It has other desirable qualities. It is possible to be critical of action because it can be measured against planned resources and objectives. Objectified processes and rational design can be scrutinized. It can be impartially assessed for efficacy of the action, where such questioning is in the interest of participants or other interested stakeholders. It may be to assess efficiency with which the action is conducted and whether it is effective for achieving desired results.

Deferred action rationality is assumed to be Simionion bounded rationality and it is primary in the act of rational design. Rational design is divided between reflective designers and action designers who differ because of knowledge of action in terms of what we can *expect* to know and what we actually *come* to know or declarative knowledge and procedural knowledge respectively. It is important for understanding and developing knowledge of design. What we know or expect to know for structural design is the domain of reflective designers. What we come to know for operational design is the domain of action designers it is a stronger in eventual design. Critical design concerns procedural knowledge so it needs to enable what we come to know more than what we expect to know.

Rationality concerns to be or being aspect of design. Reality or actuality has no ontological structure designers structure it by design. Design does not exist for action designers who act in actuality. Consequently, extent and kind of content design determinable by reflective designers is constrained by space and time of design. Reflective designer is an 'observer' and 'any system only exists for an observer' (Luhmann's terms. See K Keller). Since reflective designers are separated by space and time from the use of design there is an inherent lack of mutual intelligibility between the 'observer' reflective designer and the doer action designer. Observers cannot predict doers' actions so extent refers to the granularity of content that only action designers can determine in actual space and time. Kind refers to patterns of content, or systems architecture in systems and structure in organization, to enable deferred action rather than actual content. Action designers are agents of the observed (designed) system. They have autonomy to design responses to actual conditions as they in turn become observers of the system.

For reflective designers the kind limit is the limitation of specification design. Operational and social aspects especially meaning attribution to action are not represented well by specification design. Sufficiency of specification for operational needs cannot be determined prior to actuality. So deferred action is the proposition that design can be opened to action designers. Allowing them to do deferred design has implications for designing because it needs to enable deferred design with appropriate mechanisms. For reflective designers of organization the problem is the same but actual organizational behaviour has greater scope to deviate from specifications.

Reflective designer 'observer' is necessary but not sufficient. Since reflective designers are limited by extent of organizational and sociological (content) design they can expect to know, it is necessary to provide mechanisms to action designers to do deferred design. The focus on reflective designers' rationality undermines individuals' (action designers) rationality, intuition and tacitness and its exercise in actuality. It displaces aspects necessary for design to be successful, achieve its formal objectives.

Reflective designers require specification formalism to make representations of social action *as* organized action design. Specification formalism is necessary to design structure but has limited capability to represent emergence (operational activity). Its scope is limited to designing TSA and TOS. As deferred design provides sufficiency it is necessary to invent symbols or deferment formalism to represent deferred action and provide mechanisms for action designers to do deferred design that arises because of emergence.

Emergence

Organization is assumed to have emergent properties stemming from social action and sociality that design should reflect. So design is assumed to have emergent properties. There is no recognition of emergence in specification formalism. As a theoretical construct it is unrecognized in extant theories or formalisms for systems design but is gaining recognition in organizational knowledge management and KMS.

Emergence is the becoming aspect of design. It is the nonspecifiable property of design that is intrinsic to the social in organized action. It is an affect of interrelatedness of multifarious purposes and means to achieve them characteristic of social action. By implication emergence is the nonspecifiable constraint on design because it cannot be determined as design objects it is off-design.

Emergence has extensive implications for design, design process and types of formal models of work possible for systems design. Emergence implies that specification design cannot be symmetrical with actual organization. It constrains scope of specification design. It obliges reflective designers to create design for seeking and achieving unknown purposes, intentions and operational needs and enable emergent design.

Interrelation between emergence and future is intricate. Deferred action is inherently future-oriented as is all design. Critically, deferred action design does not predict future states of organization and systems. The problematic of determining information and knowledge requirements completely is compounded by emergent organization. Specified design as practised in IS methodologies implies an ability to predict future in terms of such requirements. It is intractable for designing.

Given emergence two types of design are possible known and emergent. Known is that which can be specified and identified to inform strategy, decisions and operations and designable by reflective designers. This is normally associated with data and information in IS and IT planning. Emergent is that which cannot be specified and identified at the time of design but becomes cognizant in actuality and designable by action designers only. Assuming a complete set of systems requirements can be voiced is contrary to emergent information and knowledge. It cannot be specified prior to design as it arises in context through interactions between people and over time. It can be addressed in specified design by deferred action.

Deferred action

Deferred action is the necessary pragmatism of human action to achieve formal objectives. Pragmatism distinguishes deferred action from planned action. Planned action is enacted as prescription by design regardless of actuality. Deferred action complies with formal objectives and arises because planned action cannot be enacted in actuality. It has implications for design and the process of design requiring radically different kinds of designs in which action designers are enabled to do deferred design.

Deferred action is an interrelation aspect of design that cannot be specified for reflective designers encompassing human traits, sociality and emergence from which interrelations originate. Researchers refer to 'social embeddedness' of knowledge and 'meaning' attribution of information and philosophers identify 'tacit knowledge' as the source of human knowledge. These cannot be formalized in design. Specification design makes the problematic assumption what we know can be objectified and formalized. Reflective designers depend on and can only know objectified knowledge to design organizational structures and systems architectures. Since 'We know more than we can tell' is at least true in the sense of non-cognitive communication, and may even be true of cognition, design needs to reflect it.

Reflective designers cannot formalize emergent organization. Knowing, expressing and objectifying purpose and action are problematical. In extant design models of human activity are based on 'disembodied rationality' or 'abstract cognition'. Reflective designers develop rational models of data and information in which purpose, intention and operations are made concrete. Whereas in actuality organization struggles with expounding purpose and direction and its dominant mode of being is that of organizing that reflects emergence well.

Rational predisposition produces contrary situations in which design seems inadequate. Deferred action is a way of achieving formal objectives that combines knowable 'rules and procedures' and actuality. It is more capable of achieving formal objectives than planned action or situated action. When called to account for how the action was determined or how it was achieved it can be explained by relating to formal objectives and specified design in which it is embedded.

Deferred objects exist. Objects that act as a conduit for emergence can be identified to enable deferred action in formal design. Just as specified design objects can be determined, it is possible to design deferred objects that can be implemented as deferred design by action designers in actuality. Deferred action models should reflect this synthesized deferred action ontology of rationality and emergence.

Design process

Interrelations between rationality, emergence and deferred action make design simultaneously rational and emergent. It is logical to express simultaneity in the design process. Structure and emergence require duplex design process. It is well expressed as a process of co-design of structure by reflective designers and emergence by action designers. Architectural or structural designs by reflective designers and operational designs by action designers compose continuous design.

For systems, continuous design combines design of TSA by reflective designers and deferred design of operational functionality by action designers. Operations or business process transforms resources. Specification of transformations in concrete terms is problematical because of variation in actual action arising from natural design. For organization design, to manage knowledge for instance, it is design of structures conducive to knowledge work that enable deferred action of knowledge workers necessary to adjust to emergence.

Design process is not discrete. It is not discrete projects of design. Social action can be demarcated into discrete design periods for structural design but not operational design. Emergence limits specification design by discrete projects because rationality cannot preempt emergence. Reflective designers cannot preempt deferred action. Since emergence and deferred action are interrelated specification design needs to interrelate with deferred action by enabling deferred design. So both emergence and deferred action necessitate a conception of design as co-design and continuous design.

Rational design is a conscious event at some point in organized social action. Rational design by specification results in the assignment problem where designed artefact becomes reality or becomes a substitute for actuality. In deferred action design the artefact is simultaneously product and process. Artefact is divided into two constituent parts. One is specification design by reflective designers as a conscious event to constitute some organized action. This is the beginning of product design. This is placed in organization to be designed by action designers as the other part or the continuation of design process.

Acquiring knowledge

The theory of deferred action is derived by realism ontology and epistemology. Plural and synthesized deferred action design perspective adheres well with realisms method of explaining phenomena. The method accounts for concrete objects and phenomenological objects.

In realism ontological entities are assumed to exist and be independent of an observer. Rationality, emergence and deferred action analytical entities are assumed to exist independently of the researcher's investigations of them. Knowledge of these entities can be developed because they are real and exist. Since they manifest regularity knowledge about them is generalizable. By understanding their 'causal powers' theoretical knowledge of design can be developed. Certain entities may not be amenable to quantification but they are still available for analysis. That analysis of subjective meaning or socially constructed meaning is possible and is consistent with realism.

The task of research is to discover entities, interrelations and explain them in terms of causality to develop valid explanatory knowledge. Entities may be simple or complex, social or material, abstract or concrete. Interrelations are characteristic of entities. Relations may be contingent or necessary, symmetric or asymmetric. Validity is assessed in terms of knowledge and practice, as Sayer explains:

> Our knowledge of that (real) world is fallible and theory laden... Nevertheless it is not immune to empirical check and its effectiveness in informing and explaining successful material practice is not mere accident. (1992: 5)

Bhaskar (1978) elaborates the basic postulates of realism. It has domains of reality shown in Table 1.1.

Table 1.1 Bhaskar's realism postulates

	Domain of real	Domain of actual	Domain of empirical
Mechanism	✓		
Events	✓	✓	
Experiences	✓	✓	✓

The real, actual and empirical are distinct. Domain of real has generative mechanisms that act independently of the observer who is in domain of empirical. Causal powers enable entities to act in domain of real. Domain of actual is where events generated by the mechanisms appear independent of the observer. Since events too are independent of the observer they can occur in the absence of an observer. When the observer observes events they are observed as experience of the entities in domain of empirical. Any system only exists for an observer is meant in terms of this realism ontological scheme.

The research task is to explain entities in terms of their powers of causality, liabilities and interrelations. Causality is not Newtonian cause-and-effect but in the sense of everyday language of causality. Organization pursues purpose, organization uses systems or systems have functions. Powers of causality are intrinsic in entities. Entities have ways of acting their causal powers. Theoretical knowledge results by explaining causal powers or ways of acting of entities. So organization organizes resources or systems process data. Such explanation is not the same as making a prediction. An explanation ascribes to the entity its capability, as organization is emergent or it is a synthesis of planned and deferred actions. An entity's liabilities are the way it permits itself to be acted upon by other causal powers. The liability of rational design is to allow emergence to influence it, or the liability of management is to be diffused because of emergence.

So formalism, emergence, deferred action and diffusion management are interrelated and can be explained in terms of casual powers and liabilities. Insight into theoretical knowledge of design and practical techniques for designing can be gained from understanding interrelations better by determining casual powers and liabilities of entities. Deferred action postulates are derived by this epistemology. Its causal powers exist in domain of real and are interrelated to rationality, emergence and management. Causal powers generate this interrelation and deferred action is the explanation. Causal powers produce events when these are observed and acted upon it is as rational design and deferred action.

There are 'emergent causal powers' in realism. Entities coming together exhibit causal powers that are more than simple aggregation. Combining organization and systems entities or specified design and deferred design entities results in emergent causal powers. Emergent causal powers of combined entities results in different structure, which is more than aggregation of individual causal powers of the organization entity and systems entities or individual causal powers of specified design and deferred design.

In an apparent paradox once data, information and knowledge is socially constructed it exists independently in domain of actual and domain of empirical. The format a customer's address or telephone number takes is a social construction. A customer experiences a telephone number in domain of empirical when making a call. It is data that exists independently of researchers or designers. Individual managers interpret salespersons performance variously. Information on the amount sold by a particular salesperson is significant in some contexts and not others. Amount sold by a salesperson exists independently of the salesperson or manager. In the study of rational design rationality and emergence are assumed to exist. Though not directly observable they are available for analysis.

Theorizing design

Structure, emergence, space and time (SEST) constitute design. Objects actual or invented representative of SEST should be modelled for design. Rationality, emergence, deferred action and diffusion management encompass SEST. SEST entities occur naturally in nature and human nature as natural design. They are final causal powers and generative mechanisms of design. Liabilities of structure are to be malleable as it permits the emergence, space and time to shape it to order things. Liabilities of emergence are to spring to occur in unknowable ways it permits space and time to influence it in unpredictable ways. Liabilities of space are to accommodate and fix action it permits or facilitates structural, emergent and temporal spatial powers. Liabilities of time are to change it permits other entities to be changed.

Significance of SEST entities is in how they interrelate to create the phenomenon of natural design. Efficient interrelation explains design in natural design. Design of physical things is put aside. SEST manifests in social action. Method of social greeting or an agreement to proceed jointly is embodied patterning of SEST. Any SEST entity only exists relative to others in any design it cannot exist independently. So structure of social greeting is its intentions, purpose and method, emergence is change in composition of individual elements of structure and ultimately structure itself, space is its physical location and setting and time is its temporal location. Order is intrinsic to nature manifested as SEST it is itself not artificial that we can create. Order in social greeting is a manifestation not creation. Interrelated synthesis of SEST entities creates and sustains design in natural design. SEST entities, liabilities and interrelations occur in domain of real.

SEST entities manifest in the domain of events but unless humans experience them they remain immaterial. When they are experienced in domain of empirical by humans they manifest as rational design particularly the life cycle. Any design in rational design is constituted as having a beginning, middle and end the life cycle. It is rational because humans do it consciously as embodied patterned design. Rational design is explainable in terms of causal powers of SEST entities and can be improved by translating natural design SEST entities into SEST properties of rational design in domain of empirical.

Humans design by nature. Crystallizing natural design as rational design improves probability of obtaining desired goals by making efficient and effective use of limited resources. So it is necessary to identify and control the principles at work in natural design. These principles stem from SEST entities and can be translated into SEST properties of rational design. The reason for emulating natural design is it is more successful in human society than rational (formal) design. Where formal design is inadequate or even fails, humans have acted to retrieve the situation and driven it towards the goal by natural design. SEST lead to rational design in accordance with being human and being social, they are natural basis for organized action design.

Figure 1.1   OM

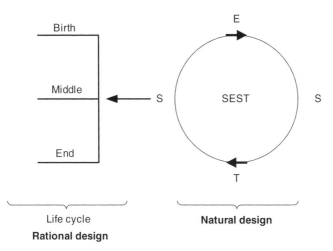

To understand design for organized action design it is theoretically divided into natural design and rational design domains depicted in Figure 1.1. Natural design is continuous so circle since it has no beginning or end depicts it on the right. Natural design is what individuals do consciously and subconsciously naturally it is governed by SEST causal powers. We all design. It can be individual or social. It serves three human purposes to be, becoming and interrelations. It accords well with free will.

Natural design has Newtonian simplicity and facility. Newton describes nature as 'exceedingly simple and comfortable to herself.' It is simple since we do not even appreciate that we design in our lives. It facilitates achievement of human desires and dreams. Design theory has to explain natural design and render it practicable for rational design in similar simple terms.

The deferred action explanation is that natural design has four properties structure, emergence, space and time shown respectively around the circle. Since action by natural design mirrors these four properties it is of four types structural, emergent, spatial and temporal. In natural design action addresses SEST either by deliberate decision or subconsciously as they are encountered in the course of some action. Since SEST is inherent in natural design acting by natural design as humans do accommodate the four properties. Natural design contains moments of conscious rational design for humans.

Rational design is an event when humans decide consciously to act rationally to determine a design to achieve some desired purpose. It is Simonian artificial design. Order though is inherited from natural design through SEST not created artificially. The left arrow emanating from continuous natural design in the Figure 1.1 depicts this rational act. So decision by an airline company to commercialize space travel or to pursue an acquisitions policy are rational acts. To govern society democratically or trade in a free market are rational acts. It is possible to design a perfect artefact one that becomes indistinguishable from natural design. Its placing in social action becomes commonplace. The Indian numeral is an example, as Laplace noted they are '...so simple that its significance and profound importance is no longer appreciated.' They have proved to be sustainable too.

Rational design results in abstract organization and systems design depicted as the three (3) the left in Figure 1.1. It is the accepted life cycle in systems design that has birth, middle and end. Rational design is pure abstract design because design objects are some orders removed from actuality where natural design is more effective. Decision to develop an IS or KMS are examples compared to the existence of information or knowledge in social action naturally. At operational level an IS management report is abstract because its form and contents are determined at a specific space (condition) and time which may not have the same structural and actual relevance when actually used.

Natural design is implicit in rational design but rational design circumscribes free will. In rational design the subconscious element of natural design is excluded formally and the conscious rational element or Cartesian rationality is deemed superior. Rational design is purposeful and explicit composition of artefact (design) to achieve purpose and objectives. Artefact design or general design is by specification. Rational design has high capability to represent the structure SEST property but is weak at representing the other properties.

Since SEST is intrinsic to natural design it is necessary for rational design to encompass it. The link between natural design and rational design to ensure all SEST properties are represented in any design is deferred action. It is interrelation between natural design and rational design. Since deferred action can be structural, emergent, spatial and temporal it is consistent with the SEST of natural design.

Deferred action design is representation of SEST in rational design. It is a synthesis of natural design and rational design with deferred action as the synthesizing agent. The circumscription of free will is removed by deferred action. Including deferment design enables free will and differentiates rational design in deferred action design from other forms. So in deferred action design rational design is composed of specification design and deferment design. It has high capability to represent emergence, space and time design properties of SEST and because it includes rational design it has high capability to represent the structure property too. A set theoretic description of these domains and subcategories is if

N = set of natural design decisions
R = set of rational, specified design decisions
D = set of rational, specified and deferred design decisions.

Then deferred action design is:

$D' = D \subset R \subset N$

As shown in the Venn diagram in Figure 1.2 intersection of the three sets is deferred action design.

David Parnas and Paul Clements (1986) rightly observe that rational development of software is not possible but because it is necessary they recommend faking it. Faking though is only necessary if the aim is to design by complete specification. Non-faked rational design is possible if SEST is accepted for both design process and designed artefact. Both require deferment to avoid the complete specification unobtainable variety of rational design.

Figure 1.2   Venn diagram of deferred action design

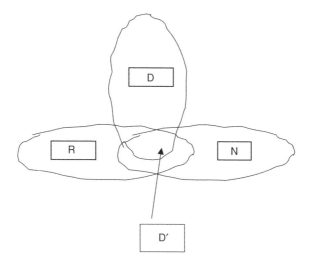

Philosophy of design

Researchers' observations of design are in domain of empirical. The subject and researcher both experience it. It encompasses domain of actual too where events occur but which may not necessarily be 'experienced' by subjects or researchers. Researchers' task is to trace experiences of humans through the events to domain of real to discover causal powers of design and how it relates to actual action or organized action.

Only experienced events in domain of empirical can be acted upon. If data, information and knowledge are to be designed it needs to be experienced first. Realism empirical experience of events is not considered in present rational design. Deferred action design is inclusive of empirical experiences the events that happen during organized action that action designers can include in design. Reflective designers cannot design such operational functionality because they do not experience it themselves in domain of empirical.

Deferred action design results in pragmatic design. It is based on the three aspects of natural design to be, becoming and interrelations they themselves are interrelated. Design has Plationian noumenal existence. Any design is created to serve human existential purpose and is intrinsic to being human. Once created design itself becomes part of being. Then like us it interrelates to other things that cause becoming to become significant because interrelating creates new dynamics.

To reflect natural design in deferred action formalism needs to reflect SEST. Natural design has three implications for deferred action design. It presupposes necessary and sufficient conditions to design, it makes the crucial assumption that design is placed in social action and it focuses on interrelation created by the placing.

Necessary and sufficient conditions

Deferred action design has two natural design sources a priori human and experiential these compose rational design. They form the necessary and sufficient conditions to design. Deferment formalism draws on both and specification formalism only on the a priori.

A priori source is a consequence of action by natural choice. Action presupposes externalization of intention that may be well structured or poorly structured. Well-structured intention contains either conscious or subconscious axioms about reality, and may contain rules of inference, similar to mathematical systems. The Web is an example. Poorly structured intention contains weaker notions of design identity a KMS and UN organization for instance.

To design it is necessary to formulate and hold certain personal constructs or axioms about the design domain (specific domain of empirical). Such collective axioms are necessary for purposeful organized action. Axioms may be subconscious, intuitive or formally established. They are presumed in acts of creativity like invention. Axioms themselves compose elements of intention. Such axioms correspond to hypotheses on things and how they work the doing tests them.

The experiential is lived it provides deep design insight as in sitting and stable base to sit whether squatting on ones feet or lounging in luxurious armchair. It is not necessary to design but it is sufficient to design. It is not necessary to have gone to space to design to travel to space. The experiential is evident as technique. For example IS methodologies in systems design and hierarchy or devolvement in organization design. It dominates rational design and it is most used to design.

Primacy of interrelation

Interrelatedness is an intrinsic quality of natural design. Any natural design is successful because it is highly interrelated internally and to other objects in fields of action. Interrelation design improves rational design and SEST improves interrelation design. Thinking of systems as interrelating in fields of action provides better intellectual constructs for designing than viewing it as some form of subordinate entity to organization. The field of action is not the same as 'environment' or 'design domain'. In structural theory and systems theory imposing a boundary creates an environment. No artificial boundary is created in deferred action. Representation of the design domain differs from enabling interrelation design in the field of action. Field of action is where rational design interrelates with other things either by design or through deferred action. The being and becoming of design happens in and is determined by fields of action. The field of action itself is determined rationally by specification as for DSS it is human and organizational decision-making.

The primary focus of deferred action design is on interrelations in the field of action. A designed artefact is composed of internal interrelations among its components which need to interrelate well internally and externally to enable becoming. It also engenders interrelations with elements in fields of action which should relate well with things in the field of action. Design becomes relevant for organized action when it focuses on external interrelations in fields of action. IS or KMS interrelate with complex humans and second order organization.

The artefact is undoubtedly an important focus but it should not be the main focus. It should serve the object of design namely organized action. Rational design focuses on the artefact, and though IS researchers have developed knowledge of the object of design it has not translated into design. HCI does not address interrelations because it focuses on 'interaction' with the artefact, as does broader interactivity research.

The primary design element in deferred action is interrelations. Interrelations between the design and humans and organization and systems as second order concepts are integral to deferred action design. Incorporating interrelation design in rational design engenders alternative conceptions of design and design types conducive to natural design or actuality.

The assignment problem

The assignment problem in rational design arises because information has artefactual roots in the work of Shannon and Weaver (1949). Thinking about design of information and knowledge as solely artefact or machines creates the assignment problem and results in preponderance of specification design. The problem concerns design of abstract artefacts (structures and operations) by reflective designers who then force it onto the real where the abstract becomes real by assignment. It masks natural design. It is the assignment of abstract structures and operations onto actual organized action. Work systems depicted in Figure 2.1 are so assigned.

The problem arises because of reflective designers requirement to know operational design. The method used to understand how something works is to isolate it and build machine-like models. In organization design it is process or workflow models, in systems design data models, informational models or class models. These are then mistaken to be real as they are *assigned*. Christopher Alexander points out this Cartesian method of modelling is 'not how reality actually *is*. It is a convenient mental exercise, something we do to reality, in order to understand it.' (Alexander, 2002: 16).

Assignment causes a tumultuous clash between rational design and natural design. In specification design assignment of designed systems models to actual organized action undermines natural design. In Figure 1.3 an actual organized action problem in the space of organization design is taken by abstraction at point A by reflective designers to a rational design clean room, labelled a design domain at point B and modelled by specification formalism at point C as a specified model (point D) that is assigned to actual situation (point E). This assignment causes incongruence between specified systems (rational design) and

Figure 1.3   The assignment problem

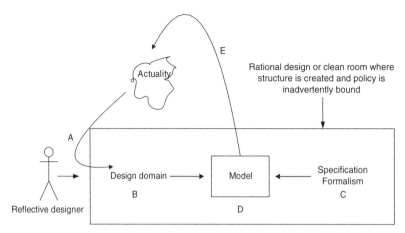

actuality (natural design) because actuality cannot be so predicted in the model and it is not stable. This kind of modelling creates problems. The model becomes a false real acted upon as observed in the actions of business workers who blame 'the system'.

Abstraction by this process makes the abstract concrete. Abstractions of actual entities for design make them real in relation to how humans interrelated to them. Business process is a concept applied to many business activities. When applied to customer relationship management and abstracted for systems design it becomes concrete. A particular system design may require abstraction of concrete and abstract entities, for example a strategic information system. Other systems design may require abstraction of concrete entities like individuals, for instance an executive information system. Interpreted in set theoretic terms the problem is this if

$N = \{ x \mid x \text{ is space of natural design} \}$ (actuality)
$R = \{ x \mid x \text{ is rational design} \}$ specified system

Then specification design assumes that the design agrees with actuality in terms of

$R = N$

In deferred action design $N \neq R$ because N has free will.

Herbert Simon rightly termed rational design the 'science of the artificial.' Systems are not natural or social. They are artefactual. This applies to organization too. Pure abstraction as practised in specification design becomes complicated because it has to represent myriad different actual entities. Entities are concrete things like individuals, groups, people and abstract things like processes, organization and markets. Deferred action draws on rational design's abstraction strength to create structure SEST property, and to represent other SEST properties as deferred design objects, not to represent spatially and temporally bound actual things by specification.

Current abstraction and systemic conception of information and knowledge is deficient to design systems for actual organized action. It lacks relevant representation of actuality and particularly of systemic mechanisms to cope with actuality once systems are implemented. Abstraction in specification design is composed of the objects of design depicted in column A in Figure 1.4. It results in strong abstraction of structure and weak and uncoordinated abstraction of other SEST properties. Axioms, physical and empirical things combine through the abstraction process in column B to form design in column C. Column B is where specification design process begins by conceptualization of physical and empirical things and its logical ordering. All design involves representation of physical things like documents, workspaces and monetary transactions. Such representation is a substitution for the real thing or in mathematical terms 'equivalence'. Empirically verified knowledge of things is not necessary to design, unverified knowledge of physical things is sufficient.

Figure 1.4   Objects of abstraction in specification design

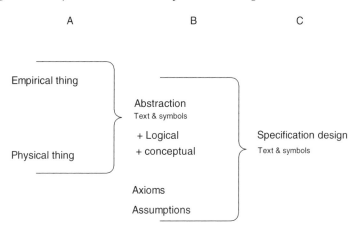

Abstraction is made of physical and empirical things as depicted in column B where design happens. Reflective designers and business workers draw axioms regarding the design domain. Axioms about the design domain are necessary to begin the abstraction process. Reflective designers make assumptions or 'constructive definitions' when designing from specification. Class, objects and interaction are examples of axioms in object-orientated design. Workflow is an example of logically connected individual group tasks. It is also a conceptualization of work.

Deferred action overcomes the assignment problem by placing and enacting rather than assigning and prescribing. Placing is the act of putting design in social action with interrelations design capable of deferred operational functionality design. Placing enables action designers to make design decisions in response to emergence, space and time SEST properties. Enacting is the act of putting design in social action with interrelations design capable of real-time structural and operational functionality design in the field of action. Enacting enables action designers to make design decisions in response to SEST. In deferred action design organization or system is placed and enacted in social action where action designers determine its operational functionality through intra- and extradeferment. They can alter its architecture (for systems) and structure (for organization) too.

The empirical deficiency of specification design is overcome in deferment design by representation of actual things as embodied patterning. Abstraction in deferment design is composed of the objects of design depicted in Figure 1.5. It results in strong abstraction of SEST

Figure 1.5 Objects of abstraction in deferment design

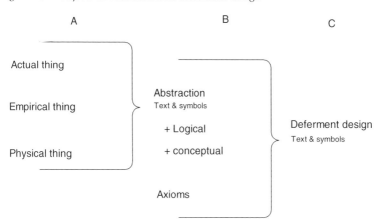

and facilitates thinking on design as composition of SEST related to deferred action. Axioms, actual things, physical things and empirical things combine through the abstraction process to form design. The critical difference compared with specification design is the recognition of actual things as objects of design in column A. Macros and web pages are examples of abstraction that well represent actual things. This removes the need for assumptions or constructive definitions from column B compared to Figure 1.4.

Placing is central in deferment formalism because rational design is interrelated with natural design. The assignment problem is avoided by recognizing that information has meaning attribution, and applies especially to knowledge too. No model assignment occurs in deferred and real systems. Deferment is necessary to account for natural design, a continuous series of imperceptible design decisions made recursively depicted in Figure 1.6. In natural design humans make imperceptible design decisions at D1, D2, D3...D∞. Each successive decision is connected in myriad connections as sequence depicted by arrow and recursion depicted by arcs. By imperceptible design is meant action taken to achieve human goals of survival, habitation and well-being. Such actions are not always rational because goals themselves are interwoven with the condition of being human with its implicit anxiety, uncertainty and emotion. Much of this action lacks forethought.

Specification design is necessary to make the imperceptible and continuous design purposeful and directed. Otherwise design is rationally aimless – it just flows according to natural conditions. Reflective designers make the imperceptible discrete to design for organized action.

Figure 1.6   Imperceptible natural design and point of specification design

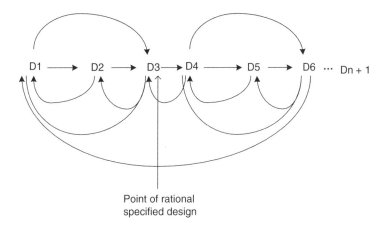

Point of rational
specified design

They create a specified structure by specification design at a fixed temporal moment in the continuous. The point of specification design shown at D3 is where the short-termism and even aimless recursive design is stopped in favour of purposeful design itself still recursive, but now towards rational aim/purpose. Imperceptible design decisions now happen within this specified structure alongside rational design decisions.

Specification design is rational design as a discrete event in the flow. It is characteristic of cultures dominated by rationalism. It is conscious and deliberate. Specification design too contains imperceptible design decisions. The difference between specification design and deferment design is that the latter enables imperceptible design whereas the former counters it, forces it underground.

Figure 1.7 Spectrum of natural design and rational design

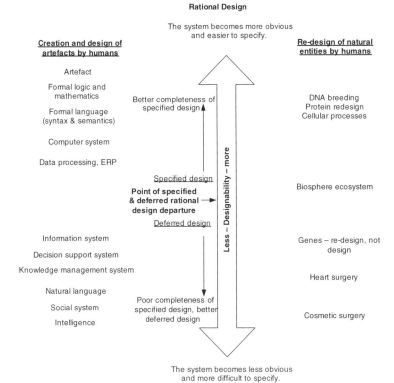

Natural design and rational design domains are mapped as a spectrum depicted in Figure 1.7. Left side above specification-deferment departure point depicts design objects catering to being aspect of natural design. These tend to be designed by specification and have a finite set of design decisions $D = \{x\}$. Design of formal computer languages and Panini's Sanskrit grammar are illustrations. Left side below specification-deferment departure point depicts design objects catering to becoming an aspect of natural design. These require deferred design because they potentially have an infinite set of design decisions $D = \{x\}\infty$. Above the point design is completely specifiable and below it is partly specifiable because it is social and natural and so requires deferment.

Rational design is suited to being aspect. Design objects are obvious, definable and designable as SSD. The set of specified design decisions is finite and there is equivalence between design and desired outcomes. Natural design is suited to the becoming aspect. Design objects are less obvious, difficult to define and design so designable as DSD and RSD. Interrelation design is difficult to specify towards natural design so it is deferred. The set of deferred design decisions is infinite. There is little scope of assessing equivalence between design and desired outcomes or $D \Leftrightarrow O$

The task mathematicians' set of formalizing mathematical reasoning is similar to the task of rational design but ironically at the opposite ends of the spectrum. Mathematics is divided into formal seeking axiomatic theory that can be mechanically proved the rational end and intuitive seeking workable propositions the natural end. Many mathematicians satisfy themselves that rational axiomatic theory is possible but do not proceed to develop one because 'it would be far too tedious, in practice, to do so (Pinter, 1971: 9). Mathematicians' choice of how to work is consistent with natural design. It is sufficiency to achieve their objectives and they accept the intuitive form because it works. Specification design is contrary to this kind of pragmatism.

Deferred action is similar to mathematicians' sufficiency mode of working. Design's axiomatic theory is equivalent to specification formalism. It would be too complex to 'capture' formally all the ways design needs to interrelate with other objects in fields of action such rational design is not achievable. Since specification formalism is sufficient to design structure SEST property deferred action proceeds to represent other SEST properties as deferrable design objects. It would be 'too tedious, in practice' to capture complete requirements of actual organized action let alone to capture its social element formally.

Specification design however seems overly concerned with formalization even though the intuitive form of design practice works. Deferred action design combines formal and intuitive forms of design practice. The backbone of design is formalism but complete specification and formalization of design is unworkable in practice. Deferred action design is the requisite compromise.

The design spectrum aids thinking on designability of design domains and design process in terms of specification design and deferment design. It depicts the problem of determining the point on the spectrum at which specified design and deferred design depart as pure forms. Specified design is associated with artefactual design encompassing as artefact, mathematical systems and computer systems that can be specified because they tend towards the mechanical. Deferred design is associated with natural design encompassing IS, KMS and social systems because they tend to be embedded in natural design so they require greater deferred design. The assignment problem exists because design objects and domains below the point of specification-deferment departure are mistakenly taken to be above the line.

Organizational coordination, integration and context design problems can be considered in terms of the spectrum. Redesign of biological and other natural entities is mapped but no parallel equivalence is intended for the right side of the figure which is depicted for analytical purposes only. Redesign of proteins, DNA breeding and cellular processes 'are generally known as *rational design* and directed evolution.' (Stemmer and Holland, 2003). Modelling proteins is similar in difficulty to information modelling 'there are a staggering number of interdependent variables that influence protein function (Stemmer and Holland, 2003). Clearly gene re-design is not the same as IS, heart surgery is not the same as natural language. Heart transplant and plastic surgery and other surgical interventions tend towards natural design because all contingent conditions are not under surgeons' control.

Organized action, formalism and design

Placing design and acquiring knowledge of design along the design spectrum is the subject of the theory of deferred action. It addresses the problem of SEST representation in any rational design for organized action. The aim is to aid conceptualizations and definitions of design objectives by conceptualizing actual situations as design types and to guide such design. Deferred action theoretical constructs and their interrelationships explain design in terms of human and organizational actuality. They help to determine what design 'ought to be' for actual organizational conditions and propose design types, processes and deferment formalism suitable to design for these conditions.

The theory's formative construction is depicted in Figure 1.8. It depicts relationship between design and actuality as involving design of SEST properties. To account for SEST the elements in columns A, B and C are necessary and sufficient. Using these constructs SEST becomes central to organization and systems design. It is present in all four constructs at C. Structure and emergence is obvious at C.C1 stemming from social action theory. Space and time are implicit in all four constructs at C.C1 and C.C2 stemming from both social action theory and mathematical theory.

Formal basis of the deferred action theory draws on social theory and mathematical theory depicted at C.C1 and C.C2 respectively. Social action theory contains conception of social and organized 'structure' and 'emergence' and mathematical theory contains conception of axiomatic 'formal system'. Knowledge of designing as formal system is needed to (a) understand artefactual design as system and (b) to reason

Figure 1.8   Formation of theory of design

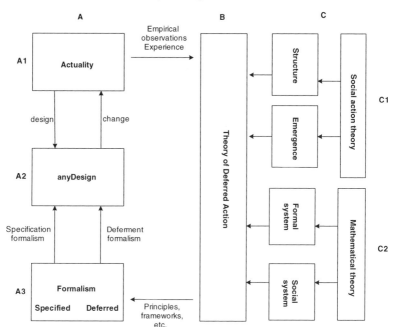

logically about it. Mathematical notation of 'system' is loosely applied to describe 'social system' but it also draws from general systems theory. These four conceptions formal system, social system, structure and emergence are the meta-theoretical constructs in the theory of deferred action depicted at B.

The theory explains empirically observed incongruence between design depicted at A.A2 based on C and actuality depicted at A both for organized action at A.A1 and designers' work at A.A3. Part is attributable to specification design. Specification formalism results in notation languages based on either rigours axiomatic mathematical systems or verbal theories seeking rigour. It is derived from mathematical theory at C.C2 or C.C1 and it is either based on theory for design (column B) or it is formulated directly as the specification formalism depicted at A.A3. Deferment formalism notation languages have similar mathematical foundation but oriented towards actual action.

Theory at B proposes deferment formalism to cater for design and design process actualities and that it should be combined with specification formalism as depicted at A.A3 to inform design at A.A2. Emergence is not yet sufficiently formulated in social theory and space and time aspects of action are not researched in social action investigations. Deferred action theory proposes that deferred design, based on empirically observed deferred action, right arrow from point A, ought to be part of design. Deferred action design addresses actual situations by enabling action designers to design in actual situations. It can be catered by specification design.

Other explanations of actual action do not make actual action designable. Actual action is termed 'means' in means-ends analysis but design mechanisms to enable are not provided. Actual action is categorized as 'complexity' in complexity theory. For design it is interpreted as contingent moves in contingency theory or simply problematical in non-theory based design approaches.

Column A also depicts design practice. There are two alternatives to understand and acquire knowledge of design and designing. Design can be done, tried out and it may if fortunate be successful – achieve objectives. This is the method of 'design research'. Lessons are learnt regardless of whether outcome is successful. This option is costly if the design is expensive as in building large systems. Another option is to use theoretical knowledge of causal powers it affords, column B. Theory is able to describe and explain things of interest, foretell what to do and what to expect. This facility of theory can enable prudent action where large expenditure is required. Deferred action compliments formal design, placed at A.A1.

Designers can make use of discipline-based theories depicted in column C. For organization design structural theory, contingency theory or structuration theory could be basis for design. Many computational and mathematical models of organization are based on such theories. Discipline-based theories could not form the basis of design theory for systems design and organization design. This is because they impose a particular perspective on the application of digital technology. Structural theory for example imposes a structural perspective on applying IT. It thus limits IT theoretically.

There are theories at C.C1 that cannot be used to inform design. Contingency theory asserts that it is not possible to provide design guidelines because design is 'situationally specific'. Despite this IS methodologies plan for contingent factors that impact on rational design, but methodologies have no theoretical basis and do not contribute to design theory being themselves an amalgam of design frameworks, principles, techniques and tools.

What design practice is suitable for organized action is theoretically explored in the following chapters. Interrelation between humans and organization and systems is arguably important for further economic and social development. Organizations are significant contributors. Yet interrelation design is at best parochially located in disciplines. In computer science it is limited to HCI studies to improve how individuals operate computer systems. There is no consideration of design of groups' interaction with systems and certainly no study of organization's interaction as second order concept.

There is no study of the S-SEI the interface between organization and systems in terms of information architecture and increasingly knowledge. IS researchers draw on management terminology of 'stakeholders' to describe people and research focuses on how project managers can use 'stakeholder analysis' to manage IS projects. Invoking social theory and drawing on philosophical work acknowledge people but there is little outcome of use for organization design and even less for systems design.

Relationship between humans and rational design is not for parochial discipline perspectives. It is certainly the domain of IS and KMS design and it should concern organization design. Cognitive science, sociology and many other disciplines can contribute to developing interdisciplinary knowledge. Deferred action contributes by focusing on the interrelation between design and actual action. It investigates closely interrelation between organized action and design and focuses on design of cohered organization and systems to achieve formal objectives.

Critical for understanding this relationship are formalism, emergence, deferred action and diffusion management. They enable description, analysis, explanation and design for actuality. Deferred action synthesis of these analytical entities is capable of examining strategic management of systems to understand how organization makes use of systems. It affords analysis of requisite simplicity to embed in design and to place design in social action, which many extant designs do not cope with well. This mismatch is a recurring problem for designers and results from the unilateral perspective that privileges specification design.

Chapter 2 is on formal organization and systems. They are significant design objects to pursue purpose formally and achieve formal objectives. On the whole they have been effective in achieving objectives. Formally assessing the success of formal design though is problematical. Catalogue of organizational failure is diverse. Chernobyl and Three Mile Island nuclear power organizations failure caused human misery. Human tragedy occurred in Bhopal because Union Carbide management failed. Exploding space shuttle at NASA seemed to shatter confidence and even momentarily shook resolve. Misinformation at Enron resulted in organization losing ethical direction and its share of market it is organization design failure. In other cases risk not properly managed has resulted in failure.

A similar catalogue of systems design failure is evident. Development of the London Stock Exchange's Taurus stock trading system was abandoned. London Ambulance's dispatch system become an operational failure resulting in tragic loss of life. Swissair's Personnel Information and Salary System and the City of Tulsa's (USA) Fiscal Impact Analysis System were design process failures.

Despite these failures, organization and systems remain efficient and effective means for organizing limited resources. For this reason we need to invest in advancing understanding and knowledge of what design is appropriate and how to design them. Understanding organization and systems is in itself valuable contribution.

Actual human activity is arguably more successful than formally designed organized action. It is the reason for our economic and social achievements. It has been aided by formal design. Developing knowledge of actual action in the context of formal organization and systems is necessary. It poses the design problems that designers need to answer. These problems and proffered conceptions of organized action are compared and critically analysed in Chapter 3.

Deferred action thesis is elaborated in Chapter 4 as an explanation of the requisite structure, emergence, space and time properties of natural design that need to be present in rational design. It is one perspective on improving understanding and knowledge of design. The theory of deferred action is a synthesis of natural design, rational design and deferred action design. It differs from other conceptions of design because it relates formal design to actuality through deferred action.

Implications of deferred action for design practice are addressed in Chapter 5. Models or types of organization and systems and how these can be manipulated to affect required change in the pursuit of purpose are proposed. Design types, constructs, principles and mechanisms are elaborated. They relate formal design to actuality and enable deferred action in formal design. Formal design types that cohere well with actual situations stem from deferred action. By enabling deferred action in formal design it is possible to create design suitable for actual organized action. Deferred action is a central feature in determining design types and design strategy.

Chapter 6 is on how to create model representation schemes consistent with natural design. It is on formalism, what it is, how it is invented, its logical basis, problems and difficulties it encounters in reconciling uncertainty and actuality. Rational design manifests as specification formalism ranging from rigorous to verbal types. Complexity of some specification formalism tends to overwhelm designers and people for whom systems are designed. Formalism for deferred action design is introduced as formalism that does not negate or constrain actuality.

A preferred quality of design is sustainability. The sustainable design proposition is valuable. Organization seeks to be sustainable. Formalism to deliver sustainable organization and systems is explored in Chapter 7. There are few institutions that have been sustained for many centuries like the university and some financial institutions. In both cases, information and knowledge seems to be the key to sustainability. Sustainability design is inherent in the deferred action synthesis.

Managing pursuit of purpose and achievement of formal objectives is the primary activity in organization. Effectively managing systems design to cohere with organizational purpose and objectives is critical to this management. Management of systems involves design, development and deployment that cohere intelligibly with organization design. Intertwined management of organization and systems design types stemming from deferred action synthesis is addressed in Chapter 8.

Empirical observation, exemplar cases and design and technology that attest to deferred action are briefly presented in Chapter 9. Deferred action design is evidenced by organization design and systems design. They have occurred independently of the theory of deferred action so its veracity is strengthened. Chapter 10 succinctly restates the deferred action thesis, draws conclusions and sets out a research agenda for further theoretical development and deferred action design.

2
Organization and Systems

Introduction

Design of organization and systems is interrelated and should encompass complete SEST. Designing requires knowledge of SEST and of SEST propensities in actuality in which design is placed. Understanding and knowledge should be developed of effect of systems on organization and effect of organization on developments in technology for systems such that it facilitates organization design as the primary aim.

A clear distinction between organization and systems no longer exists. It is now difficult to separate organization in terms of what is clearly systems (electronic) activity and what is clearly human activity. Systems are now integral to organization. Any theories of systems design needs to account for organization design too and vice versa.

Design concerns

Organization design and systems design have common design concerns. These include invention of SEST formalism, enablement of organized activity and attainment of formal objectives, relating design to actuality, fostering interrelations in the field of action, facilitation of sustainability and enablement of management of organization and systems. They are problematical when organization and systems are designed individually but become compounded when their design is interrelated. No theory of organization, systems or design accounts for all these concerns.

Invention of formalism

Organized action is formally designed and needs formalism. Specification formalism is prevalent in research and practice stemming from rational design. It is determination of purpose for organizing and the means by which formal objectives are to be attained. It forces object-ified rational predetermination of action and outcomes. It is necessary because any organized action is designed by specification. In organization design is a mission statement or strategy and in systems design it is a requirement statement or systems architecture.

Specification design involves formulation of *the* problem in a specific situation for which *a* solution is required to be delivered at specific time. It assumes that reflective designers alone are capable of creating design and designing. In organization design reflective designers are strategists and planners and in systems design they are project managers and systems analysts. Design by specification is appropriate to design structure but it is weaker for other SEST properties. It is specific to situation and time and focuses on functional requirement. The design problem and solution is wrongly construed as bound to space (situation) and time with no account of emergence. When implemented design does not interrelate well with actuality.

Not considering actual action is a major flaw. Specification design does not consider organized action as it manifests itself in actuality beyond specification bounds. Its rational design rationale forces every aspect of design to be objectified and specified rationally. How well things can be objectified and specified depends on whether reflexivity of action is possible. Some activity cannot be explicated or designed by specification but nevertheless achieves its objective. The bicycle rider learns by doing and adapting the learning design as new techniques for balance and propulsion are learnt. There is similar organizational work where actual activity cannot be explicated completely in advance of its occurring. The process of innovation is designed by specification but there is much that happens while innovating that is beyond specification bounds. Many professional practices with high knowledge content like surgery are practised and learnt by 'feel'. Practitioners cannot specify all that they do to enable design by specification or knowledge of the thing acted upon is transferable but not knowledge of the actual practice.

Specification design is limited to space and time. It cannot pre-empt actuality and predict emergence and so it cannot design responses for actual conditions. It does not recognize emergence design property so it does not cater for it. By definition specification design is abstract and in the sense that it does not interrelate with actuality. Design of operations and functionality is poor compared to actual needs. Reflective designers' designs are poor compared to actuality the things business workers actually do to accomplish tasks in workflows and processes. Working with specified designs in actuality is a hindrance.

Considering SEST, deferred action and invention of deferment formalism can enhance specification formalism. It can be supplemented with deferment design that caters to action designers who can respond to actuality better than reflective designers.

Purposeful action

Organization and systems serve to fulfil purpose and achieve objectives. Organization designers' task is to design means to achieve specified purpose whilst enabling individuals and groups to participate meaningfully. Purpose is multifaceted. Its manifestations are as various as in mission statement, business strategy and business objectives and for non-business organization in other forms. They are useful specifications because they develop shared understanding by communication with stakeholders or pressure groups.

Enactment of organizational purpose though is by individuals whose task is to achieve objectives. Individuals and groups' interpretations of purpose are varied and the means they employ to achieve tasks often deviate from specified means. Design that serves mutual intelligibility in this context is an unachieved aim but it is necessary for success.

Systems can enlarge purposeful action. Organization's scope and kind is extended by systems. Organizationally bound systems become national through computer networking and are now global through the internet and Web. This is a recognized opportunity to exploit systems by design to pursue previously unthinkable purpose and organized action. So multinational innovation teams are organized over the internet.

Significance of systems to enlarge scope of organizational purpose and enable its achievement can only materialize if interrelation design is recognized. It requires interrelation design of organization and systems and interrelation design of placed design in fields of action. Actual organization is constrained by designed systems unable to interrelate well with it. It is necessary to include interrelation design as second order concepts. This higher order of abstraction is warranted because individuals who do work do not define it, it is defined and embedded in design but they have to enact it in contexts not foretold by design. Interrelation design can help them enact in such contexts. Deferred action design types addresses this second order abstraction. Deferred action extends interrelation design to sociality and actuality in which humans attach meanings to action.

Sustainment

Sustainable design is desirable for organization and systems. Social activity lacking rational design tends to dissipate and ceases to exist. Specification design could lead to reification and loss of success, failing to be sustainable. If devoid of actuality specification design does not create sustainable organization and systems.

Design sustainability for organization is the sustainable harnessing of knowledge for marketable products or services. If sought it is usually expressed in formal documents. In business organization sustainment is considered internally and externally. Internally, it is placed in context of organization mission. Plans, projects, or systems are formalism that seeks to contribute to sustainability. Externally, sustainment is relative to competitors and in terms of markets. Sustainable organization requires designing a 'learning organization' with appropriate structures, processes and mechanism for individual and collective learning. Allowing business workers to design situations and processes or deferred design is more effective than specifying them.

Design sustainability for systems is the capability of designed artefact to continually extend its life by adapting structure and operations (functionality) in response to emergence, space and time. In systems sustainment is designed out by the SDLC. Such design philosophy has legitimated legacy systems. Whereas the most successful system ever the Web is sustainable. Sustainable IT systems are used in mission critical systems. A critical factor in sustainable IT systems is interrelation design of appropriate organizational processes and business workers actions. Internet design illustrates sustainable systems design. The organizations that govern these technologies illustrate the principle for sustainable organization design.

Sustainable design is functional synthesis of specification by rational analysis and deferment governed by actuality. It is synthesis of planned action and deferred action to design organization and systems capable of interrelating well in the field of action an intrinsic quality of sustainability. Rational analysis addresses formal aspects of organized action and deferment addresses non-specifiable aspects of social action. Formalization insensitive to social action creates unsustainable design.

Deferred action is critical for sustainable design. It seeks synthesis of abstraction from the social to formalize organized action and enable it to reflect actuality. Such design interrelates well in fields of action. It reflects non-specifiable actions in social action, human intuition, tacit knowledge, non-formal situations and contextual factors. Non-specifiable action includes actions of individuals with potential strategic and sustainability value. It enables contextual operations design and enables off-design operations to be explored for strategic and sustainability value.

Interrelation design

To make design successful and sustainable designers need to consider how designed entities interrelate. Any design is a set of interrelations composed of internal and external interrelations. These interrelations need to be determined and represented in design. Non-representation may be deliberate decision or because representation is not possible. Example of the former is limitations of technology and of the latter, competitors' actions. Externally an organization and its systems have to interrelate with partners, competitors, markets, and customers. Internally they have to interrelate with stakeholders, business processes and groups or individuals in workflows. Systems have to interrelate with the organization and individuals and groups and their tasks.

Deferred action accentuates need for interrelation design. If organized action design is a specified set of interrelated entities designed to fulfil purpose and achieve formal objectives, then it needs to interrelate with non-specifiable entities in the field of action of natural design. Deferred action improves understanding of interrelation design between formal design and its interrelation with other objects not represented in design. Such objects have significance for design's internal structure and external relations.

Interrelation design caters for relevance of design in space and progression of design over time. If structural design is not interrelated well with field of action design loses relevance. To interrelate well any design needs to allow pertinent non-specifiable objects to affect its internal structure. It fails to progress if the design is not interrelated well with emergent, spatial and temporal facets of interrelation design. Specification design does not cover interrelation design.

Managing design

Management of organization design and systems design requires equal attention. Combined they are central in the management of organization. Management concepts and ideas relevant to organization only or systems only are not sufficient. Management of organization requires managers to make decisions on organization and systems design.

Central management of design is the dominant choice of managers because it provides requisite rational basis to explain decisions to superiors or stakeholders. Choices of systems and their detailed functionality are determined by steering committees, planning committees and project managers. IS methodologies are devised to identify systems capable of 'aligning' with business strategy. They 'capture' centrally knowledge of operational functionality as concrete objects and align it with organizational purpose. Centrally managed design gives no consideration to local, socially embedded and tacit knowledge. Equally elaborate, and often complex, techniques are proposed to analyse and model current organization in terms of systems, designing 'systems models' and implementing them.

Managers have to reconsider primacy of centrally managed design and take decisions on a new category of design matters. These concern roles for reflective and action designers. Design should not be confined centrally to design committees and reflective designers it should be opened to relevant business workers. The option of diffused design is real and practised in government-sponsored educational and research systems design.

As emergence is the key in organized activity managers have to assess limitations of centrally managed design. Operational design is better managed locally and in actuality. From this perspective organization becomes organizing, an ongoing activity in the pursuit of formal objectives. Managers should consider making design open to relevant business workers.

Since all design is based on knowledge of what to design the actual is superior to any specified or centrally determined design. Establishing a complete set of requirements centrally is not feasible or desirable. It is not desirable because it undermines sociality and actuality. It negates the actual that is superior to any design. Reflective designers do not have experiential knowledge of work they design, are not involved in operational activities and cannot predict emergence so they are unsuited to determine operational design centrally.

Assumption of a complete set of requirements can be specified stems from functionalism. Complete design is contrary to actual organized activity and human and organizational capabilities. By definition actual organized activity cannot be specified by design since it occurs in the domain of natural design. Human ability to express requirements completely is limited for several reasons. People may not know what they want – people lack prescience. People only know what is required in context – when they actually undertake tasks. Peoples' and organization's requirements may change because of internal and external factors. People are unable to communicate requirements in technical terms. Theoretically, it is limited by emergent causal powers stemming from combining organization and systems and other combinations in the field of action.

Complete design is logically inconsistent with SEST and sustainment. It indicates a finality that does not exist in natural design and in practice is refuted by the need for enhancement maintenance for designed systems and rolling plans in organization. Any set of complete requirements is a closed system that by definition cannot evolve and so it cannot be sustained for social action.

Certain type of systems design is beginning to recognize these limitations and its implications for managing systems design. Decisions on what systems are required and what functions they should perform are diffused. System architectures are designed to enable local operational design decisions so that functional requirements are determined in context of actual organizational work needs. At the forefront of this kind of diffusion management is the UK government's JISC. Its vision of educational and research systems concurs well with the thesis of deferred action. It addresses the limited scope of specification design to cater for purpose in actual terms, value of interrelation design and sustainment. It could equally be applied to managing aspects of organization like knowledge work.

Organization

The space of natural design is boundless and beyond design. Some design within it dissipates not to be seen again. Some of it recurs and forms a repeatable pattern. Deferred action design of organization is such embodied patterned activity. It is readily identifiable and can be empirically investigated and designed. Organization design is determined purposefully from such repeatable patterns.

Design aids definition of organization. Organization design can be conceptually or empirically determined. It is technologically enabled and determined too. Organization composes specified and deferred sets of interrelated entities designed to fulfil purpose and achieve formal objectives. Deferred action work design is of four types: deferred, real, autonomous and specified. These design types differ significantly from extant knowledge of organization design but draw on a synthesis of previous knowledge.

Defining organization

In classical organization managers' activities form the main units of analysis. An organization has goals, a boundary and activity directed to achieve goals. It is 'goal-directed' and 'boundary-maintaining' and is conceived to be an object whose state and functions can be specified and designed rationally. For classical organization theory the problem of organization involves tasks that can be 'solved' by generating altern-ative feasible decompositions. When formal objectives are unclear or emergent it is reflected in ambiguity of design. 'Goal ambiguity' and the 'garbage can model' of organization design become explicable when deferred action design parameters and alternative conceptions of organization are acknowledged and become possible.

In socio-technical systems organization and work the main unit of analysis is business workers and their relationship with technical aspects of work. The thesis of socio-technical systems design is based on specification of technical, social and environmental considerations. Deferred action differs in two respects. The efficacy of design based solely on specification is limited and deferred action does not presently relate motivation, power and value judgements and 'optimization' to design. Optimization is consistent with rationality but should relate well with SEST. It does not consider democratic, psychological and social needs of workers work design as separate units of design. For these reasons in the thesis of deferred action the term 'systems type-3' is coined to describe the combination of organization and technical systems.

Conceptions of organization drawing on biological and evolutionary theory often neglect a critical observation of biological evolution. Biological evolution is indeterminate and occurs as random events, it seems to have no deliberate design. This is also true of design based on 'self-organization' whose intrinsic quality is assumed to be purpose and order but no such human self-organization with purpose and order can be evidenced. Such design draws on entomological studies of organization, order and survival. Proponents of this view do not account for complete SEST necessary for organized action design.

Organization cannot simply self-organize by placing people together. Design entities like determination of purpose, setting formal objectives and making structure to achieve them and enabling means for inter-relations have to be identified and designed. Organization is determinate but it should enable deferred action to permit permissible self-organization. Deferred action has propensity to self-organize too but it is not a central tenet of deferred action because it assumes rational design particularly of structure in which organized action requires complete SEST. As Brown and Duguid (2002) argue: 'The use of deliberate structure to preserve the spontaneity of self-organization may be one of humanity's most productive assets.' (p. 171).

Organization designers including strategists, planners and IT 'enterprise architects' have an expansive design domain for which they define structure and activities. It includes strategy, business processes, and workflow operational concerns with decision-making process requiring DSS and collaboration. Performance evaluation design includes considerations of judging performance over time and relating performance to objectives. Such evaluation is easier in specified organization design compared with deferred organization. Choices designers make enable or exclude activities in and enlarge and constrain the field of action as a consequence of rational design.

Design is based on available explicit knowledge and intuition is not recognized though it occurs. It excludes formal recognition of tacit and socially embedded knowledge, operational knowledge and organizational routines that derive much from tacitness. There are many aspects of design well known to academics but not well considered by designers including the need to consider requisite variety and to cater for increasing capacity.

Organization can be conceived of as generating knowledge to which KMS contribute. Resource-based theorists of the firm propose knowledge or 'core competencies' and 'core capabilities' as a defining characteristic of firms. Organizational knowledge and its management have developed into specialist research where it becomes the 'objectified transferable commodity' of knowledge management. Knowledge possessed by an organization defines what purpose it is capable of pursuing and what objectives it is capable of achieving. In this sense what organizations do with knowledge helps to define them. Teaching university transmits knowledge, research university generates knowledge. Pharmaceutical company requires knowledge of how to produce new drugs and generates knowledge of drugs. Motor manufacturer generates knowledge of how to make combustion engines perform better and less polluting.

Computerized corporate databases and knowledge bases are defining characteristics of organization. Organizations learn about themselves from 'infological' and knowledge models of themselves embedded in databases and knowledge bases. They learn what they know and what they are capable of doing from such systems of electronic activity, and make strategic and operational decisions based on information generated by them. Such computerized information and knowledge affects organization structures, processes and ultimately performance.

Just as economic markets are emergent and unpredictable, organization or emergent aspects within an organization, too has aspects that cannot be predicated and so cannot be planned. In economic markets interrelating agents jointly define a market. It is the same for organization design. Reflective and action designers jointly construct organization. Where electronic activity is a prime feature of organization as in e-Business customers are co-designers too because they determine production schedules through buying behaviour. Emergent organization is not to be confused with dynamical organization. Organization is capable of planned response to dynamic change without considering deferred action. Such planned change is addressable as change management. Emergence cannot similarly be planned or managed by specification design.

Management is a crucial factor in organization design. A single management style is not suitable for all organizations or for different kinds of work in organization. Highly emergent organizational activity needs to be managed differently from stable, routine activity. So an organization may be composed of different kinds of management suitable for different types of work and systems.

Rational and empirical organization

Systematic application of rationality to organization study is less than a century past. Empirical study is even shorter. Rationality and empiricism have been significant in developing knowledge and design of organization.

Rational design of organization seems obvious now. Organization as rationally determined entities dates back to around 1920 when Geoffrey

Vickers thought about how to improve situations in terms of systems. Researchers later focused on rationality, especially economic rationality, to crystallize conception of rational and empirical organization. Organization design was based on modelling optimization of limited resources. It considered tasks and its decomposition structure, hierarchy and appropriate suitable levels, informal networks and structures and how they affected formal design, processes of coordination and communication, models of information and decision-making and IT, and latterly information processing and systems.

Rational study of organization enabled empirical conceptions. Operations research first and management science later sought to study and define organizations as empirical entities. They aimed to develop management knowledge based on empirical quantitative data of workings of organization, and proposed knowledge free of biases, error, and subjective prejudices. Studies involved both descriptive and prescriptive research, latter based on ontology of organization and management as independent phenomena.

Empirical studies gave rise to management science and informed modelling. Models of work and processes were developed to design organization. Computational and mathematical techniques were used to develop models to represent organized action, computers and systems. Conditional analysis is applied to these models to inform design, and if used in decision support systems, to inform action.

Now rational design of organization dominates practice and much organization and management research. Business strategy, planning, technology strategy and systems are examples of rational design of organization. Research into business strategy and IT and systems strategy is by positivist epistemology logically consistent with empirical aspects of rational design. Recent research from a phenomenological epistemology is challenging dominance of rational design by questioning its scope and its claim to be objective and rational.

Networked organization

Knowledge of organization developed during the latter half of the twentieth century is insufficient. A radical distinction can be made between organizations as twentieth century human activity and twenty-first century human activity and systems of electronic activity. Organization is now described as 'networked' and enabled by internet and Web as in e-Commerce and e-Business.

Networked organizations encounter emergence. Emergent organization affects structures, processes and activities. Earlier conceptions of organization do not account for electronic activity, meaning attribution and emergence. They do not recognize organization as becoming, as 'organizing' as in formation of relevant structures as consequence of emergence and contingent factors. Organizing makes centralized budgeting unresponsive to 'a wide variety of emerging information.' (Hope and Fraser, 2003).

The prevalence of systems of electronic activity is the substance of networked organization. Data and information, and now knowledge, are intrinsic to organization, but their value is enhanced in the form of electronic activity. Organization is only possible when information related to purpose and processes, products and services, is recognized and managed. Organization is the management of information and knowledge. Organization makes information and knowledge systemic because it can then be processed and managed electronically.

Systems are standard for managing organizational data and information. Electronic information and knowledge are recognized as organizational resources, and like other limited resources, there is an imperative to manage. Information is used in determining strategy, operations and management. It also influences divergent organizational purpose as in spin-off infomediaries.

Artefactual or systemic property of data and information enables networked organization. Information is processed data. Meaning attribution property of information is embedded as algorithmic models of interpreted or 'infological' models. Speed and accuracy of electronic activity has transformed organizational work and conceptions of organization.

Conceptions of organization need to account for electronic activity and the data, information and knowledge it makes available for organized action. Electronic activity impinges on human activity. Human activity is not only enabled and supported by systems. It is dictated and constrained by systems of electronic activity that can be designed integral to human activity or independent of it.

The prevalence of databases in organization coordinates human activity and electronic activity. Databases are coordinating mechanisms which are a focal point for designing coordination. This is most visible in airline organizations. Reservation systems based on databases coordinate myriads of continuous electronic interactions and transactions between airlines, their agents and passengers' demands.

Electronic activity systems can be independent of human activity. Independent or more commonly electronic activity systems inter-related with human activity produce emergence. In autonomous electronic activity systems electronic activity is designed to happen independent of human activity. Autonomous stock trading systems had to have limits placed on them because the programmed algorithms were executed to logical conclusions resulting in stock market fallout. Research into multi-agent autonomous systems to replace many organizational human activities includes negotiation but may have to be similarly curtailed.

Electronic activity systems have made new organizational forms possible. Organizations can be conceived of as information processing entities. Some types of organization only exist to process information. Internet and Web technologies enable these infomederies. They are virtual organizations that collect and process information form various sources to sell to clients.

Complexity adaptation and evolution

Complexity and adaptation are misconstrued. In Simonion terms rational design addresses complexity with the technique of adaptation. The design subject itself is quite 'simple'. It is the environment that is complex. In organizations humans handle this complexity.

Contrary to this organization design has not been successful, as various designs have been tried to deal with complexity and environment. Hierarchical structures were unresponsiveness to market conditions and fail to harness human capital, resulting in poor product or service innovation records and customer dissatisfaction. Flat structures supported with networked organization attempt to improve responsiveness to markets and to harness intellectual capital. They diffuse more IT investment decisions to 'users', recognizing contextual needs and facilitate adaptation.

Organizational change can be intentional or responsive. Intentional change happens by business strategy or revised operations. Responsive change happens because a company needs to react to market events or competitors' actions. Change and adaptation are inherent characteristics of organization. It is termed 'evolution' by researchers and writers. Aldrich (1999: 2) defines organizational evolution as: 'the process of variation, selection, retention, and struggle that jointly produce patterned change in evolving systems.' Such explanation of organization change and adaptation is inappropriate. As noted earlier adaptation in biological evolutionary theory lacks design it is random. Humans by organizing however seek to create their own future by design.

In deferred action design complete SEST and interrelation design for fields of action are sufficient to design for all aspects of social action masked as 'complexity', 'adaptation' and 'evolution'. As deferment design and specification design are integrated aspects in organized action actual action that is not part of specified design can be catered for as deferred design. In deferred action terms by subsuming operational design in structural design rational design creates the category of 'complexity'. It becomes a design issue only because rational design seeks design by complete specification. Design complexity is a consequence of the need to account for all operational detail in organization design and for complete requirements specification in systems design.

Organization design limitations

In terms of SEST organization design is limited to structure. Emergence, space and time are off-design, beyond specification beyond specified design. Their realism liabilities do not permit design. Events emerge in actual organization for which specified information and knowledge design is inadequate. Despite systems organization remains organization without memory and in systemic terms organization without knowledge. The UK distributed police organization was unable to co-ordinate information on an individual perpetrator resulting in tragic murder of two young girls. Hiring someone to work with children requires all available information to make a decision but police checks failed. Police were unable to coordinate available information held on disparate systems in different locations. Systems containing information on the same man with different names were not integrated resulting in organizational information mismanagement. Now systems are integrated but not yet tested.

'Nothing on the system' claimed officers attempting to explain the mismanagement. They found recourse in the requirements of the Data Protection Act to delete unwarranted data on individuals. Whilst this is a legitimate explanation for some cases it is symptomatic recognition of the lack of interrelation design between systems and organization. It is a problem applicable to particular events or in general for relevance in actuality. Specification design is incapable of relating to actual conditions of work for most types of systems required in organized activity.

Whereas actual organization cannot be specified and predicted limitations of design can be addressed by deferred action modelling. Actual organization is not discoverable in mission statements, strategies, and plans or information architecture, databases and systems models. No amount of deep mathematical analysis or attention to computational detail will produce specified designs that will be successful in actuality. On the contrary it serves to reveal limits, disappointments or failure of specification design. Limitations of designed organization and systems are discovered in actual events where the action to address events happens. The problem for designers is to think of ways to overcome such limitations when they do arise in actuality. Deferred design is proffered in the thesis of deferred action.

Implicit in the self-organization proposition is end of organization design. ICT will end the need for firms or organization by empowering individuals and markets as self-organizing entities. There is no evidence of self-organizing systems applicable to human activity. In simple terms someone has to organize a place for sellers to put up their stalls and someone has to organize the structure for the market to take place. All customer-to-customer web systems are set-up and organized by design by companies or voluntary bodies. Systems can only be created, sustained and function in organization. Rather it is the current limits of organization design that cannot cope with the potential of ICT. Designers have to overcome the productivity paradox of increased ICT investment with no significant returns.

A basic contradiction in specification design is the use of static models of organized activity for systems design whereas human activity has emergent and dynamic properties and it is infinite in actuality. Systems may if inappropriately conceptualized impede human activity and in some cases be the cause of organizational failure. Design needs to ensure that appropriate ontological knowledge is embedded in systems. (For a teaching perspective on systems ontology see Patel (2005a).

Systems

There is no obvious point of differentiation between organization design and systems design. Assuming precedence of any one is simplistic. Systems for organizational work suggests organization design precedes systems but systems design can and does determine organizational work design. Systems design is organization design in many respects particularly as information and knowledge are major constituents of organization. Even strategy is of systems and enabled by systems. It is impossible to think of organized action and not to think of systems of information and knowledge necessary to make organization possible. Since systems are increasingly characteristic of organization design designers need to consider appropriate kinds of systems design for organized action.

Is organizational work intrinsic to purpose and objectives or can it be defined in design of systems and then be realized in organization designed to pursue set aims? This is a research and design question. Earlier payroll and inventory control transaction processing systems automated existing organizational work. Now systems design necessitates redesign of existing organization, organizational work, designing new workflows and business process necessary to make designed systems relevant, themselves based on industry 'best practices' coded into business process reengineering or COTS. This practice of re-designing organization to suite systems design is questionable. Researchers need to investigate its consequences and designers should question whether to proceed with this design logic.

Re-designing organization a la systems design is a consequence of specification design legitimated by rational design. Elaborate specification and diagrammatic formalisms are used to design systems on the assumption that the design constitutes actuality. There is little empirical analysis to support this assumption. Instead disappointments and failure of systems generates the search for alternative, better and elaborate specification formalism. The assignment problem is the eventual result.

As organizational demand on systems increases and becomes more sophisticated specification design is applied for which it was not conceived. A rough assessment and application of existing systemic concepts and design methods is the response of designers to meet new demands. An example is knowledge management recognized by strategists as significant and implemented by systems designers as KMS heavily dependent on explicit knowledge because it is amenable to specification design.

Early demand was for data and information processing systems that are now core transaction processing systems. Newer demand is for interactivity, text, video, and sound processing in web-based IS. Internet and web place additional demands on systems design to process commercial transactions in e-Commerce systems, and redefine business processes and work, based on radically altered business models, in e-Business systems. Newest challenge is design of KMS. These additional demands further blur the boundary between organization design and systems design.

Defining system

Of course formal systems do not exist. It is a powerful tool for developing knowledge of nature and social action. The epitome of formal systems is Newton's analytical 'mathematical systems'. Geoffrey Vickers seminally applied systems to human problems involving radical change. Since then 'system' has shaped thinking on human organizational problems for approaching a hundred years. The terms 'educational system' or 'political system' are references to organized action. The term 'sewerage system' or 'transport system' is organized activity involving technology. Both kinds of 'system' infer loosely systems theoretic but are nevertheless sufficiently linked to it to benefit from its problem framing and problem solving facility. In some cases, as in politics or education, systems are better regarded as plans in the sense that desired outcomes are known and can be planned.

Systems theoretic gel computer, IT and organization design. Digital computer technology and systems theoretic are inseparable. Conceptions, invention, design, and implementation of computer technology is intrinsically based on systems theoretic. IT and systems theoretic are inseparable too. IT is necessarily systemic as applied to organizational problems. It is not possible to think of IT in non-systemic terms for organized action design. Organizational problems concerning information, knowledge, or commerce are rendered systemically as 'information system', 'knowledge management system', 'e-Commerce system' and 'e-Business system'.

Deferred action interpretation of systems is of three kinds. The first is coined *systems type-1*. It is an intellectual tool, an abstract form for thinking of situations that are of concern to humans involved in social and organized action. It is the Vickerian 'organizing concept' to organize thinking on seemingly intractable problems. It is a formal system of explanation of phenomena. In Figure 1.8 it is introduced into the theory of deferred action at point C.C1 as social systems.

Humans experience situations where normal activity is questioned, either because of change caused by others or because of desired change to improve pursuit. Change in situations cause concern. They raise questions on the nature of the change and how it should be confronted. Thinking of such actual situations as systems type-1 helps to answer questions. In Vickerian terms it improves 'an understanding of the situation' and what is 'demanded' to act upon it. Some researchers equate organization with a system which is not meant in deferred action. Organization itself is interpreted as systems type-1 as in 'systems thinking'. Systems type-1 do not exist in actuality. In terms of systems type-1 actual organized activity is systemless.

The second is coined *systems type-2*. Examples of systems type-2 are the electronic central processor, memory store, input and output, or the hardware and software that compose a computer system. This is system as tangible artifact subject to laws of physics. It is used to design digital machines and pervades ICT. It is instrumental in invention and application of many other types of non-digital technologies.

The third is coined *systems type-3*. It combines systems type-1, type-2 and organized action. This is system as artefact too but interrelated to humans and organization (social action) that link it to actuality. It describes software engineering of systems, specification methods for systems and IS methodologies to develop systems. Deferred action theoretical and empirical object of study is systems type-3 or simply systems.

IS and knowledge management researchers study systems type-3 but their conceptualizations differ from deferred action because they lack the design link with actuality. Some UK IS researchers have proposed IS development methodology based on all three systems types, again the design link with actuality is lacking. Systems type-3 design includes within it systems type-2 design, and researchers in systems thinking would include type-1 too.

A deferred action system is any combination of these systems types for data, information and knowledge design for organized action. Deferred action design draws on all three types. Application of IT to organizational purpose is necessarily of type-2 and type-3 which are useful for applying deferred action theoretical constructs to actual situations. IS, CSCW, BPR, ERP, KMS, supply chain management systems, e-Commerce, e-CRM and e-Business are compositions of type-2 and type-3. These are socio-organizational work systems depicted at the top and bottom right quadrants of Figure 2.1. DSS, EIS or spreadsheets are individual-organizational work systems at the bottom left quadrant. They are jointly termed systems type-3.

Systems type-1 is useful in the consideration of deeper questions of purpose, meanings and interrelations between design and fields of action. It aids understanding of interrelations, their consequences and how such understanding informs organized action. Systems thinking analysis of relationships among data, information and knowledge constructs would reveal emergent properties of this 'system' that mathematical analysis or behavioural analysis would not. Systems type-1 is relevant for the emergent organization construct in the thesis of deferred action.

Deferred action conception of systems is consistent with Simonion thesis of the artificial in principle. It goes beyond to design a link to actuality so that design coheres well with actual organized activity. It differs from Simon's artificial design by enhancing social action by representing deferred action in design. It extends design decisions to action designers by redefining the role of reflective designers. Simon was aware of this kind of design and notes the radical change in design activity required to affect it.

> We have usually thought of city planning as a means whereby the planner's creative activity could build a system that would satisfy the needs of a populace. Perhaps we should think of city planning as a valuable creative activity in which many members of a community can have the opportunity of participating – if we have wits to organize the process that way. (Simon, 1996: 130).

Deferred action theory is a response to Simon's challenge. Its central design principle is to organize the design process as duplex design process or co-design by reflective and action designers. This is now possible because of the availability of ICT.

Work systems

A classification of extant systems as models of work is depicted in Figure 2.1. Its dimensions are individual and social on the vertical scale and individual work and organizational work on the horizontal scale. Plotting systems results in four categories of work systems: individual-to-social, socio-organizational, individual-to-organizational and individual. Enabling technology is shown in ovals. They are all systems type-3 with systems tending towards organizational work requiring deferred action design.

Dimensions of Figure 2.1 afford an analysis of extant systems in terms of models of individual and organizational work. It reveals that work systems are necessary but not yet extant depicted in italics. Categories themselves are possible models of work and models of systems for work. The models can be of business processes, e-Business and e-Commerce or how managers make decisions and how people work in teams. They are embedded as software models of work in systems.

The top left quadrant depicts the individual-to-social work model with few systems types. An individual designer or author works alone but needs to communicate with others. Work is individual but it is

Figure 2.1 Models of work systems

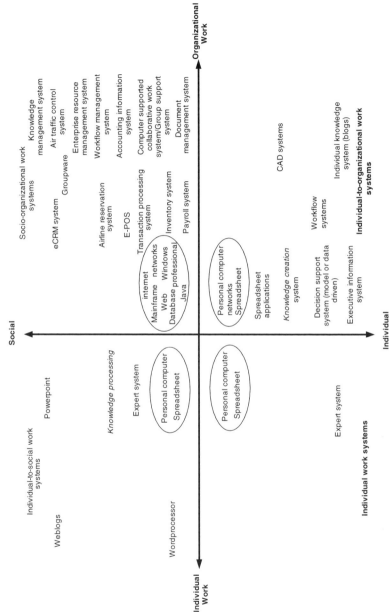

shared and communicated socially. It is not necessarily collaborative though it can be organized as an author and publisher. A word processor system supports this work. Arguably in the 'information society' there should be more systems types. Systems for individual knowledge recording and processing need to be designed as weblogs are a poor surrogate.

The top right quadrant depicts the socio-organizational work models where collaboration is the norm. Collaborative work is coordinated by pertinent information. Cyert and March's (1963) analysis of information based on structuralist theory of organization is seminal. There are many systems types to manage organizational information but comparatively less for knowledge. It suggests right kinds of system have been conceptualized for organizational work. They cover information, knowledge, business processes and commercial transactions. Design efficacy though is debatable.

KMS epitomized socio-organizational work systems for which design is highly problematical. Knowledge is 'socially embedded' and 'encultured' and requires interrelations among people to achieve objectives. Synthesis of explicit knowledge, tacit knowledge and socially embedded knowledge seems an intractable design issue. Design is unable to cope with the four types of knowledge identified by researchers: embrained, embodied, encoded and embedded. So KMS design focuses on 'ontological knowledge' for design more accessible to designers.

Socio-organizational work systems are outsourced or purchased as COTS. COTS designers draw on industry 'best practices' to conceptualize and design systems that have implicit or explicit embedded models of work. Implementation often requires redesigning existing work to match embedded models that are not intrinsic to a particular organization, its purpose, management style or culture. So redesigning organization is questionable. There are cases where organizations have failed because of such enforced redesign.

The bottom right quadrant depicts the individual-to-organizational work model. A manager or an executive's policy or decision-making work has individual elements, tacit knowledge for instance that are communicated organizationally. DSS to generate information for semistructured decision problems is an example. DSS contain sophisticated models of business activity and knowledge bases derived through ontological modelling. Other DSS draw only on data. Evidence is equivocal on their impact on decision-making. DSS design is rigid in respect to the field of action in which managers need to make decisions by interrelating pertinent entities.

Surprisingly there are few individual-to-organizational work systems. There ought to be more because the work of individual managers, executives, financial accountants and cost accountants work contributes significantly to organization. Systems are needed for personal knowledge work to exploit tacit knowledge and embedded knowledge. Personal KMS can be built from ontological models extracted from experts.

The bottom left quadrant depicts the individual work model. Inventors, doctors or surgeons mental work is individual. They communicate their knowledge to other colleagues and patients. There is paucity of individual work systems. The classic example is an expert system. More are needed too.

Systems design limitations

Three key limitations of systems design are philosophical, epistemological and technique. How design is conceptualized concerns philosophical presuppositions on the nature of design, its epistemology and ontology. Similar to organization design, realism liabilities of emergence, space and time do not permit them to be designed. Present conceptualization of rational design is inconsistent with natural design. Assumptions concerning acquisition of knowledge of design domains and artefact form epistemological constraints on rational design. Since technique is the embodiment of available knowledge, its capability and precision of associated design tools is related to philosophical and epistemological knowledge. A significant limitation of design techniques concerns effectiveness of specification formalism in actualities.

Reflective designers only can design systems type-3 is an erroneous assumption of specification design. Allied major flaw is the assumption that specification of requirements is sufficient for successful design. Search for rigorous specification design is significant limitation. Specification design is central systems ontology of all extant systems type-3 design and a prime component in all extant methods and methodologies for designing systems. Taking licence of reference to Herbert Simon out of context:

> ...discovering a programme that has specified consequences may be a difficult or impossible intellectual task. (Simon, 1957: 147)

Replacing systems for 'programme' implies that specification design by reflective designers is insufficient. Limitations of specification design manifest in actual organized activity where deferred action is observed. In other situations it is workable. Where organizational emergence and change has minimal impact on systems specification design is effective. Instances of highly effective design based on specification formalism exist for such conditions.

That successful systems can result from specification formalism is an equally erroneous assumption. Advocates of formal methods tend towards extreme formal design to cover every eventuality a system may encounter in actuality. They seek improved design quality with improved notation languages that enable precise and unambiguous specification. So specification formalism is deepened in the expectation that it will lead to relevant design but the resultant design is overly complex operationally. Specification formalism limits design to state space design and lacks adequate designed responses to actuality.

Ironically, inadequate notation languages and formal methods is a limitation. They produce improper representation of design subjects and design objects. Notation symbols and operators depict design subjects that then become systems models to inform design. Inadequacy of symbols to represent actual situations and limited scope of operators to manipulate the symbols place limits on relevance and quality of design.

Static modelling is an inherent limitation resulting in the assignment problem. Systems design based on specification design remains abstract in most actual situations. It fails to cope adequately with actuality. For simple functional abstraction for recording personal details in a CRM systems changes in actual situations do not impact on its operation. Complex abstraction involving models of collaborative work fail to address actuality and may lead to disruption of work or failure to achieve objectives.

The 'logical' machine in systems type-3 enables design of infinitely complex systems that are abstract and intangible to humans. Abstract logical machines are inherently limited in actual conditions. Design of complex logical systems based on equally complex formal methods complicates systems usage for instance extreme logical form in which explicit knowledge is captured and represented in KMS. Designed as logical paths and outcomes but knowledge workers' interaction with the system leaves them frustrated and dissatisfied. Business workers are presented with elaborate logical machines that lack relevance in actualities. A non-trivial example was the unsafe operation of the ambulance dispatch system of the London Ambulance Service.

Adequacy of design technique and tools depends on knowledge and understanding of coherency of organization and systems. Gorth (1999) extols a tool as a: 'wholly constructed expression of both knowledge and values.' It does not depend solely on understanding HCI as propounded by systems designers. Design techniques based on predetermined complete specification limit systems temporally. Limitations become apparent after implementation when detail design is found unsuitable in actuality. In actual situations the design is unable to cope with new conditions or changes required.

Coping with actuality means designing for emergence. 'Emergent organization' is beginning to be recognized as an IS and KMS design issue. Rational design assumes a static and predictable field of action which places obvious limitations on systems that operate in emergent organization. Failure to acknowledge emergence has resulted in major wasted and lost investment as systems fail and legacy systems.

Coping with actuality is a critical limitation. Lack of operational relevance is a major deficiency related to inappropriate conception of time in systems design. There are numerous legacy systems in organizations, some continue to contribute through data mining, but many become simply redundant because they were unable to cope with emergent organization. Systems design needs to interrelate with actuality particularly for complex combinations of organization and systems design.

Emergence in crises situations is significant for critical systems. Crises are defined by emergence of situation in unexpected ways which require radical systems management as existing systems become doubtful and even a hindrance. It may be necessary to suspend certain aspects or switch off systems in terrorist or natural disasters. Flooding in the UK town of Boscastle required shutting down local mobile phone networks to clear airwaves for emergency services. Switching systems off is not a normal design issue for designers of IS and KMS but terrorism, unexpected uses and integrity are considerations.

Success of organization and systems

Historically, pursuit of purpose by organizing is materially successful. Military, government, and companies organize to achieve purpose. Organization has enabled setting and achievement of technological objectives like building railways and space travel and humane objectives like providing national healthcare. Rational design is a distinguishing aspect. Purpose, objectives and limited resources, and other constraints, can be thought through in formal terms, such as mission, objectives, plans, procedure and processes.

Success of organization and systems is critical for societies that have come to depend on them for every need, progress, wellbeing and leisure. Whether successful by design and how successful they are compared to actual human activity itself is important but problematical issue to evaluate. Successful by design or not lessons for design can be learnt. Evaluating and measuring performance of organization and systems is logically consistent with designing them rationally. As organization and systems are designed rationally they can be evaluated and their performance measured rationally.

How evaluation should be done is problematical because it is not possible to demonstrate formally logical connections between individual elements of design and performance. In logical terms, it is not possible to demonstrate sufficiency. Sufficiency measures require a one-to-one relationship between individual elements of design and elements of performance or success. Sufficiency is difficult for organization and systems design equally.

Measurement is usually by collecting data on performance that seeks optimization to assess expected outcomes but there are no universal measures of success for organized acts. Kinds of measures possible are inherent in the very formal mission statements and stated aims and objectives. So measuring criteria is logically intrinsic to design itself and purpose for designing. This is true of systems design too. For organization and systems design an alternative conception of measurement is continuous improvement. It permits change to be reflected in measures but they are less favoured because they are not exact.

Organization and systems design measures can be interpretive or quantitative focusing on PEE. For organization design quantitative measures include ranking and assessing outcomes relative to needs. Measurement of efficiency concerns how well an organization is able to manage resources and measurement of effectiveness concern whether expected outcomes are produced. Qualitative measures include balanced scorecard, a quasi-quantitative technique. For systems design, quantitative measures include cost-benefit analysis. Researchers propose computational and mathematical models of organization to evaluate and improve systems design. It is problematical to measure intangible benefits of organization and systems design.

Researchers doubt the success of formal design by specification and organization as formal instruments to achieve purpose. Compared to actual human activity, or in deferred action terms natural design, formal organization has been less successful (Mintzberg, 2004). Formal mechanisms to organize have been disappointing. Company mission statements, strategies, and plans have not always materialized. Organization structure has not succeeded in producing required products or services to meet PEE requirements. There is veracity in this view and it applies to specification design and formal methods for systems design. Despite this fundamental shortcoming humans continue their effort to set purpose, organize and succeed in achieving goals. Organization remains the only credible instrument for setting and achieving goals that individuals by themselves cannot attain but collectively more likely to succeed. So to study and advance all formal forms is important and necessary.

Success of formal organization depends on availability and application of information and knowledge suitable for designing. Organizations now generate information and knowledge by systems. Like organization, measures of systems success are intrinsic to formal systems design. A system is successful if it meets its design objectives. This is the usual measure of systems type-2 design. Such intrinsic measures are limited for assessing organization and systems design or systems type-3. These entities are deeply intertwined with actual human activity and affect it in almost imperceptible ways associated with deferred action that reflects natural design.

Intrinsic design measures are not sufficient for evaluating the success of systems type-3 designs. Since systems interrelate with humans and other things measures of success is intertwined with a system's field of action. Systems function as coexisting electronic activity and human activity. Systems are intermediaries in and facilitate social interaction. So a contributive factor to success is requisite degree of coherence between organization design and systems design. Where there is coherence organization is more successful as organizing air traffic control and its enabling systems. It becomes problematical to measure success of individual components. It may be necessary to conceptualize this combination of organization and systems anew and seek new measures of success rather then measure them individually. The combination becomes clearer as a second order concept. So organization and systems type-3 are themselves two elements of a supra-system that maintains itself through mutual interrelations of the two elements and with other objects in the field of action.

Evaluating success is complicated because of the task organizations set themselves. Organization and systems are designed to change the field of action itself though this is not obvious to designers and of less concern than warranted. A system is not ineffectual in its field of action which is designed to change its field of action. Collaborative systems like the Web seek to change the way people communicate – where communication is the field of action. Decision systems change the way individuals or groups make decisions – where decision-making is the field of action.

Similarly an organization does not simply accept its field of action and act in it. A car manufacturer seeks to make its car the choice of transport – where transport is the field of action. Original car manufacturers sought to change the mode of transport radically from horse carriage to motorized vehicle. NASA seeks to make space inhabitable – where habitat is the field of action. Such rational design of organizational purpose interrelates with an existing field of action to create new dynamics and is one cause of emergence that in turn creates emergent organization, and so the need for organization and systems to respond to it. This problem of better conceptualizing organized action is discussed next.

3
Organized Action Design

Introduction

As formalism functions in actuality its appropriateness for actual organized activity is important for design. The research problem concerns inventing rational design formalism that incorporates natural design in terms of its SEST properties. Representation of complete SEST is necessary in any design for organized action so invention of appropriate formalism is required. Actual action individual or organized is not well depicted in formalism for organization design or systems design. Design research tends to focus on artefacts and design process but equal weight needs to be given to actual action because it delivers formal objectives and formal design has to interrelate with it. Formalism needs to be derived from knowledge of actual organized action in the context of rational design.

Researchers interested in constructing theories of design and practitioners interested in developing designing techniques and tools are concerned with how the design problem is framed and resolved. Rational design has not delivered expected success. Rigorous specification formalism has resulted in underperforming organization and systems because of its focus on structural design. Hierarchical structure is inefficient at facilitating communication and sharing information and knowledge. Similarly focus on information architecture has resulted in abandoned systems projects.

Designing for organized action is problematical because the obvious is extremely difficult to theorize and analyse. By considering complete SEST rational design is workable in actuality. Organized action design is constituted of SEST and designing is the representation of SEST properties. All aspects of organized activity can be represented as SEST design objects that well represent social action.

Problem and toward solution

Construction of SEST should be such that it is formalizable and formalism needs to represent SEST properties in design. Extant formalism caters for one or more SEST properties but not all. Consequently, design constrains social vigour in organized action. Rational design has not invented formalism for actual organized action and capable of embedment or placing in fields of action.

Formalism has four capabilities: description, analysis, prediction and enablement. Particular formalism may not contain all capabilities or in equal measures. Specification formalism contains all the capabilities compared with diagrammatic formalism or verbal formalism. A fifth capability of formal methods within specification formalism is calculus. Deferment formalism is underdeveloped and it should possess all five capabilities.

It is individuals who act based on task and organizational information and knowledge they possess not 'business processes', 'system' or 'organization'. Some organizational knowledge resides in all its members as service to customers or quality of production it usually is general knowledge related to purpose and aims, certain knowledge in departmental or sectional members only compiling an invoice for an order or compiling cost accounts. Other knowledge is in groups who have project knowledge and individuals in groups who have expert knowledge. Their knowledge is formally structured, emerges and varies over time which is not constant.

The problem is to represent such organizational information and knowledge in formal design. Available formalism is summarized in Table 3.1 with indication of its dominant logic but no further comment

Table 3.1   Types of design formalism

	Formalism		
	Quantitative		Qualitative
	Statistical formalism	Specification formalism (Deterministic)	Deferment formalism (Free will)
Organization Design	Statistical associative	Verbal	–
Systems Design	Functional point analysis	Diagrammatic formal methods	Context-free formalism
Logic	Deductive	Deductive	Abductive

on statistical formalism is made. Specification formalism encounters problems representing the social that organization theorists and designers classify in structural terms as 'dysfunctional' and 'informal' and systems designers as 'creeping requirements' and 'enhancement maintenance'. The structuralist remedy is more rigorous specification formalism but it results in complex designs because it attempts to 'capture' requirements exhaustively even perfectly. Deferred action design can be simple because it addresses SEST as design objects which does not require exhaustive requirements statement of operational needs.

Success of formalism and design depends on how well design interrelates in fields of action or actuality. Deferred action is a theoretic construct to enable such design. Deferred action is the proposition that actual action is superior to formal design so formal design needs to cater for it. Deferred action is actual action in relation to design. It explains actual activity in relation to design and necessitates deferment formalism to design for actuality. It needs to be a formal aspect of design. So the deferred action framing of the problem combines formal design for action with actual action. This is significantly different. It combines formal design with actual action in actuality. Action relative to design in particular actual contexts is critical because it either affirms design or rejects it.

Deferment formalism represents actual organized activity in formal design. Its invention requires better understanding of natural design, the interrelation between design and actual action, design of organized action and formalism and the interrelations between them all. Formalism needs to be capable of representing deferred action. Like natural action deferred action permits acting on belief as well as calculated (design) action, so formalism should be capable of representing belief and meaning. Deferment formalism needs to be akin to modal logic and nonmonotonic.

Actuality, organized activity and systems design

A postulate of deferred action is that natural design (actual action) is superior to rational design in all cases because it is more effective than rational design in achieving objectives. Rational design though is necessary for organized activity to formulate and achieve formal objectives. Primacy of actual action necessitates invention of deferment formalism capable of representing it in relation to formal design. Deferred action representation scheme gives primacy to actual action by business workers acting as action designers. Deferred action is actual action that affirms specified design in terms of deferred design.

Interrelation between organized action and systems design, and whether actual organized activity is permitted to influence systems design, is crucial. Organization design features systems prominently. It depends on knowledge of actual activity and knowledge of design know-how available in the form of theories, models or characterizations, techniques and experiences of designers.

Systems type-3 design requires abstraction from actual activity. Deferred action proposes representation of actual activity by symbols of deferment formalism. It permits actual activity to be a significant operator in design. As an operator it affects future design and reflexively future activity. Knowledge of actual activity, even if it is absent as in new ventures, is a critical design operator that determines whether the design, and achievement of purpose, is successful. In deferred action actual activity is an operator in design which is operationalized as deferred design.

A deferred action design principle is that rational design is a consequence of natural design (actual activity). Actual activity is independent. Most design approaches make it dependent and fixed. By so doing they create unnecessary facets of representation to compound the assignment problem. An example is unambiguous data definitions in structured design that increasingly divorces data from its context making processed information irrelevant. In general, this is the problem of inventing adequate symbols and their interrelations in fields of action to represent design domains as SEST rather than 'capture' it.

Representation in systems design is complex for non-trivial domains because formal design needs to interrelate and co-operate with actual organized activity. Deferred action addresses this problem in a representation scheme that synthesizes specification and deferment formalisms to cater for the known and the actual respectively. It is based on empirical observations of deferred action in organization and supported with the general observation that formal design generally has been less successful than human activity itself.

In the deferred action scheme specification design is to create architecture models developed by using specification formalism to cater for the structure element of SEST. Deferment design is the creation of models of deferred action developed by using deferment formalism to cater for emergence, space and time elements of SEST. The combined models form the TSA. Reflective designers design its architecture. Action designers design its operational functionality as deferred design.

Specification formalism and deferment formalism

Two issues arise in determining appropriate formalism. One is how organized action is characterized. Organization and systems designers draw on anthropological, sociological, cognitive, engineering and organizational characterizations to determine relevant designs. They can be descriptive as in some anthropological studies or explanatory as in cognitive studies. Social scientists' problematization or 'accounts' of social action and organization are different from computer scientists' and IS designers 'problem definitions' of systems designs that interface with humans in organization.

The other issue is how formalism itself ought to be conceived. Some formalism derives from mathematical formal systems and engineering design. Its form is deductive logic deployed deductively to derive a solution. Discrete mathematics and logics is basis of much specification formalism and formal methods for systems design. This kind of formalism and its notation languages is termed specification formalism. Specification formalism is an abstract set of representation symbols for deductive design that results in determinism because it seeks to specify reality by complete representation of design domains but remains detached from actuality. It contains symbols to represent design domains by one-to-one correspondence of structure, functions and dynamics and set of rules to apply and manipulate the symbols. Some kinds of specification formalism can be applied to organization design too. For example, declarative logic is applied to managerial decision-making and even rigorous formal methods like Z can be used to model organization. In general, formalism for organization design is non-mathematical and includes verbal formalisms like 'hierarchy', 'network' and 'business process'.

Deferred action design requires two types of knowledge to act. Organized action design where design knowledge is explicit, requisite knowledge to act is available. Knowledge of purpose, outcomes and how to achieve them is available and can be stated formally. Such organized action design is possible with specification formalism. The other is design knowledge of some understanding of purpose, an idea of the expected outcomes and some idea of how to achieve them. Design knowledge cannot be stated formally, requisite knowledge to act by specification is not sufficient. Knowledge of purpose, outcomes and how to achieve them is vague and ambiguous. Design for such situations is possible with deferment formalism. Deferment formalism seeks representation symbols for abductive and deductive design that facilitates free will by catering for actualities of fields of action by inter-relation design of actual action. It concurs with realism and reflects empirical observation of actual organized activity.

Organization and systems are designed artefacts that interrelate with social action and which requires synthesis specification and deferment formalisms. In general any artefact that has social action as its fields of action needs to interrelate with it and requires this synthesis. Organized action design and supporting systems is an example. Many organizational problems, especially in business, are better represented using this synthesis.

Deferred action design focuses on actual organized activity and its interrelation with design. Since complete knowledge of actual activity to inform design is not possible actual activity should be incorporated as a design parameter – the emergence, space and time SEST properties. This may be thought of in terms of parameterized functions in programming languages, where the function behaves according to the parameters passed to it. Alternatively as an object's service behaviour according to the messages it receives. Any formal design is similarly affected by unpredictable actual action.

In realism terms specification formalism is poorer than deferment formalism for addressing design issues in domain of empirical. Domain of empirical is where business workers experience interrelation between design and work. Since deferment formalism permits action designers to design operational functionality it is better suited than specification formalism for actual situations.

Formalism should maintain an active link with design domains where necessary. Whereas some specification formalism caters for structure and time well it does not maintain an active link. Its focus is on formal models or formal systems. Deferment formalism caters for SEST by maintaining an active link with design domains. Its focus is on active models or active systems.

SEST design

Action is a manifestation of SEST which is composed of SEST properties. It can be shown to have SEST properties with appropriate analytical tools. Organized action is a manifestation of SEST interrelations. In natural design, action itself is not important but how it interrelates with other things in fields of action is significant. Organized action results in formalism to structure action, it generates responses to emergence, results from spatial environment and it is time-specific.

The problem for design is to represent actuality and maintain an active link with design domains. Actuality can be represented as SEST design objects with resultant design being active systems or organization. Successful design depends on how well SEST interrelates internally and externally in the field of action. In set theoretic terms the relevance of design is determined by the $x \mapsto y$ relation.

Representing structure of action is the strength of specification formalism. As it does not recognize the other SEST properties it frames the design domain as a problem in structural representation. It therefore unwittingly intertwines architectural and operational functionality in structural terms. Its notation language symbols are invented to capture structural properties well. It is capable of intricate elaboration of structure in designs. Specification formalism does not recognize the emergence, space and time SEST properties of action so it has no symbols to represent it. Deferment formalism recognizes them as an inherent quality of organized activity it draws on this capability to specify TSA.

Physical space is accounted for in deferment formalism but not in specification formalism. Like information space has artefactual property. Specification formalism ignores actual space and its affect on action. It contains no direct or indirect symbols to represent space. Space affects organized activity. Certain types of work are enhanced by design of specific physical space. Knowledge work requires open space conducive to communication whilst production work can be compartmentalized. Deferment formalism is concerned with space and time and how they affect action and how designed artefact interrelates with it.

An artefactual relationship exists between space and time and human activity. Time is invented to initiate and organize human activity. Invention of the steam engine required re-designing time in which local regional time was re-designed to provide common national time to allow train timetables to be complied. Perception of time in design varies depending on human activity and machines. It varies according to the need to make design decisions concerning organization. In the case of organized action the need depends on actual action. In the case of machines it depends on its operational state.

IT is having similar affect on human activity. Synchronous and asynchronous digital communication determines how humans conceptualize and perceive time. It influences organizational and collaborative work. In deferred action time is a product of interrelations between design, emergence and deferred action. It is classified as deferred-time, real-time, present-historic time and autonomous time for systems design. They can be applied to organization design too.

Deferred-time is movement, ongoing design activity relative to temporal location of creation of an original design it and time are not fixed. Aspects of original design, particularly operational functionality design which may include systems architecture, are deferred. Deferred-time is deferred relative to present-historic time of reflective design, which itself suggests that design has to be concurrent with action.

Deferred-time is relevant for action designers and is relative to design decisions of reflective designers. It describes situations where action designers design operational functionality during actual action. Deferred-time design is different from real-time design. Action designers' deferred-time design decisions may not necessarily be implemented in real-time.

Deferred-time is used in high-level model-driven systems architecture to defer technical implementation decisions. It is prevalent in hardware where it is used in procedure call for memory interrupts and memory management. Another example is in software where scripting results in deferred execution of installation action. At conceptual level deferred-time is used in Model-Driven Architecture, an initiative of the Object Management Group. Rather then reuse code systems architecture is composed on ready-made models that can be combined and decisions on actual implementation deferred until the composition is complete. It is used in image processing systems to enable images to work in real-time or deferred-time.

In real-time a distinction is necessary between real-time operation and real-time design, implementation and operation. Real-time describes situations where operation of a system and organized activity are congruent. This is real-time operation of systems. An example of real-time operation of designed systems is air traffic control systems. The system reflects actual situations.

Operation of a system may include further design that is implemented in real-time. An example of real-time design, implementation and operation is modern military networked systems. These systems are designed to implement action designers' design decisions in real-time to deliver new information for operational action. Such real-time design and implementation distinguishes real-time systems from deferred systems whose deferred design may not be implemented in real-time. Deferment formalism is needed to represent deferred-time and real-time in systems.

Present-historic time describes situations where the act of designing systems is detached from the action in which systems will be used. So design precedes the action of usage in actual situations. An example is the requirement to convert pound sterling into euros in a financial system. Its operation after implementation is then expected to be relevant even though pound sterling may be replaced by the euro. Design domain representation by specification formalism results in present-historic time in systems.

Autonomous time is prevalent in intelligent and multi-agent systems. It is used when decisions about system states are made by intelligent agents, the system itself, or autonomously in the absence of human intervention. Autonomous time is used in multi-agent systems, distributed sensor networks to enable machines to coordinate network nodes based on correct time in a particular node, and in multimedia systems, particularly movies.

PASADA

Planned action, situated action and deferred action (PASADA initial letters of the three terms) are pertinent characterizations of social action. Design formalism is derived from them they inform invention of formalism and conceptions of organization and systems design. They variously combine natural or intuitive design and rational design. Each is the dominant logic in certain formalism and design approaches. Planned action tends towards rational formalization of design giving little scope for natural design. Situated action tends towards natural design giving no scope for rational design. Deferred action seeks synthesis of natural design and rational design that interrelates well with actuality. Only deferment formalism combines planned action and deferred action. Planned action and deferred action can be bases for organized action design. Situated action cannot by definition be formalized nevertheless it is used as a formal form for designing. A critical comparative analysis of PASADA is given in Table 3.2. Only pertinent aspects of PASADA are discussed and assessed for its conduciveness for design in terms of SEST in following sections.

Planned action

Plan is a device to set and achieve specific goals by describing operational details it is interpreted as predictive device. This is termed planned action it prescribes actual action as predetermined moves. The history of public projects has been one of planned action employing systems type-1 to understand policy and administration problems and devise solutions. Planned action dominates design in commercial organizations.

Table 3.2 PASADA

	Planned action	Situated action	Deferred action
Organization	Rationality – goals/plans. Rational design. Standardized acts. Accounts for structure & time but not emergence & space	'Setting', environment is important. Context, Contextual/ Situated acts, emergence, Embodied acts. Accounts for emergence & space but not structure & time.	Unique acts in relation to formal design (goals). Deferment formalism, (plans) emergence (setting) Goals/ plans/context/Social. Accounts for SEST.
	Positivism, Objective/cognizance/ Requires explicit knowledge. Can be formalized.	Phenomenological/Interpretive/ Social/Requires embodied & environmental knowledge. Cannot be formalized.	Realism/real, actual and empirical domains. Requires explicit, tacit, embodied & field of action knowledge. Can be formalized.
	Specification formalism & design includes: Strategic business plan, IT/IS plan, Strategy, Process/ Workflows, Projects. Declarative logics.	Situated formalism & design includes: Frames, Agents, feedback loops, declarative logic.	Deferment formalism & design includes: context-free grammars. Enables emergent strategy/revise strategy as required; Enable emergent plans/incorporate contingencies. Stopping failing projects is legitimate. Abductive & declarative logic.

Table 3.2 PASADA – *continued*

	Planned action	Situated action	Deferred action
Systems	Human-Computer Interaction. Specification & predetermined algorithms	Embodied Interaction. Specified algorithms with sufficient detail of environment & feedback.	Embodied Patterned Interaction. Deferred Design Decisions. Deferred algorithms; Ttools.
	Objectivity: System design based on explicit knowledge	Interpretive: System design based on embodied knowledge.	Realism: System design based on explicit, tacit, embodied & emergent knowledge. Driven by causal powers.
	Specification formalism includes: Z, E-R models, DFD. Examples: IS, KMS, DSS.	Specification formalism & design includes: Frames. Example: Intelligent agents.	Specification formalism & deferment formalism includes: deferred objects, HTTP. Example: Web, Spreadsheets.
Pertinent Differentials	Design focus on internal state space, finite states, requires explicit knowledge to design.	Design focus on setting, depends on embodied & environmental knowledge & enables its use.	Design focus on synthesis of actual action with design. Internal state & field of action are intertwined. Enables explicit, tacit, emergent & field of action knowledge.
	Rational design, specification formalism, specified models, strategy inter alia can only be designed if explicit knowledge is available. Lacks sustainability because plans/designs lose relevance in actual context.	Situated action negates planned action & formalism. Coupled with context but has no account of endurable structures, so it lacks sustainability.	Duplex design domain. Actual action is conceived to work with design. Conducive to context & sustainability because of duplex design domain.

Its basis is Aristotelian empirical rationalism, epitomized in Cartesian constructs of rationality and reductionism, so it draws on cognitive science. It characterizes organized action exclusively as rational act and is logically connected to specification formalism. Action is characterized as rational therefore objective, purposeful and intentional. It is useful for design problems that can be well structured like logistics or inventory in organization design and algorithms in systems design.

Planned action entities are formal and knowable and manipulated to achieve objectives. Planning creates new objectives, structures and means to achieve objectives. Design theory and practice based on it results in specification formalism. Design is temporally constrained and based on formalism devised to specify representations of actual entities, relations between them and operations. Consequently, complicated representations of design domain are created. Planned action serves rational evaluation of action. Explicit specified design is easier to evaluate than actual organization where no evaluative markers are laid.

Much organization and systems design is based on planned action. Its units of analysis are concrete objects. Design results in intricate detailed specification of internal states of planned entities. Organization design results in intricate plans and systems design results in intricate systems models. In organization design planned action entities manifest as strategy, plans, policy, business process and decision-making processes. They include making mission statements and devising strategy and plans to realize the mission. In planning actual objects are identified and manipulated to achieve objectives. Planned action is the basis for inventing verbal formalism used to formulate business strategy and plans, and it is used to plan IT and IS requirements. Such design requires explicit knowledge of current situations and conditions, future desired outcomes and the means to achieve them.

In systems design planned action is used to invent specification formalism to model internal states of systems. Planned action entities manifest as specification formalism, formal methods, software algorithms, systems models, IS methodologies and project management. IS methodologies assume planned action is efficacious. Explicit knowledge of artefact to be designed is necessary in systems design based on planned action, or in XP terms 'planned design'.

'The map is not the territory' is a concise critique of planned action. It accounts for structure but not other SEST properties. Design based on planned action cannot cater for events and structures needed in context or that emerge such design is not sustainable. It limits business workers' action. Since they are required to act in accordance with prescribed action and to relate actual events to plans they are unable to respond to emergent and contextual events by natural design manifesting as actual action.

Design is not sustainable because it and the specification formalism used loses relevance in context (space) and over time. Planned action is described as 'disembodied action' that does not account for richness of being, intuition, tacit knowledge or the setting things that are well represented by natural design. The plan for ARPANET (precursor of internet) was to allow researchers to share computing power to do research, but in actuality communication through email was key benefit.

There are a number of problematical assumptions with plans and planning. Planning assumes that planners have explicit knowledge of objectives, processes and required outcomes, and that perfect information is available to plan and execute it. It assumes stable future in which plan can be executed to realize predicted future outcomes. It assumes stable or frozen actuality. It implicitly assumes context or actuality has no relevance to attainment of objectives. These assumptions are problematical in practice.

Situated action

Situated action units of analysis are setting, environment and actors in it. Analysis concerns relationship between setting and how actors determine a course of action in it in response to events. Situated action accounts for action in settings or the situation in which it happens, hence accounting for the 'territory' or environment where planned action fails. It is useful for design problems that are semi-structured like mergers and acquisitions or interface design and AI systems. Action determined in settings is termed situated action.

Its characterization of human action is based on philosophical argument and ethnomethodological research. Heideggerian phenomenological situatedness accounts for action in terms of action itself, its context and emotional conditions. Unlike planned action in situated action intention cannot be explicated in terms of rules, procedures or plans because it is informed by settings. So it results in embodied action and leads to subjective conceptions of context, though objective conceptions are possible. In this sense similar to deferred action it is actual action.

In organization design situatedness is useful for recognizing contingent factors and create interactional devices for actual situations, though there is no non-trivial organization design based on situated action. Systems designers deploy situatedness to design HCI and 'situated systems' that 'participate' in the setting of interactions between humans and systems. In AI planned action is used as a resource but situated action is deployed to respond to environment. Intelligent agents are designed to draw on knowledge of environment to justify action choices. Some writers argue that 'situated action' in systems design is inconsistent because it lacks account of Heideggerian emotional condition of humans.

Situated action is strong at representing emergence, space and time SEST properties. Its focus on setting does this well. Situated action is problematical for design theory. It has no theoretical construct to represent structure SEST property inherent in natural design. It lacks theoretical account of two aspects of natural design. One it does not explain where and how action originates it lacks account of intention. Any design has to originate somewhere be intentional. The other is structure itself. It does not explain how 'enduring social organization' or structure is created, maintained and even enhanced. It is unable to explain how a setting is initially created and maintained. So situated action results in the undesirable negation of specification formalism. Since settings are found situated action is deterministic and no structure can be specified to create settings. The setting itself cannot be created. This is contrary to natural design and all rational design in which the primary act of design is the act of creating the setting by specifying structure. So not so ironically design based on situated action results in specification formalism that seeks to make rules explicit.

Pertinent for design theory is that situatedness affords no synthesis of acts of creating something artificial, rational acts, and settings that shape action. Since situatedness is naturally occurring it is difficult to reconcile with Simonion artificial design. It is unable to reconcile rational action, which motivates designing, with situated acts that are supposedly natural. This is logical contradiction of creating formalisms and designing for situated or embodied interaction. So theoretically no symbols can be invented to model structure. Though it does not preclude invention of situated formalism as seen mainly in intelligent agents research.

Phenomenological interactivity studies recognize experiential action but unlike deferred action there is no explicit recognition of 'users' as potential designers (action designers). Agile systems development and eXtreme programming focus on importance of 'users' but do not construct them as designers. Its systems ontology assumes assignment of specified design to actuality. They do not recognize designing for and in actuality. In recent studies of organization analytical subjects have been organizational members rather than some abstract 'organization'. Management researchers focus on 'stories', 'autobiographies' and 'narratives' of managers. In organization design and systems design the focus is shifting from 'form' to 'context' and from 'figure' to 'ground'. It is this context and ground that specification formalism neglects by not accounting for emergence, space and time that deferred action seeks to redress.

Deferred action

Since deferred action is constructed from natural design it caters for complete SEST. Its characterization of organized action reconciles diametrically opposed planned action and situated action in terms of SEST. It caters for structural properties of action necessary to account for intention and pursue formal objectives and emergent, spatial and temporal properties inherent in actively responding to actuality. Its core unit of analysis is SEST to design for actual organized action in context.

Deferred action is distinct from planned action and situated action. Deferred action is actual action that is simultaneously structured, emergent and spatially and temporally contextual. Therefore it caters for uncertainty and risk inherent in natural design. It synthesizes specification formalism and deferment formalism. It is useful for design problems that are structured, semi-structured or unstructurable like organizational knowledge management or networked collaborative work.

Deferred action is a paradox of formal and actual, certain and uncertain, structured and emergent, and known and unknown. It seeks working design synthesis of formalism and actuality. The 'formal informal' category created to explain lack of planned action success is not needed in deferred action. Deferred action is the so-called informal but formally recognized. Ironically, significant examples of deferred action are abandoned plans, failed projects, and ineffective system designs. Cases in which planned action fails but actual activity continues to strive towards its goal in spite of design. Trivial examples are the non-use of a KMS when it does not cater for the situation and the use of other means, or completing a hand-written sales receipt when an item is not found on an electronic point of sales system. Cases where business workers aim to achieve objectives or complete tasks despite design. Natural design supersedes rational design.

Deferred action design is enablement of actual action within formal, predetermined structures intentionally designed to achieve formal objectives. Its focus is interrelation between design and actual action. Unlike planned action deferred action does not leave actual action unaccounted. Deferred action is proposed as an intrinsic and integral aspect of invention of formalism for and rational design of organized action. It differs from situated action because it proposes that rules and procedures can be stated to design tailorable structures for actual action to pursue formal objectives. It explains how action originates by reference to abductive reasoning inherent in natural design.

In deferred action design structure is designed by synthesizing specification and deferment formalisms. Unlike situated action deferred action does not leave structure unaccounted. Structure, organization structure for organization design and systems architecture for systems design, is deliberate creation arising from intention and shaped to achieve formal objectives. Consistent with natural design structure is tailorable in response to actuality. Deferred action design is a synthesis of predetermined moves and actual action in context. Deferred action is a synthesis of rational design and natural design.

In organization design strategy is structure in systems design which is systems architecture. Deferred action systems design is a duplex design process consisting of specified TSA design and deferred objects design. Examples of deferred systemic objects are deferred-action-list and deferred-action function in emacs. The deferred action theoretical constructs TSA, S-SEI and DDD are sufficient for design to respond to fields of action in terms of SEST. There is no need to design complete representation of the design domain as in planned action and setting as in situated action.

Deferred action differs theoretically from planned action and situated action. Deferred action is synthesis of rational action (planned action, formalism) and actuality (context, setting, actual action). It combines rational design with natural design (actuality). Planned action excludes actuality. Deferred action is synthesis of knowable 'rules and procedures' and actuality to design ways of achieving objectives in context. Situated action assumes that rules and procedures cannot be explicated.

Deferred actors can give an account of action because it can be related to rational action however minimal. Actual action in deferred action bears semantic coherence with planned action. Situated actors cannot give similar accounts. Since action happens in context it cannot be predetermined rendering situated actors incapable of explaining courses of action.

Deferred action is predicated on structure (planned action) so it does not admit 'self-organization' or 'autopoietic systems', or similar conceptualizations that have potential to compromise purpose and formal objectives of design. Planned action precludes self-organization but autonomous behaviour and emergence within the designed system is permissible.

Natural design, organization and systems

Designers' problem is to devise SEST design constructs for organized action design. They base designs on one or more SEST properties of PASADA characterizations of action. This characterization is an explanation of natural (social) action. An alternative explanation is action as objectifiable that results in think and act sequence or as integral to practice that results in act and think circularity. Is all organized action an object 'disembodied' action composed of think and act sequence or is there scope for phenomenological 'embodied' action composed of act and think circularity?

Deferred action facilitates both ways of acting. Before acting it is necessary to create structures to enable acting. Humans do not simply spontaneously act. To practise medicine it is necessary to create the structure of a 'doctor', the 'sick' and 'medicine'. To practise management the structure of 'manager', 'aims', 'employees' and 'resources' is necessary. This answers how 'setting' or 'situation' arise and leads to the synthesis of rational design: think and act is characteristic of reflective designers and act and think is characteristic of action designers.

Paradigm case for rational design is think and act sequence. It is characteristic of planned action and results in specification formalism and specification design. Thinking about acting is detached from doing it. Consequently planned action is sequential. Reflective organization designers adopt it to determine mission statements, design business strategy, and devise operational plans. In designing organization to manage knowledge processes of knowledge generation and communication are assumed to be knowable. Reflective systems designers adopt it too. In designing KMS they assume explicit knowledge of operational requirements, availability of design information, stability (present and future), and relatively predictable future. So resulting in specified systems that are detached from the act of using them.

Think and act design strategy is problematical because social action manifested as organized action cannot be theorized, modelled or characterized in its every actual detail. Design theory and principles that advocate complete specification of requirements before designing that result in prescribed action are unsatisfactory for situations where design is interrelated with actuality, and where actuality (natural design) is often superior to designed action (rational design). In such situations it is not feasible to compile complete specification of operational functionality. Operational functionality, at least, needs to be deferred and it is a consequence of emergence, space and time SEST properties.

The alternative act and think circularity strategy or 'practice' compensates for limitations of think and act strategy. Thinking of how to act is simultaneous with action. Action is engaged and involved and reflection is imperceptibly intertwined. It is more descriptive of natural design and gives rise to deferred action and deferment formalism in rational design.

Reflective designers adopt it for organization design. In designing organization to manage knowledge they assume knowledge has emergent properties and design spatially and temporally related communities of practice rather than only structures. In systems design the design process has SEST properties, making act and think a better strategy for designing. Reflective designers in agile systems development adopt the act and think strategy they assume that design knowledge is emergent and embedded in business workers.

Emergence is acknowledged as a 'significant feature' of practice in creative design. Though creativity does not feature high in organization and systems design approaches it is acknowledged in the theory of deferred action and its consequent design constructs. Emergence characterizing deferred action applies to action designers whose design of operational functionality features responses to emergent events uniquely located spatially and temporally.

Reflective designers of deferred and real systems defer design of operational functionality and even structure to action designers. Similar to agile systems developers and reflective of natural design, for action designers design can be thought of as engaging with required action and simultaneously during action thinking what needs to be designed to achieve objectives. As in the practice of designing a negotiation strategy there is tacit knowledge, uncertainty, change (present and future), and complex relationships that can be facilitated by engaging with situations and formulating deferred design during action.

4
Theory of Deferred Action

Introduction

Descriptions of organized action as 'complex', 'problematical', or 'difficult' are reasons for breaking ranks from intellectual traditions to seek further and deeper. They contribute peripherally to knowledge and understanding of design. Theorists should develop theoretical knowledge of the act of design to inform invention of formalism and practice of design, predict or anticipate designed artefacts in social action and detail appropriate epistemology. They should explain formalism, its representational capacity, how it works in actuality, and how it can cater for organization and systems designs for actuality.

The theory of deferred action explains designing and usage of designed artefact in actuality. Usage in actuality is critical. Design of organization and systems is unique because it is created to alter or affect existing reality where new design intrinsically invokes change and seeks membership. Placing design in reality makes usage study critical. So a core premise is that actual action is superior to design, natural design is superior to rational design.

Deferred action explains natural design in context of rational design. It explicates relationships between rational design and requisite deferment formalism, emergent organization, and deferred action to enable natural design where appropriate. It is a metatheory of design – a theory of theories of design – as it includes extant theoretical constructs and empirical knowledge. It addresses the theoretical problem of synthesizing formalism with actual organized action and the operative power set in the theory (its subset is social action, itself a subset of human actuality, itself a subset of natural design) in terms of systems theoretic. It explains how formal design can work in actuality.

Its scope of analysis covers systems strategy, organization and systems design and systems management. It explains systems strategy in systemic terms rather than current references to management theory and frameworks. Deferred action overcomes limitations of classical rational design, from 1900 to 1990, when internet and Web radically redefined design, organizations and systems.

Designs, design practice and limitations of specification design are addressed by proposing a synthesis of extant design knowledge with the theoretical construct of deferred action. Rather than propose one type of organization or systems design taxonomy of types is created based on deferred action. Each type requires dedicated organization and systems strategy, design, and management approach. Specification design suits some types but not others. An organization may have a combination of types to account for different work required to achieve objectives.

Metatheory serves two purposes. It elaborates a set of ontological entities necessary to explain the phenomenon of design and provides epistemological methodology to develop knowledge of it. Two, it clarifies relationships between different perspectives of organization designers and systems designers by providing logical and consistent synthesized frame of the ontological entities. It organizes theoretically different perspectives on design by specifying their individual domains of application. (Tsoukas, 2000).

The theory elaborates possible design and its outcomes. It defines design, designers, and creates and demarcates roles in design process for professional designers and business workers. It explains interrelation between organization design and systems design and proposes appropriate design solutions. Extant separate theories of organization and systems are of limited use to design because they address only discipline related interests. Deferred action applies to organization and systems design because it is constructed from natural design relevant to both. It addresses how to characterize cohered interrelation useful to design, details kinds of design problems and suggests appropriate models of organization and systems.

The theory broadens design to overcome its present specification design constraint. It explains how natural design can be translated into rational design as a synthesis of formal design and actuality. It is a framework to develop knowledge of how to make formalism and organized actuality co-exist. The key is to determine synthesis design of structure to achieve formal objectives and catering for actuality. It requires sophisticated and, ironically, simple synthesis of formalism and actual action. A significant contribution of the theory is deferment formalism proposition to enable creation of designs that are well placed in actuality.

The problem of design is one of synthesizing conditions. Design has to cater for organized action, acknowledge existing reality and cater for actuality and action subsequent to design placement in fields of action. Such organization and its systems cannot be explicated in sufficient detail by specification design. Deferred action addresses design details the actuality of action that cannot be specified by synthesizing it with rational design. It concerns interrelating design with actuality. Deferred action is the explicit recognition of this interrelation as 'equivocal reality'. Individuals are independent actors more capable than any design by specification to achieve aims. All design therefore should enable deferred action. Any specified design imposed on humans and organized action ultimately fails. Theoretical constructs to enable designing for actuality stem from deferred action. General applicability and qualifications need to be considered for particular design domains.

Understanding individual and social action in organized activity is necessary to devise formalism for design. Deferred action applies to organization and systems design. It is the primary unit of analysis capable of representing the space of natural design to develop active models. Its understanding improves invention of formalism. It enables theoretical analysis of design problems in terms of natural design by accepting superiority of natural design in all cases and devising mechanisms to enable it in actuality. Other researchers can analyse or research empirically its theoretical constructs and design constructs.

Herbert Simon locates 'means' for achieving goals empirically, in deferred action terms in the space of natural design. He keeps state space design separate and proposes 'satisficing' as an alternative to unbounded rational design. So means-ends analysis does not explain how empirical means employed in actuality can be included in design. The 'means' devised to achieve objectives in the thesis of deferred action is constructed as deferred action within formal design not separate from it. Simonian 'means' is deferred action as facilitated in design through deferred design, itself one aspect of a duplex design process proposed by the theory. Similarly, 'discovery' is deferred action with the radical difference that deferred action results in deferred design a critical element of formal design. It requires inventing deferment formalism to incorporate the 'means' or deferred action in formal design.

Deferred action design does not exclude rational design. It facilitates natural design. Deferred action is natural response in context by individuals, groups or organization to emergence. Deferred action through deferred design permits the space of natural design to be addressed in organizational and systemic terms. Its ontology is actual action within formal design. Deferred action, DDD and S-SEI explain how to inter-relate formal design with actual organized action. They constitute an active link between rational design and natural design necessary to improve success of formal design. S-SEI enables design to interrelate with actuality or fields of action. This interrelation design is based on the DDD principle. They are sufficient to design for actuality.

Formalism

Formalism is intrinsic to natural design. It is necessary to invent it for rational design. Rational design formalism is the technique for defining structure and representing other SEST properties in design. It is the key to rational design. Designing itself as a rational activity is enabled by formalism. Formalism is necessary to design and to create designs that achieve predetermined objectives. Its rigour clarifies vague human purpose and objectives. How it is conceptualized determine possibil-ities in organized action design and how organized action is conceptu-alized determine kinds of formalism invented. Formalism in turn determines usefulness of design.

SEST

Deferred action design is representation of SEST by rational design for-malism. SEST is necessary and sufficient to represent all social action in any design of organization and systems. Appropriate formalism sym-bols are needed to represent SEST in models. Design for social action can be accomplished with such formalism. Organized action and systems behaviour can be represented as SEST properties.

The theory of deferred action elaborates how to determine the 'shape of design' and define the 'shape and organization of the design process' in terms of SEST. Shape and process are necessary constructs in design theory. SEST is clear recognition of goals and functions. What kinds of design there ought to be and what the appropriate design process for them to 'attain goals' and 'function' is elaborated. Elsewhere this has been set out for deferred systems design type (Patel, 2004).

Parameters of design that synthesize natural design with rational design are formalism (planned action), emergence, deferred action and diffusion management. Synthesized interrelations are depicted in the gDRASS stylized matrix in Figure 4.1. These design parameters are

Figure 4.1 gDRASS matrix design types

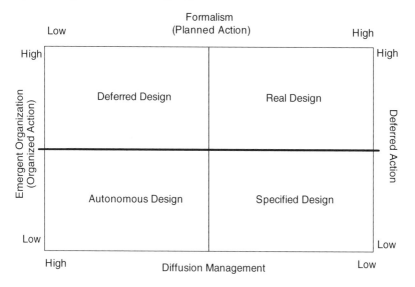

themselves correlated. The synthesis is of their individual causal powers which is sufficiently elaborate to describe organization and systems and can be generalized to design of other social action objects. The taxonomy reveals four types of possible coherent organization and systems design depicted in the quadrants: deferred design, real design, specified design and autonomous design. These are termed deferred action design types or design types. The 'high' and 'low' scale for formalism is better interpreted as specification formalism and deferment formalism respectively in some contexts.

Theorizing rational design for purposeful action where action itself is emergent is depicted in the matrix. It is a four dimensional matrix on three planes: individuals, organization and technology (systems). Its design parameters account for SEST. Structure design for all design types is achieved with specification formalism. For design types above the horizontal line it requires synthesis of specification and deferment formalisms. Emergent organization leads to emergence design accounted for by deferred action that happens in the space of natural design and accounts for space and time.

The matrix depicts theoretical constructs, suggests design principles, and development of appropriate design techniques and tools to engage with each design type. Design parameters synthesize rational intellectual tradition, scientific management and recent emergent organization to provide a plural explanation of design. The matrix can be used to describe, analyse, and explain design and design domains. It enables rich descriptive and analytical basis for design, use and management of organization and systems. Its explanatory power is the result of this synthesis in terms of realism causal powers and in terms of pragmatics of design. Design can be improved by analysing design domains in terms of the design parameters. The design types can be generalized to organization and systems. Work systems design and design in general is better conceived as the various design types that account for SEST variously.

Since the design types stem from empirical organized action they have obvious application for organization design. Analysis of organized action in terms of these design parameters reveals four types of possible deferred action organization design: deferred organization, real organization, specified organization and autonomous organization. An organization can be a particular type. Bureaucracy is specified organization type because it is centrally designed and managed and does not cater for emergence; therefore it does not permit deferred action. It is designed on the premise of planned action so it is high in specification design. Alternatively, organization can contain various design types within it. Its organized activity can be designed differently depending on kinds of work. A manufacturing organization can have sections of specified organization for production work and sections of deferred organization for knowledge intensive innovation work.

The design types are valid for systems design because systems type-3 is inherent to organization design and because such systems interrelate with humans. So analysis of organized activity that needs to interrelate with systems in terms of the design parameters reveals four types of possible systems design: deferred systems design, real systems design, specified systems design and autonomous systems design. Each type is affected by varying levels of emergence and deferred action that determines kinds of formalism required to create effective designs. Each design type requires different formalism to design, account for emergence, its management and interrelations with business workers.

Formalism is constructivist. Similar to axioms in mathematical formal systems it builds systems. An organization and its systems are constructed with formalism (A.A3 in Figure 1.8). Action is actual experience that happens in the empirical world (A.A1). It does not correspond well with designed organizations and systems. Deferred action happens in the empirical world and interrelates with such design. In these terms deferred action is adjustment of the rules of design necessitated by actual experience.

All design is necessarily constructivist. Specified systems design is assigned to the empirical world where actual experience may render it incongruent with required action. Since incongruent systems will not be accepted or work in practice it is necessary to place design in the empirical world or in fields of action and enable people to interrelate with it through deferred action. Deferred action is the necessary synthesis to place design to enable formal design to accord with experienced world. It is continuation of formal design in context.

Situated action intrinsically lacks formalism because it negates any form of predetermined structure. Situated formalism is illogical because it precludes action based on predetermined structures like plans, so it precludes the structure property of SEST. Objectives are set in situated action but contingent conditions determine action. Actuality is central in situated action. Its strength is in representing the emergence, space and time SEST properties. Situated formalism is not appropriate for purposive organization design and systems design because it has no controlling feature or representation of structure to ensure achievement of objectives. The probability of deviation is greater since by acting according to the situation solely a different course is logically possible. Discovering the Americas instead of the Indies! Not the Trukese but Columbus.

Specification formalism

Since design is by specification operational functionality is specified. Specification of functionality results in the assignment problem and disconnects specification design from actuality because actuality is off-design. Actual action, where emergence, space and time SEST properties matter, is not an intrinsic feature and no design schemes or symbols are provided to account for actuality.

Specification formalism results in design that is separated from actuality because it is focused on representation. It abstracts structure and functions as models and assigns modelled design to organized action. Its strength is in representing structure SEST property. It caters for internal digital machine states only and does not seek to represent actuality. Since design is creation it is conscious and rational which manifests as specification. Specification of structure is necessary.

Specification formalism has an unacknowledged component of abductive logic when an initial idea or hypothesis for a particular design is generated. It subsequently focuses on deduction to arrive at a resolution. It severs the connection with actuality after the initial design concept. Since the field of action for any design is composed of SEST with some stable features – structure – and other dynamic features – emergence, space and time – design based on specification only accounts for its structural features.

Deferment formalism

Deferment formalism maintains an active link between design and actuality and in terms of abductive and deductive design. It acknowledges rational design and intrinsically reflects actual action. Its strength is in representing complete SEST. Since formalism is invented and used to create designs to affect an existing reality and needs to perform subsequently in actuality it needs to reflect actual action. Deferment formalism makes actual action a dominant feature in particular for open systems.

Deferred action happens in actual situations relative to design. It is intrinsic to deferment formalism invented to enable actual organized activity. It emphasizes interpretations of business workers (so-called users). It is necessary for systems type-1 and systems type-2 design. In systems type-2, computer hardware and software design reflects deferred action as in some GUI-based operating systems.

Deferred action is necessary for all formalism invented to model organized activity as open systems. Deferment formalism contains interrelation constructs to enable design to interrelate with fields of action. It has symbols to represent objects in fields of action. DDD and S-SEI are interrelation constructs and basis for inventing symbols to represent objects in fields of action. They constitute interrelation design and the active means for representing actuality in design.

Deferment formalism recognizes abductive and deductive logics, but it differs significantly from other formalisms because of its focus on abduction. It enables design to cater for reflective designers and in particular of action designers' abductive logic. Abduction includes heuristics, conjecture, hypotheses, or guesstimates. Abductive reasoning illustrates interrelation between deferment formalism and action in terms of cognition and action. Categories devised to think about things real or creative are representation symbols stating the existence of something. They are formal or axiomatic in the sense of forming basis for action. The initial symbols of abduction to represent empirical things do not themselves exist. They are synthetic. This formal semiotic representation of the real separates the thought from the object by giving it a formal symbol. An example is the IMS Learning Design

Specification (LDS) conceptual model (IMS, 2005). It is a set of UML class models and vocabulary to describe learning pedagogies, represented as learning objects that have SEST properties.

Action is characterized as mind, body, space and time totality. It is unlike Kantian discrete process of sense perception, understanding and reason the final rest. Abduction is intrinsic to natural design proceeding by conjecture, hypothesis or design ideas generated by self. It is naturally occurring in actual action. Deferred action itself may be abductive.

For designers too the design act requires abduction and deduction. Rationality is critical to design but in actuality rational and embodied acts jointly determine design. Abduction begins the design process. It proceeds to deductive reasoning central to the process. Abduction may be likened to heuristics. It provides the creative idea then subjected to deductive reasoning characteristic of specification formalism. If desired outcome is satisfied then no further design is necessary. In its absence further heuristics are employed. Such uncertainty arises because of emergence.

Emergence

Ordering SEST in terms of dominating causal powers results in the order emergence, time, space and structure. Emergence is the governing principle of all natural design. If emergence is the dominant causal power then how is presence of structure to be explained? It is possible because space and time hold structure together but not perpetually. Since space and time also succumb to emergence structure begins to lose consistency. This set of causal power relations is true of rational design, all social action, and organization and systems design. So space and time permit social action that results in some structure. Artefact too becomes relevant by its location in space and time.

Emergence encompasses structure, space and time SEST properties. Emergence is the causal power of actuality and so it affects structure too. It is a feature of physical and social worlds. When two or more entities interrelate the result is an emergent second order entity distinct from its interrelating components. Two business people interrelate to form partnership, supply and demand interrelate to create price, data and algorithm interrelate to create information.

Emergence is a necessary property of all organized action design. It stems from social interactions in physical space and time. It may be organizational, technological or social. Emergence design is based on the knowledge that knowledge and understanding of actual action is incomplete and the future is unpredictable. Emergence in turn necessitates deferred action and deferred action design.

Rational design is not negated by emergence. It is not necessary to replace planned action. In deferment formalism planned action and emergence are interrelated, correlated and co-exist. It enables planned action and deferred action to co-exist with emergence. Deferment design by reflective designers is not design of actual emergence. It is a means to cater for emergence in actuality or fields of action. Design and emergence are synthesized to produce space of organization design where different combinations and synthesis of planned action and deferred action are possible.

Deferred action explains design in context of organizational emergence in which cognizance of purpose and reasoned thought seems unattainable. Characterized as planning in the mess with plans for the mess. The 'mess' is emergent organization. Predetermined purpose and planned action to achieve it encounter emergent factors preventing enactment of design. In this context planned action is supplemented with deferred action – action other than planned action. Deferred action design is capable of functioning in this mess.

Emergence differs from 'complexity', 'uncertainty' and 'change'. Complexity advocates assumes it is possible to design-in complexity, in deferred action complexity is off-design which is part of emergence. Uncertainty is the inherent imperfection of design, or formal system in Gödelian terms. Change can be managed. In deferred action emergence is off-design. It is the core of action and of sociality. Deferred action is the natural and possible positive responses to emergence. So emergence is correlated with action and since such action is permitted within formal design it is deferred action. Emergence cannot be pre-designed by specification which is facilitated and designed as deferred design.

Emergent organization

SEST is the nature of organizations. They have structure but emerge by specific spatial and temporally located actions. It is such actions that lead to notions of organization as 'situated', 'self-organizing' and even 'ephemeral' but misplaced because structure is a necessary property of organization. Organizations appear unmanageable, not designable and complex only because emergence is the dominant property not because they are these things.

Theories of social action and organization with structure as a unit of analysis result in notions of determinacy and inform design as specified design type. They mistake emergence for 'complexity' and 'uncertainty' implying that it can be structured. Much business organization emergence stems from interrelations with competitors' actions, changing markets and economic conditions. Rigid structure is ineffective in such conditions of emergence itself unstructured.

Similarly it is assumed all work is well structured and static. So strategy-making work is designed as planned action and explained in terms of explicative rational thinking. Its organization and the organization to achieve strategic objectives results in specified design type. From discourse analysis executives' stories of strategic moves however reveal emergent strategy and 'strategizing'. Emergence does not negate planned objectives like reducing costs or producing superior products or services, in this sense strategy is deliberate. Intricate plans to achieve such objectives remain largely unrealized in practice because emergence is negated.

In deferred action work itself is constituted as SEST with certain types of work more emergent. Work can be determined as design types. Extant theories of organization do not acknowledge emergent work but research into managing organizational knowledge is making a difference. Knowledge work particularly involving research and industrial innovation has emergence. Organizing for innovation has to necessarily consider emergent nature of innovation and is better organized as deferred design type. It is true of strategy-making.

Emergence of design occurs from interrelations in fields of action. Since any design is placed in an existing reality it has to function by interrelating with things already existing. Reflective designers cannot know specific details of this interrelation which cannot be specified hence it cannot be designed it emerges. This is interrelation design. Transplant surgery is a suitable analogy. Surgeons cannot predict how a transplanted organ will behave. Knowledge of the design only becomes available after it is allowed to interrelate in the host body it emerges. KMS design is not much different.

Business workers' interrelations create emergence. Individuals and groups generate interrelational emergence. Interrelational emergence is characteristic of much organized activity not accounted for in structural or behavioural theories of organization. Specification design is incapable of representing it. Individuals and groups overcome task obstacles not depicted in strategies or plans by interacting to seek resolutions consistent with predetermined objectives.

Emergence results in action that is abductively determined by attaching interpretive labels to emergent experience. It is deferred action when related to predetermined design. Deferred action is not Cartesian cognizant and rational determinate action. It has elements of embodied revelation not apparent during design particularly concerning operational design. It is justifiable in particular physical space and context, subsequently giving rise to emergent or different meaning.

Such 'emergent organization' is acknowledged by researches at IFIP Working Group W8.2 who invoke DSD as 'promising directions' to cope with emergent organization. Truex et al. (2000) propose 'amethodological' systems development for emergent organization. Purao et al. (2003) propose R-Form representation of emergent organization in IS and set out some requirements for inventing representation schemes.

Emergent systems

SEST is the nature of systems too. They have structure but emerge by specific spatial and temporally located actions. It is such actions that lead to notions of systems as 'situated', 'phenomenological' 'complex' 'self-organizing' and 'emergent' but misplaced because structure is a necessary property of systems. Systems appear intractable, not designable and complex only because emergence is the dominant property not because they are these things. Emergent organization requires emergent systems that cohere well with it. Since organizational emergence needs to be reflected in systems three SEST design issues are critical architecture, operational functionality and interrelations.

A defining characteristic of emergent systems is separation of architecture and operational functionality. To cohere with emergent organization structure, or systems architecture, that distinguishes between structural and operational needs is necessary. Systems architecture is designed to deliver purpose for organized action. An extant system that separates the structure SEST property from the remaining properties is the IMS LDS e-Learning system architecture.

Remaining SEST properties concern operational functionality in actuality. Design of emergent systems excludes implementation of operational functionality. Since operational functionality is subject to emergent organizational imperatives it is defined in actuality in emergent systems. Operational functionality is changeable in response to further emergence. Designers devise mechanisms to enable action designers to design operational functionality in fields of action or context and alter it as necessary. The IMS LDS enables intradeferment to allow action designers to determine actual operational functionality contextually.

Interrelations produce emergence. Among individuals and groups emergence is a prime source of awareness of operational needs involving systems. Need for information or knowledge arises from business workers' interrelations with co-workers and business partners and engagement with work. Management's awareness of these operational needs results in initiation of projects to develop systems. Exemplar strategic IS resulted from such emergence of particular operational needs. Attempts to *plan* strategic information systems remain unrealized.

An ethnographic study of systems design work in UK local government revealed emergent, interpretive and contextual domains in scoping and defining an IS development project. This is reflected in a statement made by the project lead officer at an initial meeting:

> ....So (its that) its trying to make sense of work that to take forward, the notes of the meeting reflects the fact we aren't going through what the leader's vision and we are trying to scope some of that work, and I made an attempt at trying to develop a project plan which would tell us that it is that we really needed to do hoping that other people would input to that project plan, but I haven't had any comments from anybody, so, we can go through that today to see if anybody if we could capture all the work that needs to be done... (Verbatim transliteration)

The study concludes 'emergent informational and organizational behaviour that supports the case for deferment.' (Harris and Patel, 2001). It also revealed 'tacit traces' of interaction conceptualized as 'deferment points' developed further by Patel (2005b). Emergence is more important research, innovation and creative knowledge work, such as technological innovation and scientific work. Supporting systems need to cater for human interrelations resulting in interactive emergent needs. Information needs too emerge in the course of individual or group activities.

Patel (2005a: 147) identifies six issues in specification requirements analysis that are problematical for emergent organization abstraction, objectification, specification, engineering, fixing, and replication. When each is pitted against emergent organization it lacks capability to cope. This has an impact on capability of specification formalism to represent emergent organization.

Deferred action

Deferred action results in emergence, space and time SEST properties being represented in formal design, in RSD design type it applies to structural form too. Emergence is the casual power of deferred action. Deferred action formally interrelates emergent actual action with formal design. It is relevant for CSCW and other work involving social settings but applies to individual work too.

Deferred action expresses interrelations between formalism, emergence and action in terms of design. Formalism and emergence are interrelated because formalism needs to account for emergence or actual events. Formalism and deferred action are interrelated because formalism needs to enable deferred action, action required in actuality. Formalism, emergence and deferred action form a complex set of interrelations in which each is affected by the other.

Deferred action is shaped in the context of SEST. Deferred action is active linking of natural design and rational design. Active linking is necessary because rational design is placed in actuality and interrelates with it as deferred action. Deferred action is the interrelation between actuality and design. It interrelates actuality with formal design to produce workable design.

Design that prescribes action, planned action, in an emergent organization is not successful. It is devoid of actuality, space, sociality and organizational factors. Rational design cannot determine emergent action. Deferred action is a response to emergence and it enables emergence to be the subject of design. Since emergence itself cannot be modelled or designed it is reflected in design as deferred design. Models of deferred action can aid design of mechanisms for deferred design.

Deferred action is individual, group or organizational action that interrelates emergence to formal design. It enables design of the interrelation of actual organized action and organized action design as illustrated in Figure 4.1 a richer depiction of the assignment problem in terms of deferred action. It depicts the interrelation between rational (formal) design above the horizontal line and natural (deferred) design below it. Design of structure (planned action or formal design) is depicted at point A, formal space of organization design. Emergence or events arise in the course of time depicted by the right arrow from point A to B. They manifest as actual organized action depicted by spiraling upward arrows at point C. These emergent factors need to be considered to achieve formal goals.

Deferred action is the response to emergent factors which is conceived to achieve organizational goals rationally and to enable task completion. Deferred action seems contrary to designed organizational strategies and processes and systems functionality and interactivity. The deferred action implemented at point A1 is not contrary because it is a response by business workers to actual or contingent conditions that need to be addressed to achieve planned goals. The cycle repeats at point C1 where additional actual conditions need to be considered.

Emergent organization and systems, or richness of actuality, is catered by efficient synthesis of deferred action and deferment formalism. Interrelational organizational emergence is encompassed in design by deferred action. Figure 4.2 shows emerging factors in actual organized action below the horizontal line at C and C1, resulting in deferred action within formal organized action design above the line. This combination of planned and deferred actions or rational and natural design is necessary to cope with interrelational emergence in actual situations. It enables responses to off-design situations. XP illustrates this picture of work which has much deferred activity to reduce risk but XP itself is not illustrative of deferred action design process because it avoids 'Big Up Front Design'.

Affects of formalism on action are determinable. This is true of formal methods for systems design but more difficult to gauge in

Figure 4.2   Planned and deferred action synthesis in organized activity

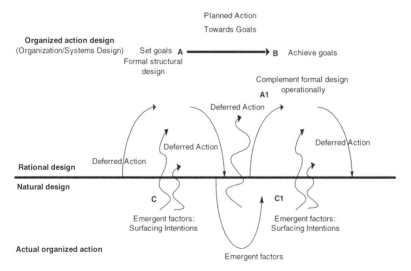

verbal formalism for organization design. Affects of emergence and deferred action are indeterminable. They are unknown quantities at the time of design. Specification formalism cannot be invented to model actual emergence but models of deferred action can be developed and appropriate symbols invented to enable it.

Emergence, space and time or actuality is off-design. In deferment formalism the DDD principle is to cope with actuality. In terms of complexity theory the principle permits designing for 'wholes', 'emergence', 'uncertainty' and 'complexity'. Specification formalism explains away emergence as 'complexity' inherent in 'the environment' borrowing from biological sciences. It does not provide design principles or actual mechanisms to enable design to cope with it.

Heuristics is characteristic of deferred action which is used by business workers. It makes use of tacit knowledge and ad-hoc action stimulated by physical space and contingencies. Heuristics is not considered legitimate action by specification formalism. Deferred action encompasses heuristic and other actions that deviate from planned action but still within formalism in the sense of being designed to achieve set objectives or complete set tasks. At present deferred action is enabled in systems type-2 and it is unwittingly implicit in many extant systems type-3.

Deferred micro-action

Action to obtain objectives is individual and group action or micro-action. Macro-action is mobilization of economic resources to achieve purpose as organized action, as in organization to manufacture or deliver healthcare. Deferred action is intrinsic in both types.

Deferred action synthesizes formal and context elements. It enables action on imperative events that cannot be decided by separation from their space of occurrence, so necessitate contextual decisions. Deferred action enables such micro-decisions. A micro-decision is an event where an individual or group make design decisions in context. Micro-action is the primary source for innovation, change, and improvements in PEE.

Successful organization and systems result from micro-action. The American Hospital Supplies' (now Baxter Inc) order system gave the company strategic advantage; it resulted from micro-action of an individual sales representative. Knowledge workers seek variety and expression which for specification formalism is a source of tension with centrally controlled actions. In deferred action it is a source of success and sustainability.

Deferred design decisions

The representation problem is framed from the perspective of action designers who determine what to design. It concerns how an action designer, or any designer type, comes to know what to design. Charles S. Peirce's semiotic abductive inference principle is relevant to understanding how individuals decide to act and design artefacts to support action. The logical conclusion of Peirce's abduction is that there is no final design. This justifies the DDD principle. It separates design activity between reflective and action designers.

Peirce argued that individuals have a 'prepared mind' that is receptive to emerging signs representative of the object of preparation. It is on this representation of the world that 'purposive action' is based. As the object is information or knowledge in organizational work the mind of action designers is more prepared to allow emergent signs representative of its need. They then determine purposive action based on this abductive representation. Since reflective designers cannot know what the object of preparation will be they are unable to represent it. Action designers themselves only know it in actuality through abductive inference, so they are better placed to represent it through DDD as deferred design.

Specification formalism represents design domains comprehensively and as 'optimal solution'. Such computational representation of organized action is problematical. Richer representations can only be gained at greater costs and additional computational intractability. An example is implementation intractability with Bayes Theorem in autonomous systems.

'Capturing' kinds of representation is not necessary if deferred action is acknowledged. To avoid computational complexity systems that enable deferred design are necessary. DDD can be implemented as an interpretive and instrumental mechanism. Necessary action that is not reflected or enabled by specification design can still become part of design through DDD.

DDD principle suggests invention of appropriate design constructs and symbols in deferment formalism. It avoids complex representational problems. It is crystallization of previous researches that investigated systems development. Its latest application was to identify deferred action in knowledge work and determine systemic deferment points (SDP) to design KMS. It rightly gives action designers responsibility for determining representation and so overcomes the assignment problem. Reflective designers' task is to design TSA and to find atomic SDP and represent them as SDO to enable deferred design.

Layers of deferment

Deferred action is characteristic of reflective and action designers. Deferment formalism consists of layers of deferment relevant to each designer type. Since deferred action is natural to all work (action) it applies to design work of reflective designers. Reflective designers have recourse to deferred action too as formally recognized in XP. In deferred action design reflective designers themselves intradefer design.

In intradeferment reflective designers design structure that caters for emergence, space and time SEST properties for professional systems designers (other reflective designers who act as action designers). They create deferrable technologies and systems architecture depicted as Layers 0–3 in Figure 4.3, each layer depicting distinct types of design activity. Examples are software components, patterns or the LDS architecture. In extradeferment reflective designers create deferrable technologies, systems architecture and DDD mechanisms for business workers (who act as action designers), depicted as Layers 4–7. Action designers respond to emergence with deferred action at various layers of sophisticated deferred design. Examples are macros and spreadsheet. In the final column Web and internet design illustrate the scheme.

Figure 4.3 Layers of deferment

Designer Type	Layers	SEST Property	Design Activity	Illustration: internet and Web
Action Designers Deferred design; Extradeferment	7	Emergence, Space & Time — E - problem solving	Design deferred systems architecture	Real-time 'on-the-edge of network' internet networking
	6		Design deferred operational functionality	XML Schemas Rich Site Summary (RSS)
	5		Design & implement deferred systems models	Content management system
	4		Deploy Ttool	Develop Website; get IP address
Reflective Designers TSA design ; Ttools design Intradeferment	3	Structure — S - problem solving	Design Ttools	XHTML; CSS; DTD; XML; XML Vocabularies; JavaScript; IP/TCP
	2		Design Tailorable systems architecture (TSA)	World Wide Web, internet
	1		Systems analysis and design; Modelling	-
	0		Invent deferment formalism, programming & scripting languages	SGML, HTTP; Java

In systems design deferred action is multi-layered. Intradeferment Layers 0–3 depict structural design and concern design of systems architecture. They cover the structure SEST property. At Layer 0 deferment formalism and associated deferrable technologies are invented. At Layer 1 it is deployed to design TSA based on systems models, including deferred action systems models, developed at Layer 2. At Layer 3 integral Tailoring Tools (Ttools) are developed for action designers to use in extradeferment layers.

Extradeferment Layers 4–7 depicts deferred design and concern design of operational functionality. They cover emergence, space and time SEST properties. Action designers using Ttools designed by reflective designers do deferred design. Ttools correspond to tailoring types micro-, meso- and macro-tailoring (borrowing socio-technical systems terminology to describe individual, organization and societal actions respectively). Layers 4–7 are differentiated by degrees of sophisticated operational functionality design undertaken by action designers. Simplest DDD by action designers is at Layer 4 where available micro-Ttools are deployed to create deferred design. Sophisticated action designers can create proprietary Ttools at Layer 5. They make DDD on contextual and emergent functionality at Layer 6 and DDD on emergent systems architecture at Layer 7.

Deferment layers correspond to systems architectural design. Layers 0–3 depict specified structural design by reflective designers, where deferrable technologies are invented and where core TSA is modelled and designed. Meso-Ttools design maybe specifically for a TSA or generic. The spreadsheet's formula bar is an example of the former and the Webs XML an example of the latter. Layers 4–7 depict emergence deferred design by action designers, where operational functionality, and in military cases systems architecture, takes shape in response to actuality and physical space of organized activity experienced by action designers.

Deferment formalism, intradeferment and extradeferment are used in practice. Internet and Web in Figure 4.3 illustrate layers of deferment. They provide all tailoring types including macro-Ttools. Reading up the final column Layers 0–3 exemplify development of structure with deferrable technologies and TSA through intradeferment by reflective developers of the Web. Application development reflecting emergence, space and time is by skilled action designers at layers 4–7 through extradeferment.

Deferment layers distinguish reflective and action designers' problem solving. Implicit in specification formalism is the assumption that design problem is solved only once by developers at the inception of a system. Deferred action design divides problems into two types according to SEST origin and frames problem solving itself as recurring in design which is not discrete. Problems are intrinsic to organized action.

Deferred action separates Newell and Simon's (1972) 'problem space' into S-problem solving (SPS) and E-problem solving (EPS). Both have elements of interpretation and construction but in different problem contexts. SPS concerns structural design at Layers 0–3 which occurs in rational design as specification design. Any design requires structure. Framing the problem of structural design and its resolution is SPS. EPS concerns emergent design at Layers 4–7 which occurs in deferred design but as an aspect of natural design reflecting emergence, space and time. Any structural design requires operational functionality design, the framing of operational functionality problems and its resolution is EPS. A flaw in specification formalism is that SPS is assumed to be minus EPS. Deferred action design maintains an element of SPS in EPS, since design by rational choice (SPS) is a prime feature of actual organization activity. In terms of natural design since structural design is continuous its design needs to be open to EPS too.

Distinguishing between SPS and EPS is not unreasonable if we accept that all design is based on designing for situations and available requisite information and knowledge of what to design and how to design. Situations and information are not limited to 'requirements analysis' of specification formalism. For information and knowledge design such situations and information is experienced only in actuality where action happens. Open source recognizes EPS. RENISYS method, other Language/Action methods too, recognize EPS by enabling 'users who have become aware of a problem' to specify 'problematic *knowledge definitions*.' (de Moor, 2002 original italics). However, it is rooted in specification design.

Active tools and Ttools

It is too simplistic to think of systems as tools but appropriate where a tool does not interrelate with its user, though it is difficult to identify such tools. Philosophically, a tool tells its user whether operation is successful and, critically, whether objective is achievable. In terms of realism, action designers in domain of empirical experience systems exist only for the observer. So deferred action design is conceptualized as existing for the observer in actuality. In this sense systems simultaneously contribute to shaping purpose and achieving it they are active in the action. This conceptualization is true of IS and KMS because they themselves provide processed information and knowledge critical for determining purpose and organizing to achieve it.

Deferred design definition of a tool is that it is active in shaping the action in which it is an implement, termed active tools. Action and tools determine purpose and are intertwined to produce desired outcomes. Action drives design of tools and tools drive action simultaneously. Tools are capable of telling us about performance of action and also provide feedback to tool users. It tells about the effectiveness of action, and if designed well, can give information on how efficiently action is unfolding. Systems as active tools cannot be designed separately from the activity they generate and foster. Operational design divorced from actuality temporally lose relevance. This is the recurring problem with specification formalism.

In deferred action design systems type-3 are designed as active tools. This is consistent with using active models to design TSA and logically consistent with organized action characterized as synthesis of planned and deferred actions. This has significant implication for conceptualizing design process in terms of three design domains which are natural, rational and deferred with the latter synthesizing the former two. It is a continuous process, existing prior to rational choice to design, in natural design domain. After the choice to design rationally and the system going live, it is a rational process in rational design domain. When the design is placed in fields of action or actuality it is a deferred process in deferred design domain.

DDD principle and Ttools activate systems. Ttools are active because they enable innovation, collaboration and flexibility to be reflected in systems which facilitate EPS. They can be designed for all application domains such as business process management Ttools, organizational knowledge management Ttools or customer relationship management Ttools. They can be specific or generic. They enable emergence to be accounted for in systems as deferred design and determine run-time deferred systems architecture.

Extant Ttools and techniques to analyse deferred design cover systems type-2 and type-3. Deferred procedure calls are used in microprocessor interrupt management. Deferred data flow analysis is used in internet-based systems. If deferred design requires coding programmes automatic code generators can be used to implement action designers' design using Java deferred classes. Class models are structural, but deferred classes enabled deferred design.

Design domains

Organized action design can be analysed as four types of systems design types depicted in Figure 4.4. It depicts how organized action can be mapped in terms of deferred action design parameters. Organized activity can be analysed and mapped to determine appropriate systems design strategy.

Each quadrant names a design type and illustrative design domains. Organized activity suitable for Deferred Systems includes organizational knowledge management and organizational learning design domains. Activity suitable for Real Systems includes air traffic control or stock trading because it is dependent on events in real-time. Activity suitable for Specified Systems includes payroll and sales involving routine data processing. Activity suitable for Autonomous Systems includes decision-making that can be fully explicated, for example in certain supply chain negotiations or stock trading, suggesting that certain design domains may be suited to more than one design type. Decisions concerning choices constitute design strategy.

Figure 4.4 gDRASS matrix design domains

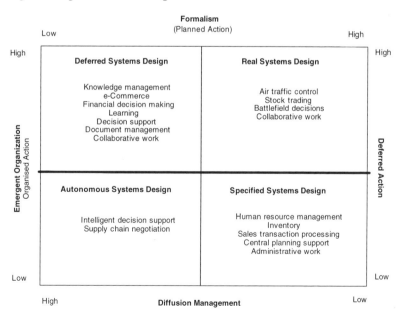

Prediction

Empirical mapping of extant systems in Figure 4.5 reveals theoretical predictive capability of deferred action. Systems can be predicted by similar mappings in terms of SEST properties before design begins to determine design type. Proposed work design can be similarly mapped. Systems in Figure 4.5 were designed independently of deferred action knowledge so improving its veracity. They map well onto the open systems and closed systems distinction depicted by the bold horizontal line. As predicted by the theory open systems above the line require deferred action interrelation design.

Systems designed with formal methods fit real systems type. As predicted these systems require action designers. Air Traffic Management System for London's airspace is designed with formal methods because a high degree of planned action is necessary to manage air space. It operates in emergent actual conditions so requiring deferred action by air traffic controllers. Systems designed with formal methods but not requiring action designers fit specified systems type. IBM's Customer Information Control System is an example of such a transaction processing system.

Figure 4.5   Predicting systems types

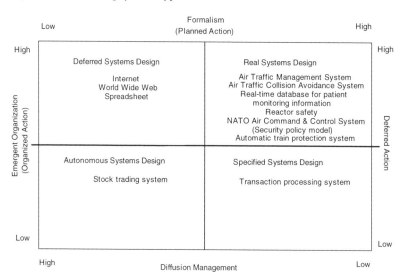

Systems designed with non-formal methods include World Wide Web and fit deferred systems type. As predicted formalisms' capacity to plan how the system is used is low because of emergence and consequent need for deferred action. An automatic stock trading system fits autonomous systems type. Its highly prescriptive algorithmic behaviour negates emergent factors and does not require deferred action. This design strategy is incorrect for organized action as witnessed in stock market crashes caused by such autonomous systems.

Interrelation design

Notions of interactivity seek specification. Interaction design is limited to what can be specified. It predetermines how 'users' will interact. Some researchers propose phenomenological interactivity in the same vein of specification. They seek to design embodied interaction but remain rooted in specification formalism. It is contradictory to design phenomenological experience by specification.

Deferred action interrelation design differs from specification interactivity of HCI. Interrelation design is central in deferred action design. It is broader because it considers designs fields of action and so it accounts for deferred design and real design depicted in Figure 4.1. It concerns interrelations arising because of emergence, space and time SEST properties and is necessary in open systems. Organization and its systems interrelate externally with partners, competitors, markets, and customers and internally with stakeholders, business processes and groups or individuals in workflows. Systems have to interrelate well with organization, individuals and groups and their tasks.

Interrelation design is individual or organized deferred action directed at shaping formal design placed in fields of action, actuality. It is the shaping of formal design as a consequence of operational and strategic needs through deferred design. It enables individuals and groups to interact by their own design with formally designed organization and systems in actual situations. It is design of active networks and interrelations formed in fields of action between formal design and actual action. Deferred action interrelation design makes Simonion 'internal structure' relates well with the 'external environment', in deferred action terms fields of action.

Deferred and real systems enable operational interrelation design. It is evident in the spreadsheet system. Action designers determine operational functionality of spreadsheet models based on actualities as when modelling company mergers. Real interrelation occurs in military networked targeting systems when battlefield personnel relay ground conditions and requirements that lead to real-time configuration of systems to supply munitions and ammunition.

5
Design Constructs

Introduction

Design is an applied science. Design constructs and principles stem from the theoretical synthesis of causal powers of deferred action design parameters. Deferred action is applicable practically as specific models deduced from the design types. Its imperative assertions concerning design are logically consistent with 'design deferred systems for situations where deferred action is observed' and 'design specified systems for situations where action is regimented.'

Design of organized action as SEST greatly improves design and its use. Deferred action design is organized goal-directed action consistent with SEST natural design. It can be applied to design structure as in systems architecture or organization structure, emergence of operational functionality or business process management, space and time covered by interrelation design. Synthesized design parameters result in four design ontology types for organized action. Different ontology synthesizes SEST properties in various combinations. Designers can draw on theoretical constructs for particular organization and systems design problems and consider suggested principles and guidelines to determine design strategy and design solutions.

Emergence is the unfolding of events beyond capabilities of reflective design which is off-design. It describes situations where designers are unable to be cognizant perfectly and completely of all things pertinent to achieve formal objectives by specification design. It recognizes social action itself as emergent since emergence cannot be predicted and cannot be specified as formal design. Paradoxically, emergence is desirable and should be encouraged by designers and managers of organization for its source of richness, intuition, latent energy and its tacitness in organized activity. It is a necessary condition for achieving formal objectives.

gDRASS matrix

Theoretical and practical design questions are: What is design for <u>actuality</u>? How should organized action be <u>represented</u> in design? Should business workers be recognized as <u>designers</u>? How should systems and organization design be <u>managed</u>? One response is the deferred action design parameters depicted in Figure 5.1. It is the synthesis of analytical entities or design parameters necessary for rational design. Though it depicts systems it applies to understanding work, work in organization, therefore it applies to work and organization design.

Theorists and designers, acknowledge and emphasize of individual design parameters or depth of synthesis expands or limits design. Specification formalism emphasizes representation solely so it limits space of organization design. Deferment formalism acknowledges the

Figure 5.1 gDRASS matrix

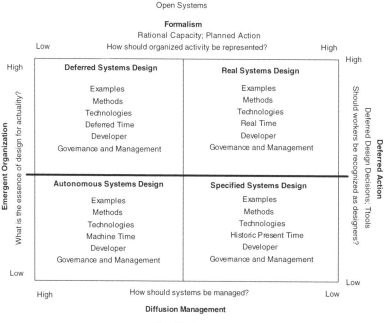

synthesized form thereby expanding design space. History of computing in organization has been the degree to which these design parameters have been recognized individually or in some combination, permitted and incorporated in design and usage of systems by designers. It is true of work design in organization.

Figure 5.1 depicts analytical generalizations to clarify knowledge of design, design process and methods and design domains. To undertake design methods, technologies, time, design process, designer types and management are necessary, shown generically in each quadrant. Design parameters are synthesized to provide insights and deeper understanding of these issues for researchers, designers and managers. Synthesis determines possible kinds of design and how designers conceptualize systems, IT, design process, design domains and devise relevant techniques, methods and tools.

Designers knowingly or unknowingly make assumptions on significance and capability of a particular design parameter. Acceptance or non-acceptance determines kinds of systems designed. Design and management of IT, IS, KMS, executive information systems, decision support systems, expert systems and other kinds recognizes variously particular design parameters. Some design and management approaches make assumptions that negate one or more design parameter, while others admit high or low levels. In actuality, designers unwittingly acknowledge varying levels of all four parameters, so the scales read 'high' or 'low' rather than ordinals.

For each design types the matrix maps design and development methods and associated organizational and management issues. It represents issues in strategy, business planning, and management for organization design and systems planning, design and management of systems. It depicts the effect of emergence and indicates design types capable of responding.

It addresses 'how' questions too. It can be used to understand how emergence can be recognized in systems design and how to frame organizational information and knowledge design problems. It can also be used prescriptively to decide what systems type is suited for particular design domains, systems development methods to use, and systems management approach to practice.

The matrix is particularly relevant for designing cohered organization and systems. Its dimensions are significant factors in design, development, and usage of systems type-3 in organization or societal systems like the Web. A satisfactory resolution to interrelation design problems has eluded designers largely because systems type-3 has not been acknowledged as requiring complete SEST made possible by synthesis of the design parameters.

Rational design

The matrix's top parameter represents rational design domain distinguished theoretically from natural design domain. Rational design reinforces the model of organized action as planned action. It is deliberate intervention in natural design that seeks to create certain structures and futures by directing actuality but actuality or emergence has overpowering tendency. The prime product of rational design is a symbolic representation of some organizational 'problem' as design 'solution'.

Rational design is entrusted to reflective designers. It addresses how to represent organized action and systems using some system of symbols or notation languages. Hence it represents formalism analytical entity. Extant responses to the representation problem privilege rationality that assumes design problem, process, definition of design and its operation all can be determined and specified rationally using some formalism. It assumes formalism can be invented to capture all structural and operational requirements, represent design domains completely and aid design process. In this connection Herbert Simon concluded: '...requirements of design can be met fully by a modest adaptation of ordinary declarative logic.' (Simon, 1996: 115) This kind of inferential logic informs invention of specification formalism necessary for rational design.

Designers and researchers assume specification formalism is sufficient. Schemas contain degrees of stipulated specification. Some admit greater scope than others for contextual latitude. In systems design structured systems analysis and design contains more prescription than its counterpart object-orientation. Software engineering is more prescriptive than XP. In some IS methodologies specification formalism is espoused but not practised. Other schemas are extremely elaborate making it difficult to practise as in formal methods. In organization design some proprietary business planning methods contain more rational prescription than classical hierarchical organization design by verbal formalism.

Some software programmers now de-emphasize elaborate specification formalism as in agile systems development and XP. They focus instead on 'people', 'stories' and 'context'. Researchers in management too are de-emphasizing rational units of analysis by considering 'histories', 'narrative' and 'discourse', and of course management consultants follow suit! De-emphasis is appropriate not negation.

Systems design

Rational design is primary in systems design. Systems type 1–3 design is possible because rational design assumes operational functionality can be predicted. Systems are characterized as objects that exist independently. Specification formalism, particularly formal methods, is invented to enable precision predictive modelling of structure and operational functionality. It objectifies and models object systems architecture and operational functionality with precision by determining complete requirements. In deferred action design inclusion of operational functionality as requirements is the design of improper structure.

Systems analysis and design processes vary for different systems ontology, specification and diagrammatic formalisms. Structured methods ontology of 'problem domains' (design domains) differs significantly compared with object-oriented methods. Diagrammatic formalism is invented to objectify objectively purpose, objectives and functionality assumed to pre-exist. It is based on objective, logical analysis. Definitions of entities and attributes compose details for designing operational functionality. Implicit and subsumed in this modelling process is detailed prescriptive definition of planned (organizational) action to achieve formal objectives. By implication actual variance in planned action is deemed undesirable.

Pure form of rational design is IS development 'methodology'. IS methodology prescribes planned action for developers and 'users'. It is a detailed plan for developing systems which structures development activities. It is a prescription on how to conceptualize, analyse, design, implement and manage systems. Some methodologies enable 'users' to participate in design process but their contribution and value is not empirically attested. It is significant for rational design and deferred action to evaluate the contribution. Methodologies themselves are embedded in another form of planned action – systems development projects. Projects are detailed plans to manage available resources to achieve project aims. The epitome of project management for systems is the CMM.

Table 5.1 comparatively analyses rational design in deferred action, systems science and IS in terms of deferred action rational design analytical entities. Rational design is a prerequisite of deferred action design encompassing SEST. Many deferred action analytical entities however are not present in dominant schools of thought within systems science and IS. They are better at representing structure SEST property and much poorer at representing other SEST properties.

Table 5.1 Comparative analysis of rational analysis

Analytical entities	SEST	Theory of deferred action	Rational design	
			Systems science	IS
Purpose (Intention)	Structure	Determinable objectively & emergent	Objects determinable objectively	Objects determinable objectively
Organization		Determinate & becoming, interpreted	Determinate & static	Determinate & static
Organization functions, process		Determinate & becoming, interpreted	Determinable objectively	Determinable objectively
Rational design (Planned action)	Structure & Emergence	Only one aspect of duplex design process	Central	Central
TSA (Tailoring Tools)		Inherent in duplex design	Unrecognized	Unrecognized
Data		Determinate & becoming, interpreted	Determinable objectively	Determinable objectively
Information		Determinate & becoming, interpreted	Determinable objectively	Determinable objectively, some recognition of meaning attribution
Knowledge		Determinate & becoming, interpreted	Unrecognized	Unrecognized

Table 5.1 Comparative analysis of rational analysis – *continued*

Analytical entities	SEST	Theory of deferred action	Rational design	
			Systems science	IS
Diffusion management		Critical aspect of design management	Unrecognized	Unrecognized
Systems (Becoming)	Emergence	Determinate & becoming, interpreted	Unrecognized	Unrecognized
Systems functions		Determinate & becoming, interpreted	Determinable objectively	Determinable objectively
Emergence		Critical aspect of deferred design	Unrecognized	Unrecognized
Deferred action		Critical aspect of deferred design	Unrecognized	Unrecognized
Reflective/ Action designer	Space	Inherent in duplex design	Distinction not present	Distinction not present
Actuality		Inherent in design and basis of action	Unrecognized	Unrecognized
Interrelations	S / T	Inherent in design	Unrecognized	Unrecognized
Time	Time	Inherent in duplex design, central	Recognized but not implemented	Unrecognized
Deferred, Real, Specified, Autonomous Design Decisions		All recognized	Only specified and autonomous design decisions	Only specified and autonomous design decisions
Description (Labels)		Bounded Rationality	Rationality	Rationality

Organization design

Organization is designed to create a new order by changing the existing order but design itself is dependent on the existing order's tendency to undermine design. Rational design is intrinsic to organization design which stems from rational analysis in operations research and the rational 'economic man' in economics. The theory of the firm is based on 'optimal' design of limited available resources.

Organization design is by specification using verbal formalism, declarative logic and simulation models. Formalism is necessary to embody purpose and devise processes. Purpose manifests itself in 'mission statements', 'strategy' and 'plans' among other strategic, tactical and operational devices of verbal formalism. 'Hierarchy', 'flat structure', 'networks', 'matrix' and 'business process' are organization structure design by verbal formalism.

Critical formalism for success of organization is management. It is central to organization design but as an occupational category it is extra to it. Schools of management and MBA qualification attest to its separate identity. Management design is premised on managers setting formal objectives and then centrally coordinating and controlling organizational activities to realize them. Much management design assumes rational managers' capability to assess available resources, determine organizational aims, analyse situations and make optimal decisions. As rational design it is crystallized in scientific management akin to specification formalism in systems design.

Designing strategy and ensuring organizational survival is pinnacle of management. Schemas for strategy work are elaborate, centred on executives' rationality and organizational capability as in core competence. Practitioners find them more credible than alternatives that characterize strategy as emergent. Managers have to justify actions to stakeholders which is easier to do in terms of rational action and more credible than the imprecise language of emergence.

Rational design is epitomized in proprietary business planning methods, process redesign and balanced scorecard. Such techniques conceptualize management as rational organizational processes. They contain more logical formalism than verbal formalism, for instance in balanced scorecard there are 'perspectives', 'objectives' and 'performance measures'.

Rational design results in abstract forms like 'process management' and 'core competency' not located in individuals but as second order concepts. Managers find it difficult to relate in terms of their own actions. Now researchers and designers focus on experience as source of design. Rational management design is giving way to 'craft', 'narrative', 'story' and 'focus groups'. Management and organization design may appear simple in narratives and stories compared with mathematical and computational formalism or other analytical schemes. Management writers claim that management is simple to devise, an example schema is management concern with planning, organizing, leading and controlling but the researches reveal intricacies of praxis.

What cannot be explained rationally is ruled to be complex, problematical and ruled out of design. In organization design it is categorized as 'complexity of management', in systems design 'creeping requirements', 'change' and 'adaptation'. Rational design then seeks further and deeper formalisms to represent these new categories. In deferred action these ruled out entities demarcate limit of rational design and only exist artificially because reflective designers expect to know all operational and functional requirements to begin design. Design need not create such dichotomy that impedes successful placing of rational design in actuality.

Emergence

The matrix's left dimension represents emergence intrinsic to natural design. Its recognition by reflective designers expands design or otherwise limits it. It is a theoretical representation of emergent events resulting from interrelations in fields of action and the design's interrelation with it. Interrelations produce expected and unexpected outcomes. Emergence is the product of the latter. It addresses the question of what composes the essence of rational design for emergence or actuality. It is the emergence analytical entity.

It maps organizational and systemic emergence. Emergence begs the question to what extent rational design is possible. Emergence ranges from strategic matters to technical and task-related operational issues. Examples of emergent situations are company mergers and acquisitions, new business partnerships and technology and new techniques to complete tasks. Emergent situations cannot be predicted to include in structural design in strategic plans or systems architecture designs.

Emergence is the occurrence of unplanned and unpredictable human events out of bounds of rational analysis and therefore off-design. Ironically it forms essence of successful design because any placed design in fields of action has to interrelate well with it. Formalism cannot be invented to represent emergence itself but it can be invented to facilitate emergence – deferment formalism. It can facilitate interrelation design. No symbols can be invented to represent objects of emergence but symbols and mechanisms can be invented as facilitators of interrelation design. They act to represent emergence when it is experienced in actuality.

Abstract models of human activity 'decision-making', 'strategy-making process' and 'business process' in organization and the use of case or class models of 'chemical ordering' or 'site safety' in systems remain abstract in all actual situations are unable to respond to emergence. This is a limitation of rational design. It is inherent in specification formalism itself detached from actuality. Recognition of emergence expands scope of rational design by redefining interrelations and boundaries between abstract products and actuality. Interrelations between abstract models and actuality become less rigid.

Scope of rational design is challenged by emergence. It encompasses issues that trouble reflective designers and managers including dynamic conditions, market and technological change. By recognizing emergence in design many of the problems in rational design can be surmounted, ironically as rational design inclusive of deferred design based on deferred action. Recent research recognizes the effect of emergence on IS and as key in KMS design. Markus et al. (2002) argue that emergent knowledge processes can only be supported by *live use* of KMS. It is not reflected in systems analysis and design methods.

Unwitting recognition of emergence led Herbert Simon to recognize the possibility of order without a planner. In deferred action 'the planner' is essential. Recognizing planning and emergence explicitly necessitates recognition of duplex design domain with its reflective and action designers. To account for emergence it makes action designers significant and accounts for planning and emergence in design by enabling both reflective and action designers.

Emergent organization and systems

Ironically, a significant gap in accounts of organization and systems concerns centrality of humans and intentionality. Intentionality is holistic encompassing objectifiable rational behaviour and deeper traits including tacit knowledge and social embedment of information and knowledge. It manifests as specific action extra to specified process action that is abstract. Deeper traits govern significantly emergent events. They are out of bounds of rational analysis and modelling through objectification required in specification formalism for systems design and mathematical and computational formalism in organization design.

Emergence is central in systems thinking the tenet of the whole being greater than the sum of its parts. Interrelating parts generate an emergent entity not locatable in individual parts. Deferred action emergence is not systemic emergence amenable to positivist analysis. Intentionality cannot be analysed in positivist terms. In recognizing emergent systems deferred action emergence emphasizes non-rational and holistic aspects of being and becoming and forming social organization. It stresses organized action aspects that cannot be formalized and are better regarded as simply natural design. In natural design creation and uses of information and knowledge differs according to situations which is not general. So systems need to be conducive to human specific purposes.

Table 5.2 is a comparative analysis of emergence in terms of deferred action analytical entities. In deferred action design emergence accounts for the emergence SEST property. Many deferred action analytical entities are not present in dominant schools of thought within systems science and IS. They do not consider this critical SEST property. Aspects of emergence are termed autopoiesis in systems science. Comparison with linguistic deep and surface structure is significant which is used in IS to develop 'deep structure' construct of meaning (Wand and Weber, 1995) and 'emergent' organization and systems (Truex and Baskerville, 1998; Truex et al., 1999). Neither describes the emergence of deferred action because the deferred action emergence is integral to the set of interrelated SEST properties, which can be extemporaneous, permanent, endogenous or exogenous. Deferred action is better at representing emergence SEST property. Systems science, IS and KMS are poorer.

Emergent organization poses new theoretical and practical problem for designers. Theorists' explanations of it as 'deep structure', autogenesis, self-reference or autopoiesis of structure are mistaken. Rational design based on specification formalism cannot anticipate emergent organization and systems. Strategic IT planning methods or IS methodologies do not account for emergence. Design that makes the design itself more complex is flawed because it fails to provide an adequate response to Asbey's law of requisite variety. Since the 'environment' is various design needs to address it and should not itself become ever more complex. Requisite variety remains unachieved in specification formalism. In deferred action requisite variety is not specifiable so it is subsumed in emergence. Emergence requires management perspective that equally accommodates necessary rational direction and recognizes and enables responses to emergence. This response is deferred action.

Table 5.2 Comparative analysis of emergence

Analytical entities	SEST	Emergence		
		Theory of deferred action	System science	IS
Purpose (Intention)		Determinable and indeterminable (Clear and fuzzy)	Unrecognized	Emergent purpose unrecognized
Organization (structure)	Structure	Emergent structure can be catered for by deferred design	Emergent structure is not possible	Emergent structure is not possible
Organization functions		Emergent functions can be catered for by deferred design	Emergent functions not possible	Emergent functions not possible
Rational design (Planned action)		Emergence can be part of rational design	Rationality has primacy no scope for emergence	Rationality has primacy, no scope for emergence
Tailorable systems architecture (Tailoring Tools)		Recognized	Unrecognized	Unrecognized
Organization (Becoming)	Emergence	Determinate & emergent	Unrecognized	Unrecognized
Systems (Becoming)		Determinate & emergent	Unrecognized	Unrecognized
Systems functions		Determinate & emergent	Unrecognized	Determinate
Emergence		Recognized, endogenous, exogenous, extemporaneous, determines formalism	Recognized, self-centric, endogenous	Unrecognized
Deferred action		Recognized	Unrecognized	Unrecognized
Interrelations		Interrelations generate emergence	Endogenous only	(Studied but not designed)

Table 5.2 Comparative analysis of emergence – *continued*

Analytical entities	SEST	Theory of deferred action	System science	IS
	Structure & Emergence		**Emergence**	
Data		Real, specifiable, deferred & emergent	Objects, specifiable, non-emergent	Objects, specifiable, non-emergent
Information		Real, specifiable, deferred & emergent	Objects, specifiable, non-emergent	Objects, specifiable, non-emergent
Knowledge		Deferred, specifiable, real & emergent	Specifiable, non-emergent	Specifiable, non-emergent
Diffusion management		Recognized	Unrecognized	Unrecognized
Reflective designer/ Action designer		Recognized	Unrecognized	Unrecognized
Deferred, Real, Specified, Autonomous Design Decisions		Recognized	Unrecognized	Unrecognized
Description (Labels)		Emergence	Autopoiesis: emergence is recursive and never ending process of social organization. (Autopoiesis; Catastrophe) Requisite variety.	Change, complexity, flexibility

Deferred action and deferred design decisions

The matrix's right dimension represents theoretical deferred action construct. Its recognition by reflective designers expands design otherwise or limits it. It is the conduit between rational design and natural design necessary for successful and sustainable design. Specification formalism prescribes planned action that struggles to deal with intrinsic SEST properties of natural design. Deferred action is the synthesizing agent or interrelation agent among SEST properties that makes rational design consistent with natural design.

It maps actions of individuals and groups as first order and organization as second order. It is the deferred action analytical entity addressing affirmatively the question whether business workers should be recognized as action designers. Individuals and groups interrelate with design in context as planned action and if context is emergent as deferred action. Deferred action is action cognizant of design that is not executable as planned action because of the lack of requisite information or knowledge. Actual action may differ from specified processes or procedures such variance is deferred action. Deferred action is a consequence of and shaped by rational design. All three systems types – one, two and three need to enable deferred design in systemic terms.

Deferred action explains much recent organization design. Redesign based on decentralization, devolution, downsizing and empowerment in flat organizations all recognize deferred action. Client-server architecture, end-user computing, component-based design and service-oriented architecture recognize deferred action in systems design. Limits of central planning have unwittingly led designers to devolve operational design implicitly recognizing deferred action.

Observations of deferred action reveal insufficiency of specification design. Where necessary business workers pursue goals in other ways than prescribed in design or when design is incapable of predicting all requirements. Deferment has a spatial and temporal quality. It is action that is undertaken in due course for a variety of contingent reasons, including, uncertainty, lack of clarity, lack of relevance of prescribed action and prescribed action that is inadequate or not required (Patel, 2005b). This is consistent with Herbert Simon's reasoning:

The sufficiency of the means is almost always empirical rather than logical. (Simon, 1977: 148)

Deferred action is such empirical means, usually concerned with operational needs sometimes influencing strategy (structure). It is consistent with realism's domain of empirical where deferred action occurs. Actual action is superior to rational design by reflective designers. It is accounted for in design as deferred design. Deferred design should be interrelated with specified design to enable pursuit of formal goals in actuality. Deferred design is the sufficient condition of specified design for actual organized action. DDD principle interrelates specified design with actual action. It is a decisional link between natural design and rational design that permits emergent, spatial and temporal design decisions.

Recognizing deferred action means specification design need not be concerned with details of policy in organization and detailed operational functionality in systems. It becomes unnecessary to design for all operational actualities, which creates the 'complexity' so problematic in specification design. Incorporating deferred action is the design by reflective designers of structure whose policies and operational functionality is designed by action designers. It is a structural case to enable deferred action as deferred design.

Table 5.3 is a comparative analysis of deferred action analytical entities. Deferred action is necessary in design that needs to cater for emergence, space and time SEST properties. It is not recognized in systems science and IS.

Diffusion management

The matrix's bottom parameter represents diffusion management. Its recognition by reflective designers expands design or otherwise that limits it. Deferred action implies management of organization and systems should be diffused within designed bounds. Diffusion management is the joint responsibility of reflective and action designers to manage organization and systems structure and operations. Managers cannot manage all aspects of design and designing centrally.

Diffusion management is the analytical entity addressing the question of how design should be managed. Systems type-3 as combined organization and systems design makes the matrix's depiction of the four questions critical management issues.

Any information and knowledge associated with deferred action cannot be managed centrally since it is embedded in natural design. Information and knowledge have certain intrinsic autonomy stemming from the logic of natural design that cannot be centrally managed. Autonomy is intrinsic to knowledge work and organizational knowledge management. The same is true of non-operational aspects of information as in strategic decision-making.

Table 5.3 Comparative analysis of (deferred) action

Unit of analysis	SEST	Theory of deferred action	Deferred action	
			System science	IS
Purpose (Intention)	Structure	Could modify purpose	Unrecognized	Unrecognized
Tailorable systems architecture (Tailoring Tools)		Necessitates TSA	Unrecognized	Unrecognized
Rational design (Planned action)		Coordinated with deferred design through deferred action	Unrecognized	Unrecognized
Organization (Becoming)		Designs organization	Unrecognized	Unrecognized
Organization functions		Designs functions	Unrecognized	Unrecognized
Systems (Becoming)	Emergence	Designs systems	Unrecognized	Unrecognized
Emergence		Deferred action is a response	Unrecognized	Unrecognized
Deferred action		–	Unrecognized	Unrecognized
Systems functions		Designs operational functionality	Unrecognized	Unrecognized
Interrelations		Generates dynamics, interrelation design	Unrecognized	Unrecognized

Table 5.3 Comparative analysis of (deferred) action – *continued*

Unit of analysis	SEST	Theory of deferred action	Deferred action	
			System science	IS
Data		Designs operational data	Unrecognized	Unrecognized
Information		Designs operational information	Unrecognized	Unrecognized
Knowledge		Deploys emergent knowledge	Unrecognized	Unrecognized
Diffusion management		Necessitates diffusion management	Unrecognized	Unrecognized
Reflective designer/ Action designer	Structure & Emergnece	Necessitates the distinction	Unrecognized	Unrecognized
Deferred, Real, Specified, Autonomous Design Decisions		Necessitates DDD	Unrecognized	Unrecognized
Description (Labels)		Deferred action	Unrecognized	Unrecognized

Table 5.4 Comparative analysis of (diffusion) management

Analytical entities	SEST	Theory of deferred action	Diffusion management System science	IS
Purpose (Intention)	Structure	Set by governing body	Unrecognized	Unrecognized
Rational design (Planned action)		Determined by reflective designers	Unrecognized	Unrecognized
Tailorable systems architecture (Tailoring Tools)		Designed by reflective designers	Unrecognized	Unrecognized
Organization (Becoming)	Emergence	Determined by action designers	Unrecognized	Unrecognized
Organization functions		Determined collectively	Unrecognized	Unrecognized
Systems (Becoming)		Determined by action designers	Unrecognized	Unrecognized
Systems functions		Determined collectively	Unrecognized	Unrecognized
Emergence		Managed collectively	Unrecognized	Unrecognized
Deferred action		Taken by action designers	Unrecognized	Unrecognized
Interrelations		Managed collectively	Unrecognized	Unrecognized

Table 5.4 Comparative analysis of (diffusion) management – *continued*

Analytical entities	SEST	Theory of deferred action	Diffusion management	
			System science	IS
Data		Structural design by managers, operational design by action designers	Unrecognized	Unrecognized
Information		Structural design by managers, operational design by action designers	Unrecognized	Unrecognized
Knowledge	Structure & Emergence	Structural design by managers, operational design by action designers	Unrecognized	Unrecognized
Diffusion management		–	Unrecognized	Some recognition is research
Reflective designer/ Action designer		Reflective designers manage structure, action designers manage operations	Unrecognized	Unrecognized
Deferred, Real, Specified, Autonomous Design Decisions		Central to decision-making	Unrecognized	Unrecognized
Description (Labels)		Diffusion management	Unrecognized	Unrecognized

In deferred action management of knowledge and information becomes an organizational process where management is done collectively. Control is still necessary to ensure achievement of purpose but operational management shifts to business workers engaged in actual situations. Deferred design necessitates that central control on systems development or work design be relaxed. It questions development of systems as a project. Table 5.4 is a comparative analysis of deferred action analytical entities.

Design types

Figure 5.1 depicts four systems types. Systems highly affected by emergence, space and time are plotted in the top two quadrants termed Deferred Systems Design (DSD) and Real Systems Design (RSD). Systems minimally affected by these SEST properties are plotted in the bottom two quadrants termed Autonomous Systems Design (ASD) and Specified Systems Design (SSD). These are second order models of design – design models for modelling actual systems. In practice, it is possible to mix these design models in one system in any combinatorial pattern for two, three or all to be synthesized as one system. It is often necessary to develop systems to reflect qualities of more than one type. An organization would have different types to suit different kinds of work or combinations of types for certain work.

Design decision-making is critical. Decision-making by reflective designers exclusively is countered by proposing the need for decisions by reflective and action designers. So metadesign design decision-making principles for each design type are deferred, real, specified and autonomous. Different combinations for each design type is depicted in Table 5.5

These combinations are termed co-design. Patel (2003) posits circles of influence on system design activity that reflect the four design para-

Table 5.5 Design decision types

Reflective design decision type (reflective designer)	Action design decision type (action designer)	Results in:
Specified design decisions	Deferred design decisions	DSD
Specified design decisions	Real design decisions	RSD
Specified/autonomous design decisions	–	ASD
Specified design decision	–	SDD

meters and two designers types. Reflective designers exclusively make Specified Design Decisions (SDD) in SSD. They make SDD concerning systems architecture and operational functionality. Action designers make DDD on operational functionality in actual situations, emphasizing the SEST properties of design in DSD and RSD. The autonomous designer makes Autonomous Design Decisions (ADD) in ASD.

Deferred systems design

The dominant SEST property is emergence resulting in the dominant design principle of deferred design decision. Deferred systems are placed and have delayed enactment in fields of action. Since deferred action is shaped in actuality and occurs to achieve objectives by natural design, organization and systems design needs to enable it through design. A deferred system is deferred until action designers decide what it becomes in actuality which in this sense is closer to natural design. Reflective designers make structural design decisions and action designers make emergent, spatial and temporal design decisions or operational functionality relating to its SEST properties. Theoretically it is termed deferred systems ontology. It represents and interrelates all SEST strongly.

Deferred systems contain minimal operational design by reflective designers. It cannot be completely predefined because of the richness of human and organizational context in which operational needs emerge. Deferred design reflects emergent functionality or SEST properties that cannot be pre-designed. It is consequent on actuality reflecting intentions of individuals and groups who interrelate with systems fields of action or context. DSD quadrant in Figure 5.1 is significant for modern organizations exposed to constant change.

Table 5.6 lists properties of deferred systems by illustrative examples like spreadsheet, Web and XML. They are assessed in terms of seven properties with ticks indicating fulfilment of property. Web-enabled deferred systems crucially have properties of needing no downloads and no DDD need to be stored on the server.

Deferred systems are co-designed by reflective and action designers who design TSA and operational functionality respectively. Operational functionality is unknown and unknowable to reflective designers. They do not seek to determine operational functionality completely for systems fields of action or actual contexts. They design TSA by specification design. Specification design draws on rational design, specification formalism and deferment formalism. For sustainable deferred systems

Table 5.6   Properties of deferred systems

Deferred system properties	Spreadsheet	World Wide Web	eXtensible Mark-up Language (XML)
Emergent	✓	✓	✓
Reflective Developer	✓	✓	✓
System-System Environment Interface (S-SEI)	✓	✓	✓
Deferred Design Decisions (DDD)	✓	✓	✓
Action Developer	✓	✓ Partially, if trained (Extradeferment)	✓ (Intradeferment)
Tailoring Tools (Ttools)	✓ (micro-Ttools)	✓ (micro-Ttools & Meso-tailoring)	✓ (meso-Ttools)
Non-SDLC Developed	✓	✓	✓

Adapted from: Patel N V (2004), Deferred Systems: Deferring the Design Process and Systems. Journal of Applied Systems Studies. 5 (1).

reflective designers continuously upgrade TSA and technology through intradeferment and meso-tailoring. Reflective designers enable DDD in TSA.

Action designers design operational functionality as deferred design in context. Deferred design draws on natural design and embodied patterning. Action designers experience operational functionality in actuality as interrelations. Since they are engaged in processes and tasks, they are able to determine required system functions better and implement them through deferred design. They extend operational functionality through deferred design.

Emergence, space and time SEST properties determine design of operational functionality and how systems are used. Systems take shape through deferred action and changes with further deferred action. Action designers can also determine some design of architecture (structure). Systems operational form cannot be predetermined by reflective designers' SDD because capability to design functionality by specification is low where emergence is high.

DSD caters for high emergence and deferred action (deferred design). Deferred systems functional form takes shape through deferred design by action designers' DDD in response to emergence. They are suitable for design domains where specification of operational functionality is ineffective and complete requirements gathering is not possible because of deferred action. An example is KMS to support innovation.

Deferred ontology of data, information and knowledge is artefactual and attributable with meaning. It is assumed to have SEST qualities. It is designed as artefact (structure) with meaning attribution capability (emergence, space and time). Therefore it is determinable, emergent and tailorable. Determinable things are explicitly known to reflective designers stock, costs, and prices. Emergent things are unknown as when competitors bring out new products or when consumers' preferences change. Data, information and knowledge are tailorable in the sense that action designers can tailor operational functionality to suit actual action required in context. They ascribe meaning to it. Tailorability enables operationalization of tacit knowledge and other deep human traits.

DDD is interrelating rational design with natural design. It results from empirical observations of deferred action in organized activity. It is the design issue of how deferred action can be reflected formally such that systems become 'means' or 'procedural' to achieving objectives, active tools. This is facilitated with DDD principle. It enables deferred action to be integral to formal design.

Action designers make DDD on operational functionality. Deferred design is not constrained by prior SDD by reflective designers. Action designers make design decisions in pursuit of objectives and come to own systems. Deferred decisions happen in context in the situation where they are necessary. Early COTS example of deferred systems is spreadsheets. Action designers decide what combinations of functions and formulae are required to process data to determine its operational functionality. They design data structures and algorithms. These DDD on operational functionality are not constrained by reflective designers' SDD on TSA design.

Real systems design

The dominant SEST property is emergence resulting in the dominant design principle of real design decision. Real systems are enactive. Action designers enact real systems in fields of action, in this sense it is closet to natural design. Reflective and action designers jointly make structural design decisions. Reflective designers make initial structural design decisions by specification design then when the system is live action designers make structural and operational functionality design decisions by deferment design in real-time. Theoretically, it is termed real systems ontology. It interrelates emergence and time well in real-time.

Action designers design and enact real systems. Real systems architecture and operations are designed and enacted in emergent actuality and in real-time. It is not used as a delivered product like other systems types. They come to <u>own</u> the system. Real systems character is high emergence, deferred action, and the importance of central planning and therefore they contain much structural and operational design ambiguity. Structure and operational functionality are minimally designed because they are enacted rather than placed in context. Real systems take shape, form and change by deferred action.

Real systems are suitable for design domains where specification of real-time structure and operations is not possible where they emerge and need to be realized in context in real-time. So they require deferred action. An example is 'computing on-the-edge of network' military systems and aspects of learning systems. Real systems are of interest to military organizations and educationalists. Modern theatre of war poses new problems for military strategists because strategy alone cannot account for the actual field and achieve objectives. Central planning becomes redundant in actual contexts because of unknown variables and emergent situations. Understanding interrelations among specification design, emergence, and deferred action and deferred design can provide a framework for designing appropriate action to achieve aims.

Real systems are co-designed in real-time. Reflective and action designers' design decisions are effective in real-time. They co-design design the TSA and operational functionality in real-time. Real systems are not designed as designed by enactment in actuality. This may be required in deferred systems too, but it is not necessary.

Systems architecture is divided into specified structure and deferred structure. Like building construction design process deferment of structure is possible in RSD. Requirements for deferment structure can be determined by specification. Structure too does not have to be specified and can be deferred. So in RSD all SEST properties can be deferred. Reflective designers design specified structure by specification design. Specification design is to achieve specific objectives as planned action. TSA of real systems emerges and requires much deferment formalism to design. Reflective designers cannot predict much structural and no operational form because capability to design for real-time by specification is minimal.

Action designers design deferred structure by deferment design. They determine design of real-time deferred structure and details of operational functionality. Deferred structure reflects complete SEST in real-time. Deferred architectural form and operational functionality is shaped in real-time in context by action designers' DDD in response to complete SEST. It determines much of the system architecture.

The focus of specification design is on TSA but real systems differ from deferred systems in the scope for specification design and diffusion management. Real systems have higher capability to design rationally for known objectives. In deferred systems scope for such design is less. Real systems differ on the kind of management required to achieve aims. Management is less diffused and more centralized because of the imperative to achieve aims. In deferred systems, though the imperative may be equally strong, diffused management may be more appropriate because of the nature of work, for instance innovation knowledge work, required to achieve aims.

Real systems data, information and knowledge ontology is similar to deferred systems. It differs because it emerges and it is determined and implemented in real-time. Design issue in real design decision is the same as in deferred design. The difference is that RDD need to be implemented in systems in real-time, using technology that delivers real-time data, information and knowledge. The same design principle as for deferred systems applies to reflect deferred action in formal systems design.

Similar to deferred systems, co-existence of specification and deferment formalisms and deferred action is facilitated by implementation of RDD principle. So RDD of action designers are not constrained by prior SDD made by reflective designers. Properties of real systems are the same as Table 5.6 for deferred systems with additional real-time design and implementation in real systems.

Autonomous systems design

Two varieties of autonomous systems can be distinguished based on so-called control given to 'users'. Reflective designers predefine systems functionality embedded in intelligent agents enabled to make design decisions autonomously and independently of business workers and reflective designers. Some designs are based on formalism derived from situated action thesis. Intelligence inside machines is dominant design principle. Presently they admit low emergence, low capacity for specification design and low deferred action. There are no real examples of such systems, but researchers and designers are exploring multi-agent systems for many organizational processes. This quadrant in Figure 5.1 has the potential as aspects of other design types in organized action not as a separate entity. Theoretically, it is termed autonomous systems ontology. It attributes power to make interrelation design to autonomous agents so making responses to SEST properties non-human.

Other variety is context scenarios or patterns used to suggest design solutions to 'users' during system use. Autonomous systems suggest embedded predetermined design choices. Design choices are predefined scenarios created by reflective designers, and action designers only have the choice to accept or reject context-sensitive design offered. Design choices are inferred from observed user behaviour actions. Context scenarios are akin to business best practice. Context scenarios and patterns are distinct from actual contexts that deferred systems and real systems action designers encounter.

Interpretation of the planned action and emergence design parameters in Figure 5.1 differs slightly for autonomous systems. Low in emergence means systems are not emergent socially but could be autonomously emergent. Autonomous emergence is distinct from emergence defined in SEST, where it is natural. Autonomous emergence is artificial, the result of human creation schemes. Low in planned action means that it cannot be planned socially, and is autonomously planned or even autonomic. (This accounts for the apparent illogical placing in the bottom left quadrant.)

Reflective designers determine predefined systems functionality in autonomous systems, which may be based on requirements specified by 'users'. Operative design principle is autonomy in context. System effectiveness is improved through autonomous design decisions. ASD does not have potential to be systems type-3 because it is not possible to design interrelations between intelligent agents world and social world of actuality that is not computationally problematical.

Ontology of data, information and knowledge is objective and specified. In ASD it is predetermined and does not permit tailoring. Character of knowledge in expert systems is explicit knowledge. In general artificial intelligence-based systems characterize knowledge as explicit knowledge, fixed and knowable. Data and information are similarly characterized. At present the scope for emergent information is theoretical in multi-agent systems.

Intelligent agents, autonomous designer, embedded in autonomous systems makes or recommends autonomous design decisions based on presumed context design. 'The autonomous designer is the artificial intelligence embedded in a system.' (Patel, 2003: 5). The autonomous designer is enabled by reflective designers to recommend design decisions to 'users' for example in office applications. In a more sophisticated example, multiple agents collaborate to determine design decisions. They determine what operational functionality or service to perform in situations.

Specified systems design

The dominant SEST property is structure resulting in the dominant design principle of specified design decision. Specified systems are imposed. Specified systems are designed and shaped prior to its operation in actuality and assigned to artificial design domains by reflective designers. Complete design knowledge is assumed. Systems architecture and operational functionality is specification design determined by specification formalism. Operational functionality is knowable, is assumed, specifiable by 'users' and there is no interrelation design, or assumption of stable systems 'environment'. So specified systems admit no deferred action and assume high capability for specification (rational) design. It is a weak form of rational design lacking interrelation with natural design. Theoretically, it is a terms-specified systems ontology. It does not interrelate SEST since it only recognizes the structure property.

Reflective designers are exclusive designers. Design is based on specification of information and knowledge needs 'captured' from potential 'users'. Hence it requires complete 'requirements gathering', 'specification' and 'engineering' by reflective designers. Specification formalism is used to develop elaborate models to represent design domains. Formal specification details systems architecture and operational functionality. Reflective designers then design systems models and implement them. Such designing is presumed capable by methodology or other practice conforming to SDLC main phases.

Specified systems confuse SEST properties. No distinction is made between structure and other SEST properties or between TSA and operational functionality. Architecture and function is logically the same. Architecture (structure) and operational functionality (emergence, space and time) are specified and fixed, as it cannot be changed in context once systems are assigned. To make organizationally necessary changes reflective designers shut systems down to make architectural and operational amendments as 'maintenance'. An example is a customer relationship management system.

Specified systems are suitable for completely specifiable, certain and unequivocal design domains that do not require deferred action. Early applications of IT to business were of this type, and most strategic systems planning is in this quadrant of Figure 5.1.

Ontology of data, information and knowledge are objects independently existing. They are knowable, determinable, stable, fixed and independent of 'developers' and 'users'. SDD are based on ontology of information as artefact that originates in the design of electromechanical systems type-2. Specified systems do not admit meaning attribution to information.

Reflective designers or qualified 'professionals' make specified design decisions, only they can design systems. Design of large-scale software particularly relies on SDD and is termed 'software engineering'. Reflective designers make all the design decisions in metaphorical 'clean rooms' detached from experiences of 'users'. The design issue is how to determine formal systems specification for reflective designers' use to code systems.

Business workers simply use designed systems. Deferred action necessary for contextual information needs from systems is constrained by prior reflective designers' SDD, which explains research that finds systems are not used or tend to disappoint. Changes required to systems to make them relevant to context are relayed and managed by reflective designers as 'change control'.

Boundaries

The horizontal line in Figure 5.1 demarcates open systems above and closed systems below in terms of general systems theory. It depicts degrees of emergent organization and consequent need for deferred action. Deferred systems and real systems are open systems type-3. Emergent organization necessitates open systems design and interrelation design with other entities and people connected directly and with other entities independent of it connected indirectly in fields of action. Where systems need to cater for emergence, interrelation and contextual design of information and knowledge boundary needs to be open and systems need to grow and diffuse. Open systems are characterized by emergence that necessitates deferred action.

Systems type-3 in deferred action design is distinct. They do not have 'users' and their development is not 'participative'. Business workers interrelate with them as action designers. Participative design occurs in closed systems where users are not regarded as designers and are not enabled to make DDD or RDD. Action designers are enabled to do deferred design of deferred and real systems.

Reflective designers develop structure or architecture of open systems and action designers develop its operational functionality as a consequence of emergence in actual situations. Embodied patterns of behaviour emerge through individual and collective interrelated action. So design process is deferred to action designers who interpret phenomena in actuality and continuously design systems. e-Business systems are an example of open systems based on such embodied patterning. In such networked organization customers' orders directly determine production organization or services provision.

Boundary is more pronounced and systems self-contained where emergence and interrelations minimally affect systems. Autonomous and specified systems are such closed, technical systems. Reflective designers solely design closed systems, sometimes with user participation. Closed systems do not need action designers but can facilitate deferred action, as in some software installation procedures. Specified and autonomous systems restrict design to reflective designers and do not permit further design by others. Time SEST property makes closed systems succumb to fields of action and become categorized as 'legacy systems', it makes them succumb to the force of natural design.

Action designers and reflective designers

Deferred action design parameters in Figure 5.1 result in distinction between action and reflective designers, based on empirical observation of deferred action in organized work (Patel, 1999 and 2005b). Deferred action implies separation of design concern consistent with natural design SEST properties of structural design by one type of designers – reflective – and emergent, spatial and temporal design by another type – action designers. These types are consistent with open and closed systems, with specified and deferred design. In open systems design activity is separated between reflective designers who design TSA and action designers who design operational functionality. In closed systems only reflective designers design. ('Reflective developer' and 'action developers' appear in other publications but have same meaning.)

Everyone designs who is engaged in action as natural design. It is intrinsic to action and an existential necessity. Individuals manipulate objects in physical space – material in general – to achieve desired outcomes a meal or dwelling. An action designer is someone engaged in organized action, needs scope to design within bounds of specified design of formal organization or system design. An action designer brings natural design qualities to organized action. As Churchman states:

> All men are system designers and each man tries to determine what in his world, is the largest system and the smallest system. (Churchman, 171: 8)

Business workers are action designers in two senses. Within organized action natural design tendency persists. Business workers encounter situations that become problems not addressed by formal design. They have recourse to natural design first. A sales person designs unique sale pitches, an engineer designs heuristics to solve maintenance problems. A teacher designs unique pedagogy, a surgeon designs unique procedures. All designed to achieve specific objectives, either with explicit or tacit knowledge. Business workers put their knowledge and systems together as action design. Only action designers can do such design. The other sense is specific to the nature of certain work where work intrinsically requires action design. Knowledge workers involved in innovation need scope to design ways to forward themselves.

Action designers work in context hence the term action designer. They engage with present and future actual organization and need to act immediately to achieve objectives. They can be business workers acting by extradeferment and other professional systems designers acting by intradeferment. Action designers are better placed to make design decisions on operational processing of information and knowledge and its communication to others, and in some cases structural design decisions too. Open systems necessitate action designers' DDD and RDD and more effective if action designers are given scope to design.

Reflective designers work out of context, hence the adjective 'reflective' to describe design work from specification. Reflective design is abstracted from actuality real organization. Real is represented with specification formalism in abstract design. Such design requires time to analyse, design and implement systems, time which divorces systems from present, future and actual organization. Reflective design is necessary for open and closed systems to design structure or architecture, in open systems necessary to enable emergent deferred design. Reflective designers who adopt deferred action design need to think differently. They have to relinquish self-importance as sole designers. They have to replace the principle of producing final design with the principle of producing structure for further design of other SEST properties by action designers.

Reflective designers dominate organization and systems design. They deploy design techniques to capture knowable and specifiable objects for design. This disregards organizational emergence by seeking only determinable objects as subjects of design. In deferred action actual action has primacy over all formal design, so it is necessary to extend design to action designers, people who experience actuality and are better able to identify contextual and emergent information and knowledge needs. In a more sophisticated example of action design an action designer is enabled to instantiate a personal version of the server.

Interrelation design interface

Deferred action is understanding of interrelations between formal design and its fields of action where actual action occurs that is off-design. It is common to emergence and sustainability. To interrelate well and be sustained any design needs to allow actuality to affect its internal structure. Interrelation design results in tailoring operational functionality and internal structure by action designers. It improves effectiveness of open systems by interrelating internal structure and functions and other external first order (individuals, groups) and second order (organization) objects. Structure should change in response to other objects' interrelational intention in fields of action.

A mechanism to enable SEST to interrelate in design is the System-System Environment Interface (S-SEI). The term applies to organization and systems. It is formal recognition of interrelation design and fields of action. Deferred and real systems are designed with S-SEI for sustainment and relevance. It is not recognized by research institutes or leading systems developers. W3C does not recognize interrelation design in terms of an interface to the Web. IEEE's context analysis is planned response, not the same as enabling deferred action.

S-SEI is necessary to enable deferred action and to permit necessary deferred action to deal with actuality relative to formal design. It allows interrelations to be enacted in fields of action in relation to formal design. It enables SEST to be reflected in design. Complete SEST is enabled by S-SEI in real systems and emergence, space and time are enabled in deferred systems. S-SEI enables interrelation design by intermediary between operational status of design and action designers needs.

S-SEI is public interface similar to public interface of classes in object-orientation. Its purpose is to enable deferred action to be converted into deferred design in systems or organization. It functions by allowing action designers to design operational information and knowledge in deferred systems and change structure in real systems. It caters for emergent and unplanned information and knowledge processing. It enables information semantics to be contextualized and knowledge to be made explicit to suit organizational needs of action designers.

S-SEI serves two vital roles. It is necessary to account for SEST in design. It enables responses to emergent, spatial and temporal factors. They affect design relations because actual action differs from planned action. To achieve formal objectives embedded in specification design the S-SEI enables appropriate response to SEST properties. The SAP implementation in IMS is an S-SEI. It permits deferred design by intradeferment. It is also a system-system interface (SSI). Other role is S-SEI caters for sustainment based on deferred action. Sustainable design needs to interrelate well with actuality to make appropriate adjustments for sustainment. Legacy systems and defunct organization result because they lack present purpose. They fail to interrelate well with actuality. Organization becomes unsustainable because it does not relate well with actuality.

gDRASS matrix planes

The matrix in Figure 5.1 is further extended in Figure 5.2 to depict three planes of deferred action and interrelation design between them. The two dimensional matrix is depicted as three dimensions to emphasize that deferred action synthesis is applicable to humans, organization and technology (HOT). The design parameters apply to behaviour of each HOT entity. A particular entity's design decisions (DD) shown as arcs affect the other two entities (E) which are interrelated. In these terms there is much scope for mathematical description of deferred action.

Each plane has rational design, emergence, deferred action, and diffusion management dimensions, consequent four design types and needs its own formalisms and toolsets. Planes are related by realist causal powers. The primary human layer is the causal power of the organizational plane and both are causal powers of technology the enabling technological plane and the reverse causal powers apply too. Design happens in the different planes.

Figure 5.2   gDRASS matrix planes

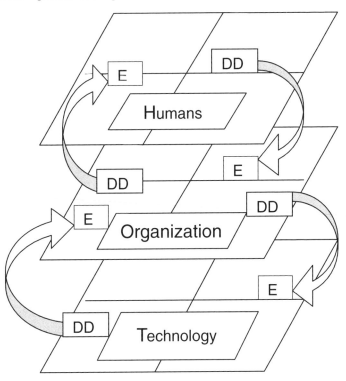

HOT planes can be considered in terms of designer types and types of design decisions. Each entity is capable of behaving in deferred, real, specified and autonomous ways. The HOT entities are linked by entity-specific design decisions that affect design possibilities in other entities. Deferment technology design like IMI's LDS design (technology plane) enables deferred design in organization (organization plane) and so caters for individual and group deferred action (human plane).

Classic problem of aligning IT and IS with business strategy is actually uncoordinated HOT planes. Mismatch occurs because organization design type is mismatched with technology design type. So knowledge work organization in deferred action terms is deferred organization (organization plane) but support and enabling systems are normally of the specified type (technology plane).

Human plane has realist ontological significance. The causal power to *be* human is to act to achieve purpose or to do natural design, which is conducive to rational design in organized action. Another causal power is discovery of *becoming*, which is subject to emergence. The third is to interrelate existence and becoming with other things. Being, becoming and interrelation are significant causal powers of the human plane.

Human plane generates intentions and defines purpose individually or in groups. Here deferred action design parameters apply to humans as first order entities. Some purpose is obvious to defend oneself or to survive. Others are less obvious such as determining personal object-ives. Design parameter synthesis determines tools used to achieve known purpose but how IT should be used in not obvious. It is itself subject to the design parameters. Some tool usage pen and paper can be specified explicitly but IS and KMS is not as obvious.

Purposeful action encounters emergent events that necessitate deferment. Deferment begins in human plane as individuals attempt to understand personal, interrelations and others actions in relation to formal design. This is termed individual deferment points (IDPs). Individual or group action can be deferred, real, autonomous or specified. It is deferred when purpose or means are not obvious when tool usage is subject to emergence or in changing conditions. It can be real in the sense that action has to occur when acting in a crisis or completing time-specific tasks. Action may be autonomous as in auto-matic reflexes.

Organization is a means for achieving human purpose expressed in the human plane. Human and organization planes compose social aspect of deferred action. Organization as second order concept is also a synthesis of deferred action design parameters. Planned action is insufficient to account for social aspects in organizing information and knowledge, where learning is integral to doing.

Organization design may be deferred, real, specified or autonom-ous or it may contain all four types for particular work. Specified organization is appropriate when purpose, objectives and means are well known and can be achieved by planned action as in production assembly line. Deferred organization is necessary where knowledge itself is uncertain as in research bodies. Real organization is structure and operations designed and enacted in emergent actuality and in real-time. It is appropriate where deferred action needs to be enacted in design immediately as in anti-terrorism response units. Autonomous organization is appropriate where human action is not required for example e-auction, except role of bidders.

IDPs from human plane transfer into organization plane where com-munication and collaboration is required to achieve objectives resulting in organizational deferment points (ODPs). Organizational collaboration and communication makes ODPs more complex than IDPs.

The design parameters apply to (digital) technology too. This is the technological aspect of deferred action. System designers can make use of relevant technology by analysing design domains in terms of design types and technology developers can use it to design required technology.

It suggests specification technology and deferment technology as kinds of technologies consistent with SEST properties and deferred action. This is a critical differentiation for inventing relevant and sustainable technology for systems type-3 design. Design parameters also suggest appropriate technology models for systems type-3 commensurate with design types. So organization types and systems types can be matched with deferred, real, autonomous and specified technologies.

Most design and development of IT is specification technology. It assumes prior knowledge of tools' actual use similar to engineered artefacts and systems type-2.

Deferment technology is evident in network and web technology but not extant in systems type-3 and systems type-2 too. There are hardware design exceptions that make use of deferment. Real technology is evident in inter-networking combining satellite, computing and mobile technologies. Autonomous technology is still in developmental stages tending towards entomology-based systems design, which is contrary to rational design and complete SEST necessary for human purpose.

These technological categories determine conceptions of systems, design of systems, methods and tools for organization plane which affect organization design. They affect human plane because they determine how individuals interrelate with technological systems.

Where systems are used to aid work then ODPs translate into systemic deferment points (SDPs) in technological plane. Current thinking on IT design does not enable complex ODPs to translate into SDPs and technological deferment points (TDPs).

Revised gDRASS matrix

Systems type-3 design using specification formalism has proved problematical. To improve success of rational design deferred action design parameters can be further generalized as shown in Figure 5.3. The matrix is refined in designing terms as the synthesis of specification

Figure 5.3 Revised gDRASS matrix

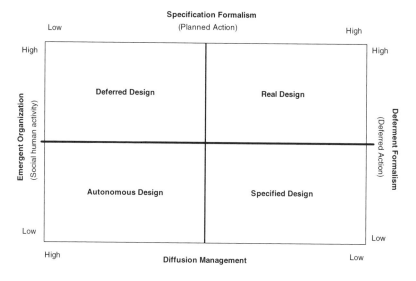

formalism, deferment formalism, emergent organization and diffusion management to improve success of formal design.

This is the synthesis of specification formalism (top) and deferment formalism (right) with emergence (left) and diffusion management (bottom). Design parameters here are in the most general form. As such they yield meta-models of design applicable to all social action design problems, including systems type-3, and can be applied to organized action to improve formal design of organization and systems for open and closed systems.

Structure and emergence

Complete SEST can be represented in design by separation of design between systems architecture design and operational functionality design. Reflective designers represent structure in systems architecture, as any architectural form is embodiment of purpose and objectives they are included in structure. Action designers represent emergence, space and time in operational functionality. Deferment of operational functionality is enabled by the DDD principle. It translates actuality or the space of natural design to rational design. It embodies interrelations between organized action and systems, space, time, planned action and deferred action.

Actuality is significant in systems type-3 design. Incongruence between formal design and natural design (actual activity) limits rational design. This problem is addressed by distinguishing DSD and RSD (and ASD if required) in terms of separating architecture and operations. Such separation is not an attribute of specification formalism and SSD design type. It concerns conceptualization of design as synthesis of specified, formal design and deferred, actual design, or synthesis of rational design and natural design. The formal, rational is designed with specification formalism and actual, natural with deferment formalism.

This separation is necessary to design relevant and sustainable systems. Many problematical design issues can be resolved by making this distinction and result in successful deferred and real systems and deferment formalism evidenced in Figure 4.5.

Tailorable systems architecture

TSA structure embodies purpose, objectives, and means and enables deferred design. It creates space for orderly deferred design and controls deferred and real design permissions. This is not the same as 'business control' since such control negates effects of natural design or SEST. Architecture is the creation of structured, tailorable space for organized action. Its primary elements are structure and deferment. TSA design and supporting infrastructure (computer network) is based on SEST to enable actual organized activity to become represented in design.

In systems architecture it is the creation of logical state space. In specified systems this state space is closed to action designers. In deferred and real systems it is opened by means of deferred and real design. This opening is achieved as TSA. TSA is composed of meso and micro levels. Meso-tailorability or intradeferment is for reflective designers to enable them to make major architectural amendments to TSA. Micro-tailorability or interdeferment is for action designers to enable them to design operational functionality.

Operational functionality

Effective design is measured by relevance of operational functionality in actuality. Deferred action is the element in actual action that needs to be translated into design as operational functionality in DSD and structure and operational functionality in RSD. Such deferred operational functionality design results from emergence, space and time elements of SEST properties. Deferred action enables action designers to design operational functionality in actuality, where elements of situation and context can form operation design.

Table 5.7   Separation of architecture and functionality

Systems type	Separation of systems architecture and operational functionality necessary?
Individual-to-social work systems	Not necessary to separate. Operational functionality of a word processor system can be pre-determined. Predetermined (specified) functionality. Functions do not need to depend on human meaning/interpretation (though can be so dependent). System is separate from human and social context. It neither converts data into information nor provide processed information or knowledge.
Socio-organizational work systems	Necessary to separate. Operational functionality of KMS cannot be predetermined for fields of action, actual context. Contextual (deferred) functionality. Functionality depends on human meaning/interpretation. System cannot be easily separated from human and social context. System processes data into information and provides processed information or knowledge.
Individual-to-organizational work systems	Necessary to separate. Operational functionality of an executive information system or decision support system cannot be predetermined for actual context. Contextual (deferred) functionality. Functionality depends on human meaning/interpretation. System cannot be easily separated from human and social context. System processes data into information and provides processed information or knowledge.
Individual work systems	Not necessary to separate. Operational functionality of a web authoring system can be pre-determined. Predetermined (specified) functionality. Functions do not depend on human meaning/interpretation. System is separate from human and social context. System neither processes data into information nor provides processed information or knowledge.
Example of KMS	System is purpose-driven and highly contextual and emergent. Therefore needs operational functionality separated from architecture. It is socially embedded. Humans interpret inputs and outputs.

An ambitious implicit principle in specification design that reflective designers are capable of determining operational functionality results from lack of theoretical knowledge. Operational design of information and knowledge in systems type-3 has been problematical to determine because no consideration is given to its SEST properties.

Operational functionality is determinable in non-information systems (NIS) mainly technical systems, with machine-like behaviours. NIS systems achieve predetermined purpose with few further human or organizational demands on them. These include word-processor systems and presentation systems. They are mostly individual-social work systems or individual work systems in terms of Figure 2.1.

Table 5.7 is an analysis of work systems in terms of separating structure and operations. DDD principle can be applied to determine whether systems operational functionality needs to be deferred to action designers. Analysts can apply it to determine whether systems need to cater for deferred action. They can apply it to determine requirements distinguished by systems architecture and operational functionality requirements.

In general, operational functionality is not specifiable for systems type-3 design, for socio-organizational and individual-organizational work systems. It is necessary to defer its design to action designers. In general, the greater the magnitude of SEST in design domains the greater the separation of systems architecture and operational functionality design.

Cohered organization and systems design

Deferred action coheres organization design and systems design. Design is cohered when actual conditions determine contextual individual or organizational action that maps onto existing formal design. Such mapping produces response or output to address present need, normally generative of organizational information or knowledge to address some problem. By cohered is meant making formal conditions created by design in which actual action occurs sufficient to enable it to obtain its expected object. The aim is to find right things to examine and understand by making design objects simple.

Based on imperative and procedural representation analytics in Moss (2005) three units of analysis are significant condition, action and outcome (CAO) to form an imperative and procedural model of cohered design based on deferred action. Figure 5.4 depicts how organization and systems can be cohered using CAO scheme for deferred action design. It is a principled way of representing deferred action formally. The UML combined with the UML Business Modelling Profile depict deferred action. It is supplemented with other non-UML symbols because the UML is not sufficient to depict intended semantics. Conditions engender certain beliefs in business actors and business workers on how to proceed. Since belief can be expressed as deferred action it can be translated into deferred design (action) with the expectation that required outcome will be generated.

The outer square of Figure 5.4 depicts conditions in which business actors and business workers (action designers) act. It contains organization design (oval) and systems design (rectangle – UML use case system). Organization's interrelations with external entities are not shown. In the oval are reflective and action designers the former

Figure 5.4   CAO scheme for cohering organization and systems

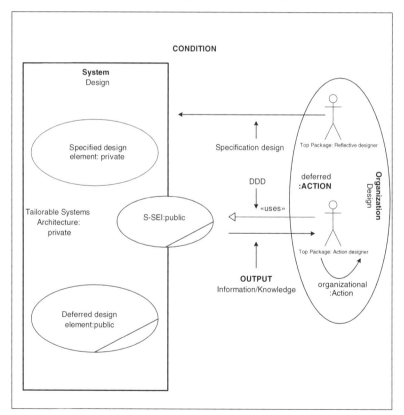

because they act to achieve organizational objectives and include out-sourcing partners or COTS suppliers. Reflective designers are shown at the top engaged in specification design TSA use case. Other elements of organization design are not shown. Systems design consists of TSA, which is composed of private specified design, public deferred design and public S-SEI business use cases. S-SEI is shown straddling system boundary to emphasize how conditions (in design terms SEST organizational factors) can be translated into operational systems functionality (outcome). The result is design for actuality using synthesized specification and deferment formalisms to deliver declarative and procedural representation, rather than abstract design.

Action designers shown in the oval are primarily business workers working to achieve task objectives involving transformations of resources, shown by arc arrow because action may not be related to systems. Action relating to information and knowledge is depicted by horizontal arrow, critical to cohere organization and systems. It is enabled by deferred action DDD through the S-SEI. Use is the special case of DDD which is deferred design.

Output is depicted with an arrow from system to action designer, delivering contextual and procedural information and knowledge. If action is according to specified organizational processes and specified systems interaction then outcome is the result of specified design. If action is response to actuality or emergence then the outcome is the result of deferred design.

Since design creates new structure axioms, beliefs and existing facts can be declared using specification formalism and how to act in actuality can be procedurally facilitated by deferment formalism. Design based on deferred action is critical for business actors and business workers because it interrelates actual conditions to powerful information and knowledge assistive tools. Deferred action as response to actuality can be represented through DDD to produce required information and knowledge.

At present no common formalism or theory is available to design cohered organization and systems. Cohering organization and systems is possible on the basis of conditional action based on deferred action. The possible cohered organization and systems types are depicted in Figure 5.5. Coherence means that the design parameters apply to organization and systems. Organization design can be determined with the design parameters applied to systems design.

Cohering organization and systems is consistent with the CAO scheme and HOT planes of Figure 5.2. Since business workers' action is

Figure 5.5 Deferred action organization types

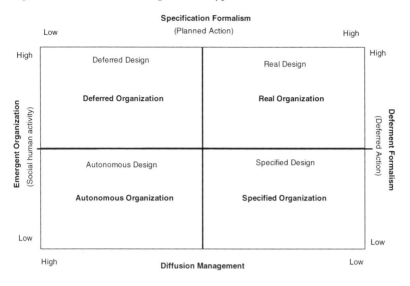

shaped by conditions or context then work organization and systems design need to be consistent. Also, particular human form of action, say deferred action, can be matched with the same organization and technology types.

Design parameters permit description and explanation of organization types coherence with systems. 'The matrix thus matches semantically theoretical systems ontology and organization ontology for four types of systems and organization.' (Patel, 2005b: 277). Each quadrant represents different organization type for types of work. Actual activity is more or less open to formal design and organization types represent degrees of formal design possible for types of organized work. Knowledge work is less susceptible to specified design so it requires deferred organization that coheres well with deferred systems. It is subject to emergent networks and deployment of tacit knowledge and extraction of embedded knowledge. Actual air traffic is contingent on weather and airport operational conditions so its management requires real organization that coheres well with real systems.

6
Formalism

Introduction

'From the moment of birth we are immersed in action, and can only fitfully guide it by taking thought.' Alfred Whitehead's observation resonates with deferred action. Our natural tendency to act is stronger than our learnt capability to reflect and much stronger than our capability to be rational. Our tendency towards natural design is stronger than our capability for rational design. This is because of realisms dominant causal power of emergence. It may be appropriate for individuals but not for organization and systems that seek to achieve purpose by design.

Some researchers reject formalism in general arguing for 'richer language of discourse'. Individual or organized action however intrinsically necessitates rational design. Organization and systems are conscious, rational design to achieve purpose, they do not happen by being 'immersed in action'. Organized action needs to be more than a fitful 'guide' because it has to embody purpose and provide enabling mechanisms for immersed action, to achieve objectives. In the absence of formal 'guide' (its design and practical value) organization capability and competency is indeterminate.

Alfred Whitehead's 'taking thought' finds its most elaborate form in formalism 'guide'. The guide for organization and systems is rational design and enabling formalism. Rational design is reaffirming conscious event of artificial design forming a beginning, middle and end life cycle that frames further action. Strategy or plan provides psychological security to executives and managers. It provides credible justification for action and defence from scrutiny by stakeholders. Executives can justify their actions because it is explicable. Systems designers use similar defense with ISDM, methods and techniques. When design fails rational baseline provides defensive rationale.

Formalism guides rational design. It is a deliberate guide to design organized action, a system for representing real things in design, creating reality and manipulating it to achieve some objective. Its basis is systems of logic ranging from mathematical axiomatic formal systems with inference rules to logical description. For organization and systems design it is of three kinds formal methods, diagrammatic (logical) and verbal.

Formalism should demonstrate analytic and synthetic generalization. It should enable analysis of various design domains since it is general notation. Synthetic generality is the veracity of its application in various design domains. Formalism is usually detailed in notation languages. A notation language is defined as a finite set of representation symbols. Their logical interrelationships to represent real social and technical problems and rules of interpretation to manipulate symbols to propose a solution design that guides action. Mechanical and electro-mechanical machines are based on specification formalism and the design of digital computer epitomizes formal methods. Once design is created adherence is paramount because it provides direction and means for realizing predetermined objectives. Action that is not in-design is not permitted.

There is a rich tradition of rationally designing organization and systems. Public organizations were subjected to statistical formalism early. Humans, their action and conditions were analysed statistically mainly as probabilities. Economic models of rational choice and competition were developed, and still are developed, and used to guide company and government policy, with game theoretic gaining more credibility. Computational and mathematical models of organization inform organization design.

Despite this rich tradition success is debatable. Success of specification formalism for systems design is better as it has led to the powerful general digital computer and associated technologies. It has not produced equal success in applying computers and now ICT to organization. Despite this mixed profile of success specification formalism is necessary. Systems can only be designed with specification formalism because the digital machine is a finite state machine.

Rationality, primacy of action based on logic and reason and evidence-based action over other forms of action epitomize formalism. Formalism stems from rationally identifiable entities and subjects them to rational analysis. Real entities are abstracted and reconfigured into work and systems design that is assigned to organized action. Abstraction results in selecting details considered relevant to resolve problems and removing other details more descriptive of actual problems, principally removed because they do not succumb to rational analysis. The result is complex structural forms with embedded operational functionality resisted by actuality.

Spaces of action design

To improve formalism and understand what can be designed spaces of action design are demarcated in Table 6.1. It depicts spaces of design in rational design relative to natural design or actuality. All the spaces of action design can be rationally designed except space of natural design. What can be designed efficaciously is a design quality issue. Quality of design and its relevance in actuality depends on how representative formalism is of the space of natural design. In general specification formalism is dominant for state space design and deferment formalism for all other spaces as depicted in column three.

Space of natural design is human action in its entirety the population of design. It is daily actions, moments of thought, thinking of future and myriad other things humans do to exist and survive. It cannot be known to rational design so it is not subject to rational design. It contains the other spaces of design and can represent them but they cannot represent it completely and perfectly. It is not simply the sum of the other spaces. It is natural and unbounded. Relative to it organization and state space design are artificial adhering to Herbert Simons thesis of the artificial.

Space of formal design is for individual action. Appointments diary and task lists are examples of formal action. They are used to structure space and time formally. Design is very flexible as entries can be changed and subsequent action can immediately reflect change. It is limited to what rules can be imposed on humans through personal choice, law or societal norms. It is larger than space of organization and state space design because human action does not have to adhere to strict formalism and can be adapted easily. Formal design is able to reflect space of natural design better too.

Space of organization design is the design of organized action. The other two spaces of rational design are contained within it and enable it. Organization design includes systems type-3 design. A job specification and business process model are examples. National laws and local

Table 6.1 Spaces of organized action design

Space of action design	Design domain	Dominant formalism	Description	Formalism
Space of natural design	Natural design domain	–	Intrinsic to human action. Limited by physical laws and human laws.	Natural formalism (by inherent human condition)
Space of formal design	Rational design domain	Deferment formalism	Design of individual action. Limited by personal, social and societal norms.	Deferment formalism (by inherent human condition)
Space of organization design		Specification formalism	Design of organized action. Limited by legal, societal norms and culture.	Specification formalism and deferment formalism
State space design		Specification formalism	Design of finite state machines. Limited by physical laws, limits of digital machines and scope of specification formalism.	Specification formalism (logical formalism) and deferment formalism

culture place limitations on design. Organization design is not true to the space of natural design. There is latent conflict between it and natural design.

State space is the design of unambiguous and algorithms for finite digital machines. Algorithms or UML activity diagrams are examples of state space design using specification and diagrammatic formalisms respectively. State space design is limited to what can be designed with specification formalism and intrinsic limitations of digital machines. It is the smallest space of design because it is the least able to reflect space of natural design. Design is generally inflexible. It has the potential to incorporate deferment formalism and so expand its design scope. In deferred action design specification formalism and deferment formalism are distinguished but both are necessary to interrelate formalism to space of organization design.

Extant specification formalisms for state space design are formal methods and diagrammatic formalisms. It is logical, diagrammatic and mathematical. Formalism for space of organization design is verbal and diagrammatic formalisms. Deferred action introduces the notion of deferment formalism for state space and space of organization design.

In set theoretic terms the spaces of design are the sets:

N = space of natural design   F = space of formal design
R = space of rational design   O = space of organization design
Then F = { x ∈ R } and O = { x ∈ R }

Design decisions are the sets:

A = all design decisions   S = specified design decisions
D = deferred design decisions

In terms of design decisions if A is the set of all design decisions then the set of specified decisions is:

S = { x: P(x) }
   = { x ∈ A: x is a specified design decision by reflective designers }
S ⊂ A

and the set of deferred design decisions is:

$D = \{ x: P(x) \}_\infty$
   = { x ∈ A: x is a deferred design decision by action designers }
D ⊂ A

Specification precedes design in rational design it is a statement of design requirements. In deferred action design specification formalism has two properties common to both sets S and D. Its primary property is creative. Any design specification is a statement of creation. The secondary property is abstractive, since creating begins from an existing social and physical base things are abstracted from it.

In systems design others detail 'function', 'timing', 'performance', 'structure', and 'communication' as properties of formalisms. Clarke et al. (1996) define specification as process for 'describing a system and its properties' containing verification formalism, model checking, theorem proving and simulation. In organization design specification is confined to work required to achieve objectives and how it is done. In both cases confusing what is to be designed with how design works in actuality creates the assignment problem.

Specified organization design

In classical theory organization is an outcome of rational design, it is synonymous with rationality and embodies Weber's 'rational legal authority'. Its design is possible because of specification formalism. Specification formalism for organization design is not highly formal. Symbols and rules for applying and manipulating them are not formal, precise and logical compared with formalism for systems design, so it is termed verbal formalism.

Verbal formalism tried in practice includes plans, hierarchy, task related analytical entities, networks, matrices and process models. Dominant verbal formalism presently is business process. In all organization design since 1960s information has been significant analytical entity and now knowledge has become important. Focus now is on design of business processes, information and knowledge, and how these contribute to the organizational triad of PEE.

Verbal formalism is representation of organized action by rational identification of analytical organizational objects, interrelations definitions and their relations with business workers and customers. Principle analytical objects include business process, information and knowledge, and others include collaborative work, tasks and workflows. It is problematical to represent meaning or emotion so verbal formalism generally does not include them. In verbal formalism notation symbols and rules to apply and manipulate them are based on some theory of organization or management. Analytical generalizability of verbal formalism is not empirically verified. Computational and mathematical methods are popular with academics their analytical generalizability is better because of quantitative representations.

Analytical objects in classical verbal formalism are task, agents, and structure. In management it is decision-making. Organization is represented as design models of structural interrelations among them. Models are developed as relations among agents or between available resources and agents. They are ambiguous in practice because their identification varies within organization, over time and across organizations, so it is difficult to generalize. Information processing and decision-making were secondary objects in classical formalism but now data, information and knowledge are primary design objects.

Table 6.2　Verbal and diagrammatic formalism for organization design

Verbal formalism	Description
Strategy	Determine organizational purpose relative to competition.
Business model	Determine purpose, revenue stream, competition strategy and operational structure of organization.
Plan	Detail objectives and means to achieve them constrained by resource and time.
Business process reengineering	Redesign organizational operations radically as process.
Matrix	Decide structure & operations organization. Based on workers' capability.
Network	Decide structure & operations organization.
Hierarchy	Decide structure & operations of organization. (Organization chart)
Workflow	Describe task oriented interrelated work.
Job specification	Determine individual work.
Diagrammatic formalism	
UML Business Profile	Analyse, model and design business models that cohere with systems models.
IDEF	Analyse, model and design processes maps of organization for representation in systems.
Role Activity Diagrams (RAD)	Analyse, model and design business processes for representation in systems.
Flowchart	Describe individual and organizational workflow for representation in systems.

Table 6.2 details verbal and diagrammatic formalism for organization design. Kind and depth of analysis ranges from whole organization design as in business process reengineering to individual job specification. Modelling formalism includes IDEF or RAD used to model business processes and UML Business Profile to model business systems.

Organization is designed by modelling. Modelling entities include individual work as in task performance to collaborative work and organization-wide work as in workflow and business process. Group work focus is on understanding organizational collaboration and communication and to improve design of collaboration and groupware systems. Business process focus is on improving PEE and competitiveness. Key is model of information and knowledge.

Formalism contains checks for empirical relevance. Computational and mathematical models of organization are 'verified'. Verification is a test of empirical relevance of the representation in the model and its output. It seeks to check whether abducted logic of a model relates to experience to determine how well it corresponds to observation. In verbal formalism 'validation' of the representation is verification.

Forty years of formal analysis and rational design of organization has not resulted in a best design. Rather contingency theorists' view of organization as immediate task performance under prevailing conditions is veracious. Natural design suggests there is no best design. Initial focus of organization theory and research on optimal organization had shifted to satisficing and now to networked organization. New focus is managers' biographies, organizational stories and narratives, admitting the phenomenological and subjective in descriptions of organizational work with implications for design.

Business models depict revenue stream, competitors and organization structure to achieve objectives. It may involve proof-of-concept. Focus is on necessary organization design to attain revenue stream and compete with competitors. It involves determining product or services to sell, determining and incorporating competition strategy, and devising revenue streams. Business process design and systems are significant elements. Business models are becoming normalized as networked organization that exploits revenue stream and competitive advantage afforded by ICT.

Business plans and systems plans constitute formal organization design. Strategic plans are pinnacle of hierarchy of plans in organization design. A plan is a rational device or an instrument for action. It is an articulation of time-specific purpose, objectives and means of execution. It seeks optimization of limited resources and is normally documented. Plans are usually formulated to implement business strategy as planned action and project plans form specific task plans.

Planning is central to management. Organization structure is planned for future action necessary to achieve set objectives. Planning removes details of context and actuality and requires prediction of expected outcomes on which successive stages of a plan can build. Plans are implemented on assumption of considered factors remaining constant at the time of execution. Extraneous factors are categorized as contingencies, which plans can cater to before further planned action is implemented.

Formal computational and mathematical modelling is used to understand and design organization. Models enable conditional or 'what-if' analyses for business analysts to assess scenarios with certain conditions attached. Business and systems analysts manipulate models to assess changes to or failure of technology or introduction of new technology. Models are useful in managing risk too. The logical basis of modelling varies. Autoepistemic logic is used to represent beliefs. Modal logic is used to qualify empirical entities.

Computational and mathematical formalism is epitomized in management science. Central analytical object is optimization. Modelling subjects include crisis management, incident management and restructuring to improve PEE. It focuses organization design on modelling quantities of empirically verifiable entities. The emphasis is on what will happen and whether representations are valid.

Computational models include simulation. Mathematical models include stochastic models and models of growth and diffusion. Operations research, including supply chain management, focuses on optimization models. Model types range over general organization models, organizational engineering models, distributed artificial intelligence models, social network models and logic models. Verification of the models is integral to the modelling process.

Practical relevance of rational action and optimization premises of computational and mathematical models is weak. There is no evidence of general applicability of particular models to organization design. Consequently, to cover context-situated action, satisficing and contingency is used in other models that seek to account for actual human action.

Analytical objects in social and behavioural theories include conflict and negotiation, power and politics, organizational control, motivation and leadership. Theorists seek 'richer' explanations of social action. Social and behavioural theories of organization have had little impact on invention of formalism for organization design and less on organization design itself. Tools stemming from theory such as role analysis and group composition are used for organizational analysis. Often theoretical richness makes it difficult to apply constructs in design. So such verbal theory of organization is less formal but more sophisticated explanation of the space of natural design. Structuration and Actor Network Theory are examples of social theory applied to organization and IS. Situated action from ethnomethodology is largely applied to intelligent systems. No clear implication for design is drawn in the form of design principles or formalism from social theory but situated action does form the basis of design of intelligent systems. Generally, validation is not sought in verbal theories.

Specified organization design limitations

Specified organization design limitations include the need for exhaustive specification, rightness, precision and relevance. Critically, they are concerned with the extent to which specification design can represent SEST. Simulation and decision-making models confuse distinct SEST properties as the one structure property. In general, in classical units of analysis like strategy and decision-making, improvements in PEE, task and adaptation to task environment, task decomposition structure, hierarchy, informal networks and communication and coordination processes structural design subsumes all other design properties. Devices have focused on structure in which operations is subsumed with no consideration of emergence, space and time design properties.

Specification of any type mathematical, logical, diagrammatic or verbal is intrinsically limiting of organization design. It separates design from the actual by demarcating abstract from real, rational from the natural. It is specification of the way something should be rather than design enabling actual action that succeeds in achieving it. Specification contributes greatly to designing structure but because it separates design from the actual it is weaker at representing other SEST properties necessary.

The search for the right specification is mistaken and limiting. It supposes a generic organization to which all organizations should fit. Henry Mintzberg details generic forms for strategy design, planning, positioning so on. Organizations that require exactness like NASA strive for right specification but this is not necessarily appropriate for art, music and film organizations. In between are commercial, governmental and voluntary organizations to which generic forms do not apply. Analytic and synthetic generalization of verbal formalism for organization design is weak. Its verbal character makes it difficult to assess empirically within and across organizations.

Inherent limitation of specified state space design or systems design has impact on space of organization design by constraining it to specification of 'function', 'timing', 'performance', 'structure', and 'communication'. It concerns lack of correspondence with space of natural design, the force to comply with specified systems compounds it. Such specification design is weak at accounting for actuality of organizing. It relies on context corresponding to specified design rather than design corresponding to context. Business workers are forced to interpret actual events in terms of imposed design (the assignment problem) and when design is unable to provide direction their action is constrained and in some cases organization becomes mortified.

Lack of provision for sustainable organization is a critical limitation of specification. Sustainability is key business concern. Since plans and business models are static they are unable to cope with complete SEST. Business models seem relatively more successful than plans. Plan implementation is problematical because actual context differs from contents and assumptions made in plans. Realization of expected outcomes is poor but can be improved if plans and planning are re-conceptualized to account for SEST.

Specified systems design

Specification is what a system should do not how it will do it. Specification formalism for systems design encompasses formal mathematical methods, semiformal diagrammatic formalism and informal methods like Structured English or pseudo code. Systems design by specification formalism is rigorous and relevant but limited to state space design. Systems type-3 design is by specification of state space functionality, where it exists partially (it exists in human actuality too). Formal methods and diagrammatic formalism reflects state space requisite logical structure, capability and capacity. Designers still have to interpret design problems and design domains to propose an initial design. This is important for systems type-3 design relevance because it partially negates business workers intrinsic knowledge of work.

Specification formalism is necessary to design systems much of it resonates with mathematical formal systems. It is strong in representing structure but weak in other SEST properties similar to formalism for organization design. It defines human and organizational problems as design domains and represents it as conceptual architecture and functions with no active connection to the real. This results in machine-like behaviour of systems. Minimally, formalism contains techniques

Table 6.3 Formal methods, diagrammatic and verbal formalism

Formal methods		Specification formalism
		Description
Z	NC	Systems and organization modelling. Used in data processing, specification of sequential systems
VDM	NC	Systems modelling. Safety critical systems.
Petri Nets	NC	Deductive reasoning is possible, used in business process management
Pi Calculas	NC	Deductive reasoning. Used in business process management, mobile systems
Statecharts	CN	Specification of behaviour of concurrent systems
Normalization	CN	AKA Relational Data Analysis and Third (Fourth and Fifth) Normal Form Analysis.
Diagrammatic formalism		**Description**
UML	CN	Systems modelling. Software analysis and design. Defines syntax and semantics. Has deferred elements because it permits stereotype and extensions defined by modellers in context. For all deferred action design types.
UML Business Profile	CN	Business systems modelling. Facilitates progression from business process models to systems models. Business models form basis of Model-Driven Architecture.
Data Flow Diagrams	CN	Process modelling in terms of data. A DFD depicts how logical data move around in a system. It describes data at rest, moving, and transformed or processed.
IDEF	NC	Business process modelling. Process analysis and design.
ER data modelling	CN	For data analysis in structured systems analysis and design.
RAD	CN	RAD is a special case of Petri Nets.
Structured analysis and structured design	CN	Systems modelling. Structures data for algorithmic processing.

Table 6.3   Formal methods, diagrammatic and verbal formalism – *continued*

Specification formalism		
Verbal Formalism		**Description**
SDLC	NC	Its prescribed phases for systems development have evolved from rigid sequence to part iteration between phases to full iteration and many other versions. A case of solution to fit new problems as discovered.
StoryCards	CN	Used in ASD. A story by a 'user' is recorded as specification for designers.
Other		**Description**
Simulation	NC	Used to determine specification prior to specifying.
Informal	C	Structured English, pseudo code

Key
NC = Non-Constructive notation; CN = Constructive notation

for representing properties of software, interpretation rules, inter-connection rules for combining techniques and heuristics for applying techniques (Wieringa, 1998).

Table 6.3 details some rigorous formal methods and semiformal diagrammatic and verbal formalisms. Verbal formalism has design principles or prescribes design approaches like the SDLC. Diagrammatic formalism has notation language with finite symbols and rules for abstraction and composition. No formal reasoning is possible in verbal and diagrammatic formalisms. Specification formalism emphasizes the use of proper syntax but semantics is more explicit in formal methods. Formal methods differ because it is formulaic, and logical it enables mathematical deductive reasoning and proof with formal calculi.

Formal methods like Z and Object Control Language draw on mathematical concepts of abstraction and composition and emphasize unambiguous and formulaic mathematical expression. It aids software engineers to specify and construct reliable systems, particularly safety critical systems where reliability is crucial. Formal specification can be used to check correctness of systems and to predict systems reliability and performance. Z and Pi Calculus contain calculus to check error, omissions, correctness and completeness. They enable model checking, theorem proving and verification to analyse systems design for required properties. Axiomatic definitions and inference rules are used to prove properties based on formal logic systems. Formal methods like Z are non-constructive because the specification is not executable directly. Directly executable specification in code is constructive similar to programming languages.

Z is also used to design organizational routine transactions processing systems. It has the potential for infinite symbols defined by designers so it differs from other formal notation with finite symbol sets. Z formal reasoning can be applied to organization design and systems design. Organization hierarchy can be modelled as sets of people and so formal reasoning can be applied to organization design using Z. Formal methods manifest as notation language derived from mathematical deductive logic and formal logic systems with symbols, rules for abstraction and composition, techniques and tools.

Specification formalism has notation language to develop models of design domains. Notation languages require invention of 'symbol systems' to represent design domains, operators to manipulate representations and logic necessary to consider imperatives in design. Notation languages are symbol systems that facilitate design analysis and aid problem solving by structuring problems and systematically deriving resolution. In general notation languages make design work possible and make it concrete. For designers it enables mutual sharing of knowledge of design domain and design through communication that accepted symbol systems enable. The claim that mutual understanding extends to 'users' is less defensible because they have less technical knowledge and different non-systemic ontological beliefs.

Notation languages representation capability is determined by invention of appropriate symbols based on inventors' ontological systems beliefs. For instance, object-orientation is systems ontology and UML its notation language. Notation languages identify objects in human and organizational problem situations and represent them as systemic abstract design objects. Manipulation of these objects in accordance with interpretation rules generates design solution.

Design domain representation by formal methods differs from diagrammatic formalism. Formal methods notation language is mathematical and logically rigorous. It reduces design ambiguity by making specification explicit. Its main purpose is to design correct models by specifying and verifying systems models. Its use of mathematically defined precise symbols results in condensed expression capable of expansive coverage of design domains in shorter expressions. It makes use of operators to build formulae from basic declarative expressions and predicates. It often includes calculus to predict, analyse and check goodness and correctness of design, which is not possible in diagrammatic formalism. In UML model correctness is checked by reference to the UML metamodel, which describes correct, well-formed models.

The benefit of using formal methods is that systems design can be analysed formally. Internal consistency can be checked and other design elements derived that may be overlooked otherwise. Formal methods can be combined with logical formalism, particularly in requirements analysis, refinement and testing. Formal methods were used to develop UK Civil Aviation Authority CCF Display Information System for London's air traffic management.

Diagrammatic constructive notation language examples in Table 6.3 are DFD and UML. Its main analytical objects are data and information. It is used to structure data and information for state space processing. Structuring means to design formally human and organizational information or knowledge as 'system'. It is practised as 'systems analysis and design', based on the ontological belief in systems and set of techniques and tools applied to data and information, and now knowledge, to design systems. Notation symbols in structured systems analysis and design differ from object-oriented analysis because of different systems ontological beliefs of inventors. In structured methods each design activity is related to the next in sequential dependency, usually depicted by an arrow ($\rightarrow$) in representational diagrams. In object-orientation diagramming techniques can be applied contingent on events.

Some notations focus on database and program design they exclude organization design. ER modelling and DFD notations used in structured systems analysis and design and some ISDM are examples. They aim to 'capture' existing tasks and workflows for computerization. When systems design affects organization it is disrupted or changed ad-hoc to suit new systems design. The UML notation is capable of representing organizational aspects better because it has business modelling capability for organization design called 'business systems'.

Diagrammatic formalism does not produce efficacious representations of organized action as systems for actuality. It produces abstract structural and functional representation often inconsistent with actual organized action. It results in structural-functional representation stripped of inherent sociality of organization or emergent, spatial and temporal SEST properties. Resultant information or knowledge management 'system' is inadequate functional representation of actual human information and knowledge construction and its communication as organized activity. The system is assigned to create new reality but lacks interrelation with existing reality. It is a product representative of information theory to which business workers struggle to attribute meaning in existing conditions. Systems type-3 is erroneously regarded as functional. Misrepresentation stems from specification formalism's basis in information theory in which information is an artefact. It is better to think of systems as 'social software' requiring both artefactual design and meaning attribution design.

During 1960–1999 diagrammatic formalism focused on data and information processing with tangential consideration of its effect on organization design as in information provision for management decision-making. There is no similar formalism presently for individual and organizational knowledge but greater awareness of effect of design of KMS on organization design. Formalism for KMS is not yet sophisticated. Predicate logic and inference engines are earliest example of logical formalism in expert systems that make expert knowledge accessible organization-wide. Importance of formalizing knowledge is recognized but extant specification and diagramming formalism is insufficient to define and conceptualize organizational knowledge and KMS.

SDLC is verbal formalism because it presents no notation language, system of underpinning logic or mathematical deductive proof. It stems from engineering design methods and prescribes sequentially dependent phases but later versions abandon sequential dependency for iteration. ISDM combine verbal and diagrammatic formalisms but emphasizes verbal formalism termed 'methodology'. Methodology is prescriptive and encompasses human, organizational and technological aspects of socio-technical IS development. It is composed of SDLC and extant specification notation languages, with few methodologies inventing bespoke notations. Methodologists are concerned with relevance of prescription for systems design for organized action and underpin it with systemic constructs and latterly philosophical argument.

ISDM is an elaboration of SDLC phases as prescribed detailed planned action to develop IS in which sequential dependency is significant. Boehm's (2002) term is 'plan-driven methodologies'. ISDM prescribe how IS should be commissioned, aligned with business strategy, defined, developed and deployed. Focus is on conception of system and application of IT for organized (business) activity. Methodology use in practice is sporadic as contingent events are difficult to reconcile with planned action. Some ISDM contain much diagrammatic notation like Information Engineering and result in highly specified systems others are less rigorous.

Importance of organizational information has elevated ISDM to strategic planning. So a prime phase in many ISDM is strategic planning of ICT and IS necessary to manage organizational information. Successful strategic plans are Singapore's ICT infrastructure and Indian software companies' attainment of CMM level five certifications. Attainment results because of regimented compliance from business workers negating the human plane primarily and organizational planes of Figure 5.1.

Developing and executing strategic plans pose practical problems that have led to amendments to ISDM or alternatives like Critical Success Factors analysis to ensure top executives information needs are met. Where formalisms' limitations are admitted in ISDM the focus shifts onto contingent factors. Contingencies of actual development situations have led to including 'contingency planning' and incremental design. Contingency is slipped through the methodology backdoor which is the alternative informal formal formalism.

Failure of or disappointments in systems is attributed to poor formalism and lack of planning knowledge. So effort is made to improve planning and plans resulting in stringent standards, newer formalisms, modelling techniques or ISDM. Shortcomings have led IS researchers to social theory to understand organizational information and knowledge in human terms, but it has not added to systems design principles and techniques.

Modelling is intrinsic to specification formalism and formative in conceptualizing information and knowledge to design as systems. It is key in ISDM, software engineering and MDA. Modelling from 'specification' means to 'capture' organized activity in terms of 'systems requirements'. System models are built with notation language symbols by abstraction, description and analysis but most notations result in static models. Static models are abstract description of and unconnected to design domains. Implemented systems models are an assignment of this abstracted formalization to organized activity, which potentially curtails actual action because of organization's dependency on formal systems.

Conceptual model of organization's operational data developed for database design is an example of embedded descriptive model of organization. It contains business rules, policies, procedures and business processes and is used in IS algorithms designed to process modelled data into information. Analytical models of data are enabled directly by adapting databases for OLAP and data mining, recognizing importance of conceptual models to analyse organizational information. Analytical data models are developed using specification formalism for multi-dimensional data structures.

Specification formalism limitations

In terms of SEST most notation languages are limited to designing structure only. It is does not address other properties. Design serves to achieve goals in actuality but it can become an obstacle if SEST properties are not included. Actuality is systemless in systems type-1 and systems type-3 senses. Since actual action supercedes design in this sense its contribution depends on effectiveness of formalism to account for next actual actions.

Designers cannot defend their action solely on the 'truth' of formalisms they adopt to design. Gödel's incompletability theorem demonstrated no formalism proves its own internal consistency. The theorem precludes an absolute test so properties of formalism can only be tested with meta-formalism. Designers only have a subjective choice of formalism. Nevertheless for practical purposes some technical limitations of notation languages are significant. There is a lack of formal validation of design problem as solvable by notation. Design problems are given by business workers and accepted, and even modified, by designers for resolution. Design solutions are arbitrarily pronounced in similar fashion there is no formal check, except in formal methods or by reference to metadesign models as in the UML. In the same vein sufficiency of rules to manipulate notation symbols is not formally checked for external validity.

A limiting assumption of specification formalism is availability of complete prior knowledge of structural form and operational functionality. Modelling process is composed of objectification, abstraction, and specification of structure and operational functionality. In formal methods this process results in mathematically and logically sound models composed of axioms and logical proof, which can be further reasoned with calculus. In diagrammatic formalism it results in diagrammatic models that cannot be so reasoned. Since knowledge of design, particularly operational functionality, is imperfectly available certain axioms about the world become embedded in systems models, resulting design and implemented systems. Its truth cannot be verified until experienced in the domain of empirical. Often, when these axioms are confronted by actuality the system's view of the world overrides it to the detriment of success.

Specification formalism does not account for abductive reasoning required to commence modelling. It does not extend to designers' initial design decisions concerning shaping problems and ways to solve them. Ironically, in arriving at good designs designers defer many design decisions by leaving out details and trying different designs. In deferred action this is deferment in the design process itself.

Specification formalism separates systems design from implementation. Systems models of organized activity are determined prior to implementation, and from the perspective of deferred action form actual use. In database design conceptual models are regarded as representative of organizational activities but are actually spatially detached and temporally located pictures. Implemented systems drawing on databases therefore contain predefined organizational activity, on which business workers base subsequent actions thereby constraining actual action.

Converting specification into design and implemented system is problematical design issue in specification formalism. As Jonathan Jacky (2001) notes of formal methods such conversion requires additional knowledge of the application domain and knowledge of the application or 'constructive definitions of the application', that can result in executable code. In structured diagrammatic formalism designers use an additional step called 'transform analysis' to convert analysis into design and implementation. The conversion problem is acute for systems type-3 design, since designers and coders often assume knowledge of application domains to complete design and implementation. Such knowledge is not available to them by experience that resides in business workers' experiences. Design of formal models requires thorough understanding of requirements complicated by inadequate means of communication between designers and 'users'. Designers clean vague and inadequate requirements by making assumptions to develop systems models so reducing the SEST veracity of systems. Making such assumptions is a major weakness of specification formalism.

Systems built from descriptive and analytical data models, and conceptual models in general, in formal organized action create further formalization complexity. Often formal organization and formal systems are in conflict because actual organization conforms to natural design or when organization is changed through strategy or in response to markets commensurate change in systems is problematical. Introduction of new systems though causes no problem and is even erroneously embraced as 'change management'. Conceptual models constrain actual action by binding action to formal systems design sometimes threatening sustainability of organization. Decision-makers acting on information from inappropriate conceptual models and systems architectures have unwittingly directed organization into bankruptcy. The problem is compounded because formal systems are incongruent to actuality. Specification formalism results in rigid systems architecture and static systems that reify organized action.

Internal validation of systems models is strong in formal methods and less so in diagrammatic formalism, there is little formal business or organization validation. Conceptual models are checked only for internal consistency, not validated in terms of business and organization. Correspondence between organization design from verbal formalism and specification formalism for systems design is not checked. It results in systems determining organization design. Design research and designers should evaluate its appropriateness, should systems formalisms override organization design. Its value is questionable and may inverse the logic of designing for organized action by making the tool dictate the problem. UML Business Profile for business systems seeks to redresses this imbalance but only peripherally.

Specification formalism in general inadequately characterizes information and knowledge ontology as rational objects that can be objectified, modelled with precision and checked for correctness. It limits rather than expands application of IT to organizational information and knowledge problems. ISDM planned action models of systems has had severe limiting effect on deployment of IT and conceptions of IS. Rationalism in knowledge ontology is having similar effect on conceptions of KMS. Rather than exploit IT to expand space of organization design planned action models limit it thereby constraining pursuit of purposeful action.

Embedding best industry business practices in COTS for enterprise resource management distance COTS from actual organization. The argument that best practice of an organization is unique to it not easily transposed to other organizations gains weight when considering COTS usage in terms of competing organizations within industry. Best practice modelling equalizes rather than differentiate competing organization. Certain industries regulated by government can greatly benefit from best practice systems design as in pharmaceuticals.

Since rational design is necessary condition of organized action it should be conceptualized in ways that account for natural design or actuality. A successful form of rational design in gaming computer programmes is based on heuristics. This is consistent with deferred action in which heuristics can be employed by business workers to achieve formal aims. Inadequacy of formalism in general is indicative in emergence of agile systems development and XP. Its practice differs radically from accepted design norms by pioneering new systems ontology yet to be identified but certainly closer to deferred systems ontology. Success is yet unproven but if open source code is any indication, which has been accepted by government and industry, the movement should contribute new understanding radically different from specification formalism. It will push further the boundary of potential of systems in organized action.

By modelling actuality specification formalism amasses symbols that over complicate representation. Rather than searching for better specification formalism as primary means of representation deferred action acknowledges its limits. It reveals computational, mathematical and logical limits of specification formalism. Rather then focus on inventing symbols to 'capture' organized activity specification formalism needs to invent symbols to design TSA, S-SEI, and deferment mechanisms (Ttools) as SEST objects to enable interrelations and deferred design. Notation languages need to extend to social action symbols that can be used to design the S-SEI to embrace sociality of organized activity as interrelation design.

Mathematics requires finite abstract elementary predicates and operations to represent and explain its objects. Specification formalism attempts to model space of natural design with a finite set of symbols and operations of composition. This desirable property of formalism is the aim of deferment formalism too. Specification formalism is flawed though because it seeks blindly to 'capture' the space of natural design. Deferment formalism seeks to provide interrelation objects instead that interface well with it. Such objects do not capture but enable natural design. It utilizes specification formalism, revised to provide such representation of the space of natural design in SEST terms.

Deferment formalism

Theory of deferred action explains how to make space of rational design conducive to space of natural design. The problem concerns representing deferred action in design as SEST properties. Examples of deferment formalism in practice are DDD implemented in a banking application, Java deferred classes, and deferred data flow analysis for networking. Deferment formalism is an ongoing research and development theme. Its broad parameters are sketched out here.

Is it possible to specify systems whose actual operational definition is deferred to action designers? Deferment formalism defines real problems as design's field of action and represents it as conceptual architecture with active connections to fields of action by deferring representation of functions and if required architecture too, resulting in semiotic behaviour of systems consistent with abductive logic. Its significance is its catering to natural design as an aspect of rational design. Natural design itself cannot be a design subject but formalism can be invented to facilitate it. Extant formalism like the UML has elements of deferment. Network protocols like TCP/IP, Web http and scripting languages like XML have deferment elements too. These techniques make SEST properties accessible to action designers.

Deferred action is acknowledgement of specification formalism limitations. It proposes realism combination of specification design and deferment design to reflect SEST properties. Instead of increasingly abstract rigorous specification formalism basis of modelling organized action, deferred action merges rational design into natural design, formal design into actuality. It proposes theoretical constructs and design principles to better organize in actuality.

Formalism differs in forms of abstraction and composition particularly common to all formal methods. Deferred action explains difference in terms of natural and rational design causal powers. Difference can be nominally measured on the spectrum of design (Figure 1.7). Most formalism tends towards rational design some inadvertently represents natural design. In deferred action design veracity of notation language is its creative, abstractive, compositional and communicative capability to represent actual organized action.

Deferment formalism is inferred from deferred action and seeks representation of complete SEST. Deferred action necessitates invention of ways to interrelate actual action with representation by rational design. Deferment formalism preserves integrity of actual organized activity in relation to formal design, does not constrain actual action, or undermine existing design. The Indian number system is an exemplar. Its use in mathematics, statistics and everyday calculations is contingent on new developments and actual conditions. Neither its design nor actual action (in which it is put to use) is compromised. Similarly, design is not compromised and actual action is not constrained by deferment formalism. By so designing for social action the assignment problem is overcome.

Deferment formalism is based in realism to emphasize that rational design is of use only in the domain of empirical. It seeks understanding of causal powers relevant to empirical design tending towards natural design. It utilizes specification formalism to account for structure SEST property, acknowledging abstraction and composition but it emphasizes deferment formalism to account for other SEST properties stemming from natural design. Deferment formalism in turn defers abstraction and composition to action designers. It seeks to enable design of interrelation objects to cater for complete SEST to reflect actual action in formal design. Further characteristics are detailed in Table 6.4. No such formalism yet exists but elements of it exist in extant techniques detailed in the second part of the table.

Table 6.4 Defining deferment formalism

Deferment formalism	Description
Realism	Epistemology consistent with natural design reflected in models and design.
Free will	Maintain free will of natural design. Not constrained by specification.
Rational design & natural design	Open rational design it should reflect complete SEST.
Specification & deferment formalisms	Synthesize specification accounting for structure and deferment enabling deferred design. Abstraction and composition by specification formalism and deferment of abstraction and composition to action designers.
Duplex design domain	Design structure & defer structure in RSD – do not specify run-time architecture. Defer operational functionality – do not implement functionality or specify run-time operational functionality.
Designers	Reflective designers design structure & action designers design for emergence, space and time.
Design decisions	Distinguish specified and deferred decisions reflecting SEST properties, and other decision types real and autonomous.
Interrelation design	Provide notation symbols, mechanisms/deferred objects enabling run-time architecture design & operation functionality design. Apply abstraction & composition to interrelation design too. Symbols to represent actual action are not one-to-one representations but enable interrelation design in fields of action. They are context-free similar to context-free grammars.
Rigour & relevance	Draw on abstraction & composition technique of specification formalism. Provide symbols capable of abductive and deductive logics to represent design domains.
Scalable	Applies to standalones systems design & Web-based systems. Applies to design of systems type-2 and -3.
Generalization	Principles can be generalized to formalism for other types of design especially organization design.

Table 6.4 Defining deferment formalism – *continued*

System	Example deferred object
Internet	TCP/IP
Web	http, SML, XHTML
IMS	RDF
UML	Stereotypes, extensions (specification formalism) as system
Spreadsheet	Formula bar
Context Free Grammar	DTD
Programming Languages & Scripting systems	Java, SGML

Systems code is empirical. Suppose this specification at time Tn: System for customer account that shows current account balance permits deposits and withdrawals. Code below is typical implementation of the specification in an imperative programming language like Java. In this design customers can make deposits and withdrawals to a current account.

```
public static void main (String [ ] args) {
      class CurrentAccount {
      private in currentAccountBalance = balance;

      public void deposit (int amount) {
            balance = balance + amount;
            }
      public void withdrawal (int amount) {
            balance = balance – amount;
            }
}
```

What actual (deferred) action is possible? A possible deferred action at time Tn+1could be: To attract new customers and retain existing ones the bank decides to combine current accounts with mortgage accounts, and allow customers to transfer surplus monies from current accounts to repay mortgage loan. Customers decide the surplus amount conditional on remaining in credit. The bank's decision is a policy change which is emergent consistent with natural design or deferred action that necessitates change to operating procedures and commensurate change in systems operational functionality.

What formalism and design enables response to such emergence? In specification formalism, the change would be categorized as enhancement change and done by reflective designers under change control policies. Components and patterns are based on specification so would need to be predicted, but emergence and therefore deferred action is unpredictable – the space of natural design. Specification formalism alone is insufficient to cope with the space of natural design. It inherently limits representation of the space of natural design. Extant specification formalism is limited because it does not account for emergence and deferred action. In design based on deferment formalism, action designers would be able to change existing systems through DDD.

Deferment formalism makes it possible to represent actual organized activity better in formal design. Organized action is created, sustained and principally achieved by rational design with natural design or deferred action as its subordinate functionary. Since it is not possible to design space of natural design deferment formalism is necessary to represent its SEST properties in formal design. It is the conduit between design and actual organized activity. It is necessary because organization design is embedded in space of natural design and does not work as an abstract form resulting from specification formalism. Formalism should incorporate symbols for interrelation design of space of natural design, symbols based on understanding deferred action. They will be less in number compared with expanding specification formalism to model actual human problems and work.

Much of discrete mathematics concerning finite states is not useful to develop deferment formalism but set theory has utility. It can be adapted to invent deferment formalism for organization and systems modelling. Its axiomatic character enables simple axioms and inference rules to be defined, which is necessary for planned action aspect of design. These axioms and rules can also be devised to model deferred action.

Data, information and knowledge

Analysis usually proceeds by seeking some principles or mechanism to convert or process data into information and information into knowledge. It unwittingly assumes that information (and knowledge) is artefact. Some writers identify 'organizational knowledge' in systems that were prevalent before it became significant. Some of these systems in Table 6.5 clearly process data to produce information, for example EIS and CRM.

Table 6.5 Defining KMS

System type	Knowledge attribute: accessible & develop capture, exploit
Decision support systems	Capture and exploit managers' knowledge, support decision processes.
Executive information systems	Make information accessible to executives.
Expert systems	Capture and make expert knowledge accessible organization-wide.
Group support systems	Capture and exploit community knowledge to complete tasks.
Workflow management systems	Capture knowledge to process high volume of 'cases' in parts of processes.
Document management systems	Make accessible organizational knowledge by sharing.
Customer relationship management systems	Develop core marketable knowledge of customers' behaviour.

Indicative modelling techniques

Heuristic or rule-based systems; case-based reasoning; constrain-based reasoning, model-based reasoning, diagrammatic reasoning.

Indicative implementation technologies

Data mining, intelligent agents, neural networks, evolutionary algorithms, fuzzy logic.

The concept of knowledge management 'system' is not yet clear. Data mining verbal formalism like CRISP-DM methodology is used to design knowledge discovery systems based on databases and AI techniques like context-based reasoning or concept maps are used to design systems that capture knowledge. Knowledge ontology is used to design IS but not KMS. Companies have attempted to manage organizational knowledge through bespoke KMS. There is no independent study of them but practices include capturing workers knowledge, exploiting existing knowledge and making expert knowledge accessible.

In deferred action data, information and knowledge have artefactual and meaning attribution properties. Data, information and knowledge reflect SEST properties by being tailorable and deferrable that enables its representation. Physical space is part of social actuality in which knowledgeable action happens. Physical space of operating theatres is different from boardrooms resulting in different knowledgeable actions. Knowledge is spatially dependent bodily action relating directly or indirectly to material things in physical space based on subconscious or rational reflective capacity. It is not simply derivative of data and information. They are its components. Whilst data is processed into information, information is not 'processed' into knowledge.

In deferred action knowledge's physical or natural design trait is significant. Knowledge is located physically and in space and time. It is stored in physical spaces like documents, digital media and human brains that combine to constitute organizational knowledge. It is actioned in physical space by manipulation of objects and results in physical products or service. In these terms tacit physical properties of tacit knowledge become clearer.

Knowledge is a consequence of the physical space in which organization happens and in which organization manipulates physical objects through research, innovation, manufacture, engineering and service like healthcare. Knowledge not used in physical space cannot be organizational knowledge. Socially embedded knowledge is thus explained because the social can only happen in physical spaces of offices, units or departments with conjunct and enabling facilities.

Knowledge is a product of reflection for individuals and collectives in organization. Design activity affords reflection because of its rational component. Data and information are produced by design in which meaning attribution is possible. Information and knowledge become defined and useful in actuality through reflexivity.

Duplex design process

Herbert Simon demonstrates (specified) rational design limitation by reasoning that 'state space' design negates actual action, which is empirical. In deferred action terms it is in the space of natural design or actuality where events or 'action' that is pertinent to achieving purpose is observed. Philosophically, systems exist only for its observer. This has radical implications for conceptualizing design process and design of organization and systems, resulting in theoretical design process constructs of deferred action. It questions the sufficiency of conceptualizing design process as unitary domain restricted to reflective designers.

Simon's observation is realisms construct of domain of empirical. In realism experience is consequential on causal powers in domain of real that give rise to events in domain of actual, which depending on the presence of observer may or may not result in experience in domain of empirical. In deferred action terms, purposeful action is only evident in actuality, space of natural design, rather than rationally during reflective design. This is consistent with realism.

Empirical experience necessitates dividing design process into duplex specification design domain of reflective designers for planned action and deferment design domain of action designers for deferred action. Theoretically, planned action and deferred action are constitutive of design but separated spatially and temporally. Duplex design process ensures design is based on reflective capacity of rational thought and empirical actuality of embodied action. Reflective design and deferred design constitute design process. The same argument applies recursively to specification design domain. Since it is organized activity reflective designers can know certain things in advance of design but experience others in domain of empirical. Problem and design in specification design are emergent too.

Specification design domain is prescriptive design or planned action by reflective designers. In organization design it is the province of strategists, planners and business analysts and in systems design project managers, systems analysts, designers and programmers. In systems design specification design domain is limited to designing TSA – state space design of structure capable of enabling deferred design. Since systems architecture is designed space for action, rather than design of prescribed action, it can be the subject of rational design. Specification formalism is particularly apt at SPS or state space problem-solving and systems architecture design. Specification design needs to cater to TSA design.

Vennevar Bush's Memex system proposal resonates with duplex design process. Hypertext technologies become available much later, when Tim Berners-Lee invented HTTP, a deferment mechanism to implement deferred action, for the World Wide Web with phenomenal success. Duplex design process is quintessential in its design.

It consists of reflective designers' design of Web systems architecture (TSA) and action designers' design of content (operational functionality) during purposeful action or in actuality.

Theoretical question in deferment design domain is extent to which operational functionality can be specified. In terms of natural design its specification is from a sample of all design domain action that by rational design is made into abstract repeatable processes. The question of whether so-called 'users' should be permitted to design is evaded by researchers and practitioners. Deferred action characterization of natural and rational design domains questions the effectiveness of specification design and viable scope for reflective designers. Design is deliberate intervention in the space of natural design but specified design of operational functionality constrains actual action. Its focus on organizational processes or systems functions marginalizes actual

action. It aims to shape desired future by design but when implemented it is confronted by emergent actuality that reflective designers
cannot predict in design. The confrontation requires reassessment of
primacy and scope of specification design.

Specification design aims to 'capture' and 'specify' organized activity
as structural, functional and dynamical 'requirements' it is the anti-
theses of deferment design domain. Actual action cannot be formalized
intrinsically. Deferment design domain overcomes limitations of
specification design by seeking symbols to represent emergence, space
and time SEST properties. It caters to actuality by making space of
natural design accessible to action designers by interrelation design.

Duplex design process is a necessary and sufficient condition to
design organization and systems for actuality. It implements the theoretical focus on rational design in specification design and natural
design in deferred design as primary interrelated deign issues for organized action. The artefact is secondary. It is based on understanding
actual action and organized activity since design ultimately becomes
real in context when confronted with actuality.

Deterministic and free will formalism

Deterministic formalism is any notation language that seeks by
specification canonical representations of design domains' structure,
functions and dynamics. It generally has natural science bias and
draws on axiomatic mathematics though this does not define its determinism. Much of it is derived from engineering design principles. Its
determinism stems from predicating design domains that binds them
to its predications. It binds actual action by assigning designed rules
embedded in models of organized activity. In this sense it is deterministic because systems are 'inserted' in application domains. This is true
of formalism based on predicate calculus.

Free will formalism is any notation that seeks interrelational representations of design domain in duplex design process. It pursues
purpose by rational design that enables actual action characteristic of
natural design. Deferment formalism recognizes action designers by
enabling DDD in models of organized action representable as duplex
design process. Modal logic is one basis for inventing free will formalism, necessary because of natural design SEST properties.

Design that works in actuality requires free will formalism. Duplex
design process prohibits deterministic formalism from binding actual
action. Since formalism should depict imperatives, given duplex design

process specification design is unable to bind actions in deferment design. Deferment design should be free to implement its own imperatives. This concerns how interrelation between specification formalism and actual action is defined. The usual definition is:

Verbal formalism → action   (α: organization design)
Specification formalism → action   (β: systems design)

The arrow → depicts dependency. In (α) action is dependent on verbal formalism or organization design, and in (β) action is dependent on specification formalism or systems design. In each space of natural design is bound by rational design because design is assigned to or 'inserted' in it. This mode of rational design is termed deterministic formalism which is problematical in actuality. It is the cause of relative underperformance of formal design (rational design) compared with actual human activity (natural design).

The problematic in designing for actuality is this: Organization is designed to achieve purpose (1) in which action is directed and controlled (1.1). In actuality events occur independent of formal design (2). Independently occurring events are interpreted relative to design (3). Further action it is not contingent on the observed events because design binds action (1.2). Failure to acknowledge independently occurring events as requiring contingent action (4) means that action is bound and curtailed by design.

The declaratives (1), (1.1), (2) and (3) constitute conditions and outcomes of specification design. This is accepted in duplex design process. Deferment design in duplex design process rejects declarative (1.2) and adds declarative (4). Therefore deferment formalism is:

Verbal formalism ↔ action   (Ω: organization design)
Specification formalism ↔ action   (π: systems design)

Here the bi-directional arrow (↔) depicts determination and enablement. In (Ω) action is directed by organization design but actual action can determine or affect change in organization design (operational aspects). In (π) action is directed by systems design but actual action can determine or affect change in systems design (functionality and some cases structure). This mode of design is termed free will formalism.

Figure 6.1 is a stylized set of theoretic depiction of deferred action free will formalism. The rectangle represents the space of natural

Figure 6.1   Free will formalism

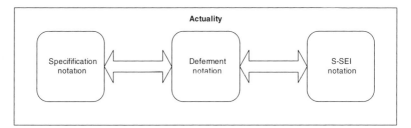

design (actuality) – universal set. Within three rounded rectangles are subsets of specification formalism, deferment formalism and S-SEI. Interrelations between them are (1) intra to design because they relate to design or particular purposeful action, and (2) extra because design needs to respond to actuality. Formalism of any kind for organized action should be composed of notation capable of modelling these three elements structure, actual action, and interrelation design or SEST. Interlinked bi-directional arrows between them signify conjunction in actuality of design and actuality or planned action and deferred action.

Specification formalism is to represent structure and enable deferment design. Structure embodies intentions, purpose and objectives – the plan. It is a prerequisite to and necessary for organized action. In systems it is systems architecture and in organization statutes, laws and relations formally defined between people. Structure is amenable to specification design because it is based on formal statement of purpose.

Deferment formalism is to represent actual action – deferred action in response to emergence, space and time. The structure is placed in actuality to shape and change it – to achieve purpose. Actuality though is not sympathetic to design and may reject it. The placing creates different new sets of interrelations and because the design cannot be fully appreciative of them, it needs adjustment mechanisms. For this reason actual action is enabled through deferment design, which responds to actuality by interrelation design to achieve purpose. Deferment notation depicts actual action in organized activity and contains notation for active model design.

Deferment formalism enables design to emerge, take shape in context. It caters to SEST properties of natural design. Sanskrit is an example of deferment in formal language. Its structure or grammar is designed to allow human expression in its infinite form. Speakers construct words to express feelings and observed things to express ideas (Briggs, 1985; 1986) as other SEST properties. SGML is formal language, an example of deferment in computer languages. It specifies rules for tagging elements as structure. It does not specify formatting; designers interpret it in context as other SEST properties. In Sanskrit and SGML construction is done in context and according to actual conditions. They are context-free grammars. Deferment formalism similarly separates structure from actual use so it is non-constructive. This separation can be generalized to all rational design that seeks to encompass natural design.

Interrelation design is enabled through the S-SEI, a significant proposition. By recognizing SEST the S-SEI serves to enable actual organized activity to be part of formal design. It caters to the richness of social action, being human, insight, expression of human intention, and intuition. It links actual organized activity with systems (design).

Since the space of natural design is infinite compared with finite space of rational design (state space design and space of organization design), the S-SEI should enable abstraction and composition of symbols to interrelate with it. Interrelation symbols enable the space of organization design and state space design to connect with actuality perpetually. It allows formal systems design to maintain an active link with sociality and actuality and contains the Ttools to enable action designers to do deferred design.

Deferred action design principles

Theoretical understanding should contribute to techniques and principles of design. They should treat organization design and systems design as an integrative activity drawing on natural design and maintain distinction between organization and systems, because there are philosophical, systems theoretic and practical problems with equating human organization with systems. Design principles can be used to develop deferred action models to inform design modelling. Similarly, systems analysis techniques based on linguistics analysis of knowledge work demonstrated by Patel (2005b) apply to design of deferred and real cohered organization and systems. They are tentative techniques to analyse and account for emergence in systems design.

Rational design should enable space of natural design because of deferred action's primary design principle. All rational design is inferior to natural design. Design principles summarized in Table 6.6 stem from it.

Table 6.6   Deferred action design principles

Design principle

Primary

1   Human action by natural design is superior in all cases and supersedes any space of rational design in all conditions. The corollary is rational design is inferior to actual organized activity.

Secondary

2   Duplex design process is composed of specification design and deferment design as process and as components it separates tailorable systems architecture design (TSA) for structure design and operational functionality design for emergence, space and time design.

3   Designers compose reflective designers who designs TSA and action designers who design operational functionality.

4   Specification design by abstraction and composition is identification by reflective designers of SEST objects to represent in design based on specification formalism that is effective for design of knowable certainties and creating TSA – structure.

5   Deferment design by deferred abstraction and composition is identification by action designers of SEST objects to represent in design based on deferment formalism that is effective for design of emergent objects and operational functionality– emergence, space & time.

6   Interrelation design relates rational design with natural design through S-SEI that enables DDD with Ttools to allow action designers to design operational functionality in design's fields of action.

7   Since SEST is constitutive of data, information and knowledge they need to be tailorable and deferrable and SEST properties interrelate to form basis of deferred design.

These principles are sufficient to generate rational design conducive to natural design. They create sustainable design capable of interrelating well with actuality. The DDD and RDD principles link formal design with actual conditions.

Active models

Deferred action systems are realism *active* systems in two senses. One is when action designers observe it in domain of empirical. This is the basis of the other sense of active interrelation with natural design or actual conditions of action in design's field of action. Space of natural design, realism's domain of empirical, cannot be modelled deterministically with specification formalism as 'problem domain' (systems) or 'structure' (organization). Emergence itself cannot be modelled because it cannot be predicted but some management scientists think the opposite! Modelling objects to convert emergent process and states into design is necessary. States emerge and do not simply pre-exist. Multifarious nature of emergence, space and time require active models in which responses to emergence can be modelled in terms of deferred action related SEST properties.

Deferred action active models are analytically derived embodied patterns from natural design. Active models are enabled by duplex design process. Modelling from specification is representation of structural properties and deferrable objects by reduction of details through abstraction and composition determined by reflective modellers. By structure is meant interrelations between objects in systems and interrelations between systems and fields of action. Structure is the set of internal and external interrelations interwoven with emergence, space and time.

Specified structure becomes active when it is linked to its field of action through deferment that enables action modellers to abstract and compose design objects for operational functionality. This is embodied analytical patterning of SEST properties. Deferment design links empirically abstract structural analytical pattern to embodied analytical patterns in fields of action. So SEST is sufficient description of system properties because structure is interwoven with emergence, space and time occurring in fields of action. This prevents simple disembodied abstract structure, systems architecture in systems design and organization structure in organization design.

Deferment formalism for active modelling is future orientated and seeks to represent embodied patterning. Active models are both declarative and imperative. Embodied patterning focuses on actuality and context and its relation to design. It is empirical to action designers as arising patterns in actuality translated into deferred design. It requires deferring abstraction and composition of systems' operational functionality. Example of embodied patterning is XML Vocabulary – presently not designable by action designers – or spreadsheet and word macros.

To enable active modelling deferment formalism should be capable of representing systems deferment points (SDP) and enabling DDD. SDP can be determined by analysing deferred action in organized work or by empirical study. Then design of operational functionality is possible through SDP and DDD that can be depicted in UML Business Systems models.

Stereotypical active model is based on the (Ω) and (π) definitions of formalism and action in the previous section. It embodies actuality and can be altered by action designers. An example of active data and information model is airline reservation systems. Its active model of seat availability on scheduled airplane flights mirrors actuality. It does not allow 'users' to change any aspect of operational functionality but deferred action active models permit action designers to do so. Since systems are placed in actuality active models allow deferred action to be translated into deferred design.

Figure 6.2 is an active model for KMS design depicting duplex design process domains. Reflective designers model determinable specified objects that compose the TSA as specification design. Action designers determined deferred objects enabled by SDP analyses and do deferred design of operational functionality by DDD as deferment design. Point A shows systemic deferred objects (SDO) emerging from actuality and converted into deferred design with Ttools at point (B) the S-SEI. S-SEI is the empirical link enabling DDD.

Figure 6.2   Stereotypical active model of systems

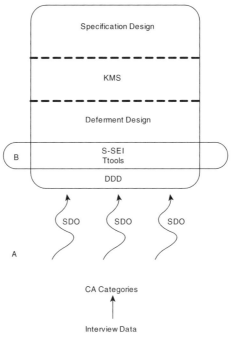

Source: Patel, 2005b

Specified element contains TSA, architecture able to host deferred design and provide deferment mechanisms. In SEST terms it is the structure property or plan enabling any subsequent deferred action. Examples of TSA are internet and Web and of deferment mechanisms IP and HTTP. Spreadsheets have TSA. Its model of numerical data processing enables design of formulae, functions and algorithms particular to workers' situations. Like the Web its TSA contains, in terms of deferred action, a model of systemic deferred objects (SDO) that action designers configure according to operational needs. It is possible to use Z to specify a TSA for deferred (design) action.

Deferred element formalizes actions of skilled and knowledgeable workers, know-how to make operations successful that normally is not modelled or designed. Building on IS research drawing on language theories and linguistics, deferred element of an active model is composed of SDOs shown in Figure 6.3 empirical example of the CAO

Figure 6.3   Linguistic analysis of systemic deferred objects

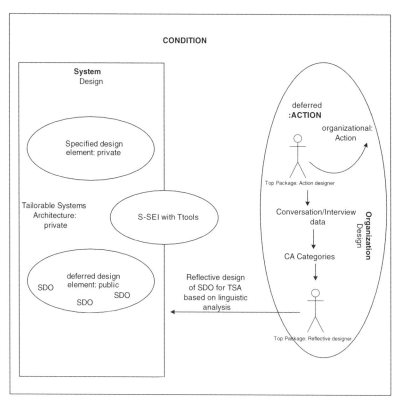

scheme. Reflective design of TSA and SDPs is based on linguistic analysis (Patel, 2005b). Here the CAO scheme is stylized UML notation illustrating context of such analysis. It depicts reflective designers in organization using conversation analysis to elicit SDO from action designers to model TSA to enable deferred design.

Reflective designers deploy reproductive SPS stratagems. Since systems serve actual informational and knowledge problems, action designers rather than reflective designers are better placed to address them because social and organizational structures emerge as much as they are planned. Action designers are better at solving emergent problems that arise in the space of natural design through EPS stratagems. Such enablement avoids deterministic models and leads to active models.

Problem framing and solving informational and knowledge problems as deferred action ontology encompasses rational and structured problem solving or specification design. It enhances rational design by deemphasizing prescribed behaviours or planned action and by not seeking final 'solution'. It recognizes occurrence of events outside the rational solution, and a willingness to allocate resources to be able to act on them. Deferment, intradeferment and capacity of action designers to address problems is recognized by other approaches discussed next.

The unified modelling language

Since the UML is extensible it can be used to model deferred action and develop active models. The UML itself is an example of synthesized specification and deferment formalisms. Its deferment element is the stereotypes and tagged values definitions that modellers can define for unique situations accounting for the space of natural design. As the three amigos state: 'These mechanisms can be used to tailor a UML variant by defining a set of stereotypes and tags and adopting conventions for their use in order to build models. (Rumbaugh et al., 1999: 106). In this sense the UML is based on deferred action model of design work but the UML itself assumes specified systems ontology.

UML could be extended to model deferred action in business systems models. Its notation symbols are passive – use case symbols like actor, business actor and business worker. To develop active models new active symbols are required to depict interaction between business workers and systems and symbols to depict deferred design in terms of SDPs à la the CAO scheme. Deferment symbols could be invented for use case, class and object, sequence, activity and collaboration diagrams.

In active models the 'use' aspect of actors would need to be refined. UML does not model actors actively as part and partial of systems but as 'users' of specified systems, so they are not modelled *in* use cases and class diagrams remaining external to systems. Actors and business workers need to be modelled as active and integrated with systems.

Figure 6.4   Spaces of action design

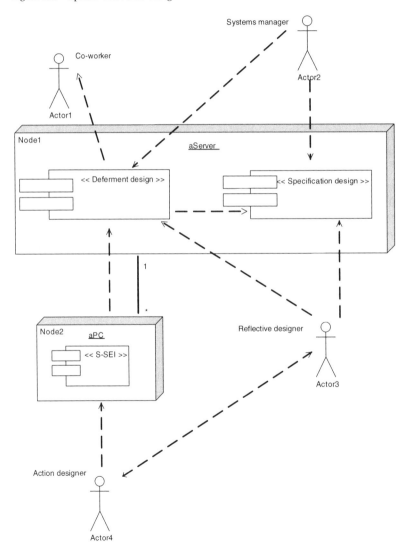

This is necessary in open systems types. Since action designers make DDD they should be modelled doing it thus integrating organization design and systems design, the aim of the UML's Business Modelling Profile. It can be used to model deferred action for systems type-3 design. Notation symbols need to be developed to depict deferred action and DDD. Other modelling conventions used for active models are deferred data flow diagrams reflecting deferred time but remain incomplete in terms of all SEST properties.

Figure 6.4 is UML descriptor-level deployment diagram of deferred systems design based on deferred action design constructs. It depicts specification and deferment design duplex design process in terms of SEST properties and deferred action. Synthesis of specified design of state space by reflective designers and deferred design by action designers in organized action caters for emergence, and their interactions, the bi-directional arrow between reflective and action designers depicts human communication, produce systems that interface well with actuality (space of natural design) through the S-SEI.

Active UML models should depict structure, functions and dynamics in terms of SEST properties of classes, objects and their interrelations. SEST also permits constructed models to be evaluated for veracity of representations created. Since any systems design either replicates something actual, as in automation, or creates something new it is not simply a case of inventing formalism capable of complete representation. It should also enable invention or creation of new structures. http enabled creation of Web and TCP/IP the internet. Most systems are new inventions.

Implementation

Deferred action design constructs, principles and system types can be designed and implemented with extant formalisms, techniques and technologies termed deferrable technologies. In general, implementation of deferred action design is latent in extant technologies. Deferred action can act as a catalyst to make it explicit and spur specific development of deferrable technology. Deeper implementation requires invention of specific deferment formalism and deferment technology.

Exemplars discussed in Chapter 9 and depicted in Figure 9.1 were designed with extant formalisms and technologies. Formal methods are high in specification but ironically the basis of RSD and SSD. Design of SGML and other Web technologies extend principles of context-free design found in context-free grammars for instance. They are significant to cope with highly emergent design domains requiring deferred action. Dedicated deferred data flow diagramming techniques is used in networking.

Programming languages like Java can be used to code deferred action based systems. Aspects of active model implementation are possible with Java deferred classes. XML and DTD are deferred technologies capable of enabling deferred Web-based IS. In one sense of deferment programming languages are deferred because they are implemented in context but formal languages are grammars for structural only definitions of systems.

7
Sustainability

Introduction

In general, the more rational design reflects natural design the more sustainable it becomes. Sustainment is intrinsic to natural design. Its theoretical and practical implication in rational design is reflected in deferred action. It should be included in deferment formalism as SEST properties. Sustainable systems, generally sustainable IT, is necessary for high performance organization.

Investments in specified IT systems result in unsustainable legacy systems. They are incapable of response to emergent business needs. Admittedly some systems have limited life and become defunct, others KMS for product innovation need to be sustainable. Systems connect to core databases and knowledgebases that should be sustainable. Systems strategy and design needs to include sustainable organization as critical design principle.

Sustainable systems like the Web and technologies like the internet are desirable themselves. Web systems sustainability is achieved because it inadvertently recognizes deferred action and deferred design in the internet it is achieved by design. Internet exemplifies intradeferment. Reflective designers at one layer defer design decisions to reflective designers of computer inter-networks at another. Web exemplifies intradeferment and extradeferment as design decisions are deferred to action designers in organizations and individuals. Organizations that govern the internet and web are exemplars of sustainable organization.

Planned action and designing sustainablity

Notions of sustainability assume rational and objective direction where reason and evidence are primary over other forms of action. This is reflected in management of organization and commissioning of systems. Pursuit of goals and its successful implementation depends on plans but it does not deliver sustainable organization. Planned action is not sufficient for sustainable design because plans and specification design lose relevance in context and over time. Critical feature of sustainability is appropriate responses to emergence, space and time properties of natural design. Dominance of rationality in planned action precludes these SEST properties.

Since situated action gives no account of 'enduring social organization' it is intrinsically of limited value for sustainment design. It lacks plan and therefore explicit direction. If all action is situated how can something be sustained when situations change? Organized action is often required to be sustainable by intention, by design. In the words of the UK Higher Education Funding Council for England (HEFCE, 2004) sustainable:

> .....implies a system that is efficiently run – one that makes good use of scarce resources. It should be a flexible, responsive and sustainable system where new needs are actively identified and met. It should work with equal vigour and creativity to meet the needs of all its client groups, building lasting relationships with them...

A research programme director of the UK JISC not so lightly described the problem as: 'building an airplane while flying.' It is seemingly an impossible case of organized action as simultaneously planned and emergent. Another example is the ARPANET. It connected various government and related agencies' computers. Its design aim was to sustain US government administration in case of debilitating enemy attack and to preserve integrity of information passing between agencies. These are not specified systems. They are deferred and real systems that are evidently sustainable. It is paradoxical to use the term 'system' in deferred systems, since the system is 'deferred' in the sense that it is still to take shape. Plans cannot be predetermined to make such systems sustainable.

Deferred action design constructs and principles deliver sustainable systems. Natural design SEST properties identify character of design interrelatedness with human and organized action. Design encompassing these properties is sustainable. Web and internet have these properties. Java possesses them too. The IP/TCP and Web https protocols display the properties.

Design focusing on structure is minimally interrelated and less sustainable. CRM and HRM systems have structure SEST property but lack others. Design that lacks all these properties is least interrelated and unsustainable. It resists natural design at every turn. Early systems lacked even structure as coding was considered a 'craft' resulting in proliferation of GOTO commands. Calls for its demise signified importance of structure and deliberate 'structured analysis' and 'structured design' was invented. Now structure needs to be supplemented with the other SEST properties to deliver complete design.

Formalism and sustainability

Formalism should contain symbols for context and actuality for design to be sustainable and enable contextual elements to *become* part of design. It needs to cater to sustainment of organized action. Systems of formalism should reflect natural design SEST properties so that organization and systems can respond flexibly to actuality. Since business workers encounter actuality in context deferred action design should facilitate it. Relationship between formalism and sustainment is broken in specification formalism when non-SEST design is assigned to context. Assignment results in inability to respond to actuality or imposition of rules that threaten organization's survivability.

Sustainment is composite of planned and deferred action formalisms their synthesis for sustainment design is weak. Isolated systems incorporating the two well as SEST properties can be identified. IMS Learning Design Specification enables intradeferment. Ironically, design based on formal methods and rigorous specification formalism tends to be sustainable as internet and Web attest they contain elements of deferment formalism and unwittingly reflect complete SEST resulting in sustainable design.

Specification formalism based on discrete mathematics, set theoretic and predicate logic lacks symbols to represent actual organizational activity. It has declarative symbols for organization but lacks imperative symbols for organizing. Focus on existential categories leads to categorical predicate statements that deny becoming, which is much of an organization's life reflecting natural design. In this respect as aspects of natural design abductive logic and modal logic are better able to reflect actuality.

Emergence, sustainability and deferred action

Key to sustainability is emergence SEST property. Sustainable systems are emergent systems same for organization. To achieve sustainability response to emergence is indispensable. Open source code illustrates direct relationship between emergence and sustainability. Linux operating system is sustained because it draws on emergent problem formation and resolution (EPS) by its myriad developers. Duplex design process of development and the system in Linux both respond well to emergence. There is low level of central planned action.

E-Business models process information for organization sustainability. Customers can personalize products or services resulting in emergent information, gathered from customers' purchases to allow organization design to emerge commensurately by re-design business processes based on such purchases. Design is based on emergent or actual information hence it can be catered in deferred design. Deferred action is requisite for sustainable design. Deferred action is the result of such emergence which is contextual rational acts or peoples' rational capacity in actual situations. It is necessary to respond to emergent information pertinent to sustainment. Formal design acknowledging it is successful and sustainable.

SEST properties of deferment formalism are conducive to sustainable design. Sustainability is consequent on natural design responses to actuality. Linking design to actuality creates sustainable design, it facilitates peoples' natural design tendency to respond to emergence appropriately. Tread of sustainability encompasses knowledge, organization and systems. Sustainable organization presupposes sustainable knowledge – creation and application of knowledge that contributes to success – both presuppose sustainable systems. Creation of knowledge relevant to achieve purpose is prerequisite for sustainable organization. Explicit knowledge can be formalized, modelled and prescribed as planned action. Sociality that engenders tacit knowledge and socially embedded knowledge is off-design which can be enabled as deferred action in design.

To sustain design create tailorable space. Deferred action synthesizes planned action *and* indeterminate actuality and sociality that are off-design. Organization is both planned and emergent. Indeterminate factors need responses to achieve set formal objectives. Objectives and response mechanisms form TSA in systems design and TSO in organization design. It enables application of deferred action rationality and choices available in actuality to people better able to interpret and act on it. Reflective designers' problem is to identify methods, tools and techniques to enable emergence sympathetic to sustainment activities.

To sustain design enable deferred design. Context of deferred design is rational acts, embodied skills and mutual intelligibility. It may modify or alter expected outcomes necessary for an agile organization or agile systems. Since reflective designers cannot design for these off-design aspects, their occurrence in actuality in collaborative work and supporting knowledge systems affect design. Deferred design is an enabling response.

Sustainable organization and systems

Sustainability design is facilitated by systems open to SEST and cohered with organization design. Figure 7.1 maps sustainability design. Design above the horizontal line is more sustainable than below it. Sustainable systems are open combining SDD and DDD. Open systems are more likely to be sustained than closed systems that are susceptible to entropy. A commercial company must respond to competitors and markets.

The figure depicts research institute and university as deferred organizations because they operate in highly emergent conditions. Their knowledge generating functions require much deferred action because of emergent property of knowledge. By ensuring work design and systems design is based on deferred action design parameters coherence is achievable. Other organization works types are mapped according to design types.

Figure 7.1   Organization design and sustainment

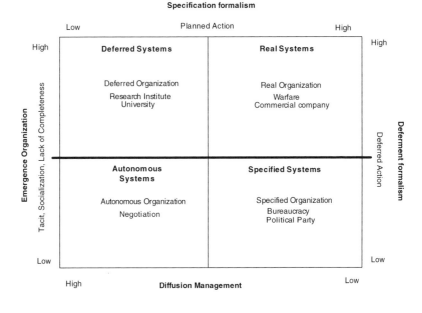

Figure 7.2 KMS as specified and deferred design decisions

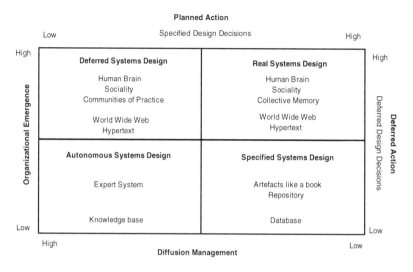

Detailed example of cohered design of work and systems within design types is shown in Figure 7.2. It depicts representation of knowledge as deferred, real, autonomous and specified with each design type showing appropriate knowledge storage mediums and enabling technologies. Analysing knowledge creation and sharing processes and knowledge artefacts in terms of deferred action design parameters improves understanding of appropriate design types for knowledge work. Knowledge work involving innovation, design, analysis and other types can be analysed in terms of these design types.

Design of KMS is an illustration involving specification and deferment design. Managing organizational knowledge is predicated on achieving sustainable organization. Since knowledge resides in human brains, emerges through sociality and practices of communities of practice specification can only be minimal. As the DSD quadrant in Figure 7.2 shows DDD is prominent for KMS design. Objectification of knowledge occurs but in context through deferred design. The other quadrants show other kinds of knowledge, storage and enabling technology.

Disjoint design is unsustainable. Organization and systems design should be cohered along same deferred action design parameters. Cohering with deferred action is then a logical, natural fit ensuring reciprocal sustainability as shown in Figure 7.3, resulting in coherent sustainable design of organization and systems for knowledge work

Figure 7.3 Cohered organization and systems design for sustainment

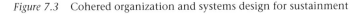
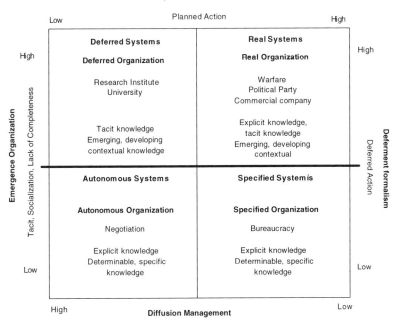

with available design knowledge rather than assumed knowledge. Cohering results in improved core competency activities, improved communication channels by reducing costs of communication, better flow of communications and reduction of need for controlling activities because of better coherence.

Design knowledge itself can be analysed in terms of design types. Organization or its sub-organizations concerned with innovation or researching new knowledge cannot be designed as if complete design knowledge were available to designers. A university or R&D sub-organization in a company cannot be specified for design, its actual strategic and operational work emerges. So elements of its design need to be deferred.

8
Management

Introduction

Extant systems management principles and frameworks draw on management theories and principles characterized as centralized management or planned action. They include techniques like applications portfolio analysis that assume primacy of rational and analytical direction. Planned action is criticized by various researchers of management who propose significant alternatives like strategizing, histories and context, stressing difference between exploitation and exploration. Systems developers too question efficacy of 'plan-driven methods' and propose alternatives like agile systems development.

Organizational information and knowledge is simultaneously design and management. Information pervades all organizational activities being critical for operations management and having potential strategic value. Knowledge is used for product and service innovation possessing greater strategic and competitive value. IS and KMS raise questions concerning how to manage technology and design, its impact on organizational structure and organized activity, how individuals and groups relate to it and how they use it to address EPS or actuality. The key is managing relationships between IT professionals and business workers. These questions and issues are addressed in terms of strategic design (specified design) and operational relevance (deferred design).

Deferred action has implications for developing knowledge of organization and systems management and governance. It stems form synthesized deferred action design parameters. Managing open systems requires different management and governance constructs compared with managing closed systems. Managing cohered organization and systems types requires radically different management approaches.

Management is effective when predetermined objectives are achieved within set constraints. Managing organization and systems as separate entities is problematical. Managing cohered organization and systems is key. Cohered management poses new challenges. It requires new and unique perspective of diffusion management design parameter depicted in Figure 4.1. Diffusion management uniquely synthesizes specification formalism, emergent organization and deferment formalism. It is synthesis of planned action and deferred action.

Management issues

Management knowledge of IT, systems, design and relations with organization stem from innovations in systems development, particularly software development, and from researches. Developers encounter and resolve problems that have general applicability. IT management researchers, fewer compared to IS researchers, seek codifications and generalizations.

Management knowledge is lagging with increasing demand and complex applications of systems. Inflexible management structures and systems governance is based on planned action that assumes organization is rational and can be optimized. Managing inflexible IT and systems poses significant overhead costs. Research on governance and management reinforces planned action and drives invention of further plan-focused management techniques. It is insufficient for design management and management of cohered organization and systems.

Managing design and positioning organization and systems are significant strategic issues. Managing deferred action systems design requires management techniques that are extant but not yet codified. Deferred design has implications for how systems are budgeted requiring a shift from project-based budgeting to include operational budgeting. Corporations do not put them to practice. Managing deferred action organization design requires invention of new techniques and use of existing ones.

Positioning of organization and systems is concerned with strategic responses. Responses need to be non-trivial because of open systems and IT intricacies. Corporate strategists' challenge is to utilize inherent benefits of IT and systems to design organized action. Ancillary management issues are recognizing design types, cohered management, managing particular development needs, recognizing actuality and allocating responsibilities to different designer types. These are important strategic and design management issues that ensure relevant system types are identified for information and knowledge needs for different kinds of organized work. Strategists and systems designers can make better choices based on clearer understanding of these issues. They are significant in terms of systems design capability, relevance and usage.

Extent and variety of deferred action in organization varies typically resulting in mix of design types. Managing specified design and deferred design as combinations requires conceptual changes in management. It limits the role of projects and project management to specified systems. Project management techniques cannot be used for deferred design. Each element of combination requires dedicated management techniques.

Managing design

Managing design involves three activities determination of design's field of action and required artefact or work patterns, deciding design processes and determination of correspondence between design method and required artefact.

Diffusion management is a plural perspective on managing design. Web and internet suggest that both high and low diffused management lead to successful systems type-2 and type-3, where identification of design's fields of action is located in actuality rather than determined by abstract centralized planning. Cohered organization and systems design can strategically be determined as design types. Deferred action design parameters help to map organized work commensurate with design types. Then cohered system types can be decided for particular fields of action.

Figure 8.1 Mapping design domains

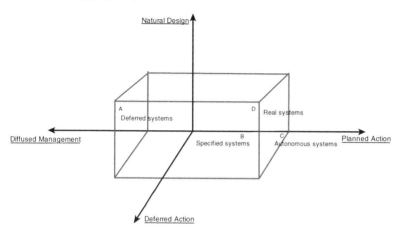

Characteristics of organized work can be determined by mapping it on deferred action theoretical constructs as depicted in Figure 8.1. There is direct correlation between the necessary scope for natural design in organized work and need for deferred action. This plotting then determines type and scope of formalisms and management required.

Determination is assessment by reflective designers of levels and kinds of possible formalism, emergence, diffusion management and deferred action required in design's field of action. Systems analysis teams model work in terms of deferred action. So production work requires less deferred action than innovation work, former can be supported with specified organization and systems and latter with deferred organization and systems. Figure 7.3 shows the stereotypical SSD and DSD mappings with other indicative application domains.

Deferred action has implications for design strategy – determination of what human activity can be designed and supporting artefacts. 'Emergent strategy' is acknowledged in the literature but it does so by countering planned strategy, which is central to deferred action. Rather than negate plans and planning deferred action correlates and synthesizes plans with emergent organization. So this acknowledges value of planned action and emergence in identification of strategic design domains. Deferred action analyses suggest various strategies and design types based on plans rather than an all-encompassing 'IT/IS strategy'. Some design types are more suited for planned action than others. Since action designers do deferred design they are capable of identifying design domains, better placed in actuality to identify design domains than reflective designers.

Problem of 'aligning IT/IS strategy' with business strategy is misconstrued because systems type-2 is assumed rather than systems type-3. IT is not solely strategic management issue it is a socio-organizational design issue. Deferred action reframes it as problem of identifying design domains and design types relative to natural design and as a problem of cohering organization and systems design.

Design process is managed as planned action bound by projects, time and budgets in rational design. This is necessary but should consider natural design and open systems. Managing deferred action design parameters is the rational management of design processes for natural design. Since design domains vary strategically and operationally design process varies too. Identification of design domains and suitable design process are cohered through deferred action design parameters. Each design type has its own design process type.

Recognition and management of duplex design process is necessary. It composes central body responsible for governance, core systems architecture design and development for specification design process and deferred design management by local action designers for deferment design process. This framework is used to manage internet and Web and is appropriate for other public and private organizations. Central body manages design types and invention of technologies. Design types are constrained and facilitated inherently by enabling technologies. Specified systems deploy IT that does not interrelate well with emergent organization. It allows minimal or no scope for deferred action. Deferred and real systems deploy IT that has better interrelation design with emergent organization. It provides Ttools to enable deferred and real-time design.

Design types have either dedicated design methods or borrowed methods. Particular methods reflect deferred action design parameters to varying degrees. Specification formalism and systems project management reflects planned action. Open source code reflects deferred action. The aim of deferment innovation is to enhance relevance of formalism, emergence, and deferred action in design's fields of action.

Greater cost of design has more organizational risk attached. Since risk is taken to allow reflective designers to design it is plausible, given appropriate technology and duplex design process, to allow action designers to take similar risks. The outcome is likely to be a reduction of risk because action designers are operationally more informed than reflective designers.

Primary design management responsibility is to determine correspondence between method and performance of design in actuality. Previous work proposes techniques to evaluate development methods but it is limited to planned action. Deferred action correspondence is based on synthesized design parameters. Suitable techniques should be developed. Methods must correspond with particular levels of emergence and deferred action determined for organized work.

Emergent organization poses new theoretical and practical problem for design management. An important aspect of this correspondence management is the quality of information provided and management of design knowledge in emergent organization. It requires management perspective equally capable of accommodating rational direction and enabling responses to emergent situations. This is possible by the diffusion management design parameter. It better explains how to combine social, organizational and technical factors to achieve aims and cater for actuality.

Diffusion management also caters to space and time SEST properties operationally significant. Deferred-time for deferred systems enables operational design in actuality during systems usage. Real systems are designed and implemented as actual events happen in real-time as present space. Design is shaped by real-time events and deferred action in context. Autonomous systems use autonomous time. Software agents' pre-programmed response to events is separated from human action but actual agent behaviour is in real-time. Specified systems are designed in historic-present time. Design happens in present space and time for future use. Specified systems result in poor investment returns because they lack operational relevance in many actual design domains.

Positioning organization and systems

Corporate strategic responses to emergence require clear understanding of organization design and systems design. Design of organization and sub-organizations of work need to be positioned strategically and be able to respond to emergence. Work analysis by deferred action design parameters enables decision-making on strategy and design of work. Analysis is to position organization or sub-organizations strategically and operationally. A car manufacturer or software company need to determine what deferred action design type to position themselves for core activities. Positioning is also to cohere work organization and systems in terms of deferred action design parameters.

Positioning is of two types. Supra positioning is determination of design types for kinds of work. Purpose and types of organized work necessary to achieve it can be determined in terms of design types. Modern military strategy and operations against non-traditional enemies depend on action taken in response to emergent events and intelligence (deferred action) but purpose remains to defeat the enemy by deploying strategies and tactics (planned action). It can be positioned as real organization design type. A religious body is better positioned as specified organization type since it allows no responses to emergent factors and no action (deferred action) that is counter to cannons. Such supra positioning in terms of deferred action is a logical, natural fit.

The other type is subordinate positioning which is positioning of sub-organizations in terms of design types. Operational organization is not monolithic in design. It has sub-organizations requiring dedicated subordinate positioning. Positioning is cohering sub-organization and systems in terms of deferred action design parameters. A car manufacturer can position its innovation or knowledge work as deferred organization and deferred systems design types and its production work as specified organization and systems design types.

Diffusion management

Thinking of organizational work and systems design in centralist terms has limited conceptions of its management. Diffusion is a quality of work and systems as active tools. Diffusion management questions centralist assumptions thereby expanding conceptions of organization and systems management. Growth of design is central to deferred action design. Since organized action draws on unbounded natural design its design needs facility to grow and diffuse. Diffusion management is the facility.

Figure 4.1 depicts high- and low-diffused management for different design types. High-diffused management is used in deferred and autonomous design types because outcomes are ambiguous and uncertain. They require high-diffused management because reflective designers cannot know eventual, emergent operations and outcomes. High-diffused management is used in deferred systems because systems need to grow and allow action designers to do deferred design. Action designers know what is needed operationally. This is true of organization design management too.

Low-diffused management is used in specified and real systems design types because expected outcomes are predetermined. In real and specified systems reflective designers determine core architecture but in real systems they cannot know all details of operational requirements and in some cases they lack knowledge of structure too. In specified systems core architecture and operational functionally are centrally directed. Project management is used to maintain direction and control in specified systems. This is true for organization design management.

Deferred design is managed as diffusion management. Deferred design can be either accumulative and discrete or accumulative and interoperable. Management of former is simpler since each separate deferred design is stored and retrieved uniquely. In the latter diffusion management is necessary. Diffusion management is used for interoperable systems as in IMS Learning Design Specification.

Strategic management of systems and related technologies is ineffective because it lacks suprapositioning of growth but it is centrally planned operational functionality. Diffusion management consistent with deferred action can improve strategic and operational management. It requires reflective and action designers to co-manage structure and operations.

Diffusion management is synthesis of strategic planning and deferred action for design types. Its level depends on organized purpose, work and desired outcomes. Where this is pursued as emergent organization central body can direct structure strategically but operational design should be deferred to respond to emergence. Reflective designers can determine centrally systems strategy, systems architecture and Ttools design. Action designers design and manage operational functionality. Suprapositioning and subordinate positioning of work in terms of emergence determine how much operational functionality is deferred.

Diffuse means appropriate location of SEST properties design in the course of actual organized action or work. There is no sharp demarcation between design and its management in deferment design process. It should cater to needs that arise from emergent operational activities through diffusion management enabled by deferred design in the specification design process. Design for open systems type-3 requires central structural design but it should enable deferred action to encompass emergent design. Organization that fails to recognize emergence also fails to exploit opportunities and so endanger sustainment.

Diffusion management is suitable for open systems but levels of planned action vary. Real systems are highly strategic, planned and centrally managed. Deferred systems suggest low planning potential because outcomes are not known. Closed systems pose different management problems. Project management and its associated techniques is an example of managing closed systems.

One model of open systems management is W3C. It controls the structural aspect of Web design by planning centrally and releasing high-specification formalism to design Web-based systems. Individuals and organizations determine actual operational use locally. Its Web technologies are Ttools designed for deferred action. This model of systems management can be applied to all organizations where structure or architecture is centrally planned and operational application determined locally. Organizations utilizing internet and Web technologies in intranets and extranets or use it to link with customers could emulate this model. It is particularly suited to knowledge management KMS can be managed effectively with high-specification core design and deferring design decisions to knowledge workers – action designers.

Diffusion management is not decentralized management or federal management. They presume high capacity for organizational planning and capacity to predict outcomes. They do not acknowledge emergent organization and deferred action. Diffusion management compliments strategic or central management rather than pose as an alternative like decentralized or federal management.

High-diffused management for open systems is necessary where there is ambiguity of purpose and eventual outcome, caused by organizational emergence that requires commensurate deferred action. Providing strategic direction, conducting central planning, designing structures and developing structural technologies that enable deferred action are characteristics of high-diffused management.

Web is a deferred system exemplar that makes successful use of high-diffused management. Its structural SEST property is centrally planned and other SEST properties locally designed and implemented. Reflective designers at W3C provide strategic direction, centrally design Web architecture (structure), set standards and release technologies. It is successful because it has TSA implementing DDD to enable deferred design. Strategic planners and reflective designers at W3C have no knowledge of local purpose or operational use of adopting organizations or individuals. Their design is context-free. Web inadvertently reflects complete SEST and actuality by enabling DDD by action designers. Web-based document management systems make effective use of this model.

As Europe's largest organization the UK government's National Health Service is high-diffused management structure. All its activities cannot be accounted for by one design type and management strategy. A strategic body decides its strategic purpose centrally. Making strategy work a real design type. Medical diagnosis is well supported with deferred design types and high-diffused management to cater for consultants' differing expertise, knowledge and differing contexts. Drug prescriptions are suited to specified systems and low-diffused management. Mid-wife support, counselling, or alternative therapy exhibit differing deferred action, resulting in differing levels of diffusion management.

Low-diffused management for open systems results when there is cognisance of purpose and eventual outcome is clear, with high emergent organization and much need for deferred action. Providing specific strategic direction, central design and enabling deferred action to counter emergence are characteristics of low-diffused management.

Internet is real system exemplar it has made successful use of low-diffused management. Real systems can be planned centrally and successfully deployed with low levels of diffusion management to enable deferred action. ICANN controls technical management system for the internet, deciding its strategic purpose. Reflective designers centrally design protocol address space allocation, protocol parameter assignment, domain name system management, and root server system management functions. Actual network connection, the internet, emerges in a global setting through deferred design.

Complex deployment of IT in organization can benefit from diffusion management. Networked organization, distributed organization and e-Commerce have properties of diffusion management. They require strategic vision and central planning but success depends on accommodating emergent organized activity of consumption behaviour, markets, competitors and economies. Management involves setting strategic goals, planning and enablement of deferred action.

There is low planning capability and high need for deferred action in emergent organization. Mass customization requires flexible and emergent organizational processes and systems architecture. Organizations with embedded e-Commerce systems and eCRM are emergent, designed to reflect emergent consumer behaviour. They enable customers to determine business processes, products and services because business models focuses on customers' needs. Business processes are designed to enable personalization and adjust to customers' sales patterns. Supporting systems reflect high-diffused management to cater for emergence.

Systems development and management

Management of systems is not well developed compared to management of organization. Management of systems type-3 is even less developed because meaning attribution quality of information and belief attribution quality of knowledge cannot be determined by specification design.

Deferred action design parameters raise a variety of management issues. They range from catering for meaning attribution in IS and belief in KMS, determining how IT strategy and business strategy can be co-designed and cohered, how organizations design IS and KMS for speedy responses to emergence and market needs, how design domains and systems can be classified to enable strategic planning that results in appropriate systems designs, and how systems can be managed effectively.

Mapping organized action in terms of design types can improve systems design and management. Each design type raises different management issues. Determination of design types prior to development improves likelihood of success because of logical links afforded to choices of formalisms, methods and techniques and recognition, if required, of action designers. Where different subordinate positioning design types need to be developed commensurate logical choices of formalisms, methods and techniques arise to improve success of development.

Systems management is the dual problem of diverse systems development and its integration in organization. Sullivan (1985) provided an earlier explanation of managing complex systems positing diffusion and infusion dimensions of technology management. Diffusion is dispersal of systems in organizations and decentralization of decisions concerning them or 'decentralized technology management'. Infusion is the degree to which organizations become dependent on systems to survive, and therefore need high central planning. Sullivan's consequent matrix depicts four types of technology management environments: opportunistic with high diffusion and low infusion; complex with high diffusion and high infusion; traditional with low diffusion and low infusion; and backbone with low diffusion and high infusion.

Focusing on complex type Sullivan prophetically raised five planning issues: the effect of information on products and services, the role of systems executives as change agents, the role of systems in organization redesign, the impact of systems on networked resource management, and the development of information architecture. Sullivan concluded complex type is difficult to manage because of the lack of suitable planning methodologies.

Deferred action overcomes this management limitation. It does so by (a) reframing the problem as synthesized design parameters, enabling interrelation design and positing diffusion management; (b) classifying design types and designer types resulting from the synthesis; (c) acknowledging emergent organization and deferred action; and (d) acknowledging systems strategy and systems design as synthesis of reflective (central) design <u>and</u> deferred design. It thus explains Sullivan's complex type and accounts for human and organizational impact on systems. It enables strategists and system designers to classify existing and new systems and to incorporate the 'dispersal' of system design decisions or operational functionality into systems plans.

Sullivan's matrix does not explain how diffusion can be achieved operationally. Deferred action design enables operational diffusion. Technology diffusion in organizations has increased through different stages of software conception since Sullivan's contribution. Packaged software, end-user computing, fourth generation languages, networking and internet and Web technologies are some diffusion developments. So-called users assume budgetary and systems design responsibilities. These developments support the action designer construct.

Managing code design

Defining features of open systems design are central management body and local development. Central body for open source code is OSI, for internet ICANN and for Web W3C. These organizations are concerned with governance and technological facilitation rather than operational design. W3C avoids operational functionality design. Tim Berners-Lee comments on the Web:

> The Achilles' heel of the HTTP space is the only centralized part, the ownership and government of the root of the DNS tree. As a feature common and mandatory to the entire HTTP Web, the DNS root is a critical resource whose governance by and for the world as a whole in a fair way is essential. This concern is not currently addressed by the W3C, except indirectly though involvement with ICANN. (Personal note by Tim Berners-Lee, W3C)

Principles of code design for deferred and real systems are given in Table 8.1. These principles cover creative sources of design – planned and experiential – placing and interrelations. Diffusion management covers these principles. They suggest development of deferment formalism, its synthesis with specification formalism, reflect SEST, and enable deferred design for deferred action.

Design principles for specified design of TSA ensure its integrity and enable deferred design. Design of deferrable technologies is included. Since specified design is constrained by actuality design principles for deferred design enable deferred action but the principles prevent compromising integrity of TSA by action designers' deferred design. They ensure that deferred design is of variable (data code) and not TSA. Variables can be free or bounded variable similar to set theory which is a specified design decision. Access to data code determined by specified design constitute bounded variables all others are free variables. Variables compose operational functionality of systems. They can be thought of as data code – the basic processed unit in systems type-3. It is similar to compiling operational functionality for particular problems and information output as data processing algorithms in spreadsheets.

Design principles for S-SEI enable action designers to design operational functionality. These principles are based on natural design commutative tenant that practice is design and design is practice. The

Table 8.1 Principles of code design for deferred and real systems

Design principle	Elaboration

Specified design of TSA – Specified design decisions

This set of five principles covers structure SEST property which is concerned with being. The source of design is strategic and creative or planned action. Designing is concerned with placing design in actuality.

S1	Reflective designers design TSA based on minimum necessary specification.	TSA design decisions are domain of reflective designers as S-problem solving. Specified design is limited to knowable structure. Identify what is necessary to enable organized action – and deferred action. Structure is the basis for deferred design. Action designers can contribute to TSA design with their work practices, patterns of interaction, embodied patterning.
S2	Design deferrable technologies.	They can be incorporated into TSA for deferred design.
S3	Design deferred classes.	They are instantiations of deferred objects based on SDP
S4	Design Ttools.	They enable deferred design. Enable design of SDO by action designers. SDO are determined during systems analysis and compose deferred design they can be enabled through Ttools or action designers' code.
S5	Control access to TSA (source) code.	Do not permit action designers to change TSA (source) code. This is true of all DSD/RSD systems – Internet and Web.

Deferred design – Deferred design decisions

This set of four principles covers emergence, space and time SEST properties which is concerned with becoming and interrelations. The source of design is experiential. Design is primarily concerned with interrelating placed design with other objects in actuality or field of action.

D1	Since emergence, space and time are necessary conditions of rational design enable DDD.	Deferred design is to cope with unknowable emergence, space and time, 'equivocal reality'. Innovative deferred action should be translatable into deferred design. It enhances innovation. DDD may be through Ttools or action designer's code.
D2	Action designers design operational functionality.	Action designers frame and resolve work problems encountered in actuality as E-problem solving. They can deal effectively with emergent challenges by designing operational functionality. Action designers design not 'participate' in design.

Table 8.1   Principles of code design for deferred and real systems – *continued*

Design principle	Elaboration
D3 Implement DDD at run-time or real-time depending on need.	In deferred systems DDD is implemented at run-time and in real systems in real-time. Real-time DDD may be enabled to change TSA or structure.
D4 DDD should not change the TSA and functionality of existing code.	Exception is real systems where reflective designers enable such change by strategy. Macros do not change existing functionality. DTD not change Web architecture.

Design of S-SEI

This set of three principles cover mechanisms for interrelation design.

I1 Design an interface for action designers' DDD.	It is the place to do deferred design. Deferred action is the view that parts of design occur in actuality in the field of action, enabled through the S-SEI.
I2 Design ways of locating deferred design.	Similar to name box in spreadsheets; provide a trace of deferred design.
I3 Design palette to display Ttools.	Similar to formula palette in spreadsheets or visual programming.

Reflective designers

This principle recognizes strategic, planned source of design either as individual or as a body.

R1 Reflective designers design TSA, S-SEI and Ttools.	They are the architects and expect to know structures and models prior to design use. They know the predetermined parameters of design.

Action designers

This principle recognizes the operational, deferred source of design either as individuals or as a body. It is experiential or existential particularly focusing on becoming.

A1 Action designers do deferred design in actuality within formal parameters of specified design.	They come to know the eventual and actual parameters of design in actuality. They design operational functionality as embodied patterns in the field of action.

design process is inseparable from its outcomes (Churchman, 1968). Since actual organized activity cannot be specified it can be accounted for in design through the S-SEI.

Design principles for reflective designers concern their role as TSA architects and toolmakers for deferred design. They are concerned with knowable purpose and strategic choices. Design principles for action designers concern their role as designers of operational functionality in actuality and interrelating with natural design. They accentuate the becoming aspect of natural design.

Managing deferred and real technology

Deferred technology is defined as software systems or hardware with complete SEST that can be shaped in context through deferred design by action designers. Knowledge of managing deferred technology is scant and limited to few organizations that manage global deferred technologies like the internet, Web and open source code very success-fully. Inadvertent recognition of limitations of specification design has led these organizations to invent deferred technology.

Deferred technology is of two types. One is its degree of coupling with design domains. Coupling concerns how well SEST propensities of a particular design domain are reflected in design. Tight coupling indi-cates strong deferment. IMS Learning Design Specification is tightly coupled with learning and teaching which is strongly deferred. Second is how well technology caters for emergence. The more it reflects its emergent design domain or field of action the more deferred it is. Generic deferred technology like the Web caters well for emergence in any design domain.

Invention and specification of deferred technology is inseparable from deferred action. Since deferred action is actual or active it reflects natural design or work. Such action is based on lived experience. When it is converted to design it is embodied patterning. Active specification is derived from embodied patterning. HTTP is Tim Berners-Lee's embodied patterning or his recognition that colleagues repeatedly asked him for same information. This led him to design an IS to make his personal information publicly accessible.

Reflective designers can design for embodied patterning. Macros and Java deferred class enable embodied patterning. Java has deferred classes defined when there is no default implementation. This is com-mon in organized activity where there is emergence of actual events. Ironically scheduling resources is indicative. Embodied patterning in macros is of action designers' contextual need to process data in par-ticular sequence relevant to work. Other examples of deferred techno-logy are listed in Table 8.2. Deferred technology can be for micro, meso and macro human action.

Table 8.2 Deferred technology implementations

Term	Description
Deferred-action-list; deferred-action function	Used in emacs-development. *Check* http://lists.gnu.org/archive/html/emacs-devel/2005-02/msg004303.html
Deferred Execution Custom Actions	Used in scripts for Windows installer. See http://msdn.microsoft.com/library/en-us/msi/setup/deferred_execution_custom_action
Deferred Procedure Calls	Microsoft uses DPCs to manage hardware interrupts At micro-processor level: Microsoft's response to this problem is to use Deferred Procedure Calls (DPCs). http://www.nematron.com/HyperKernel/index.shtml
Client side deferred action with multiple MAPI profiles	This is a patent at: http://www.patentalert.com/docs/000/z00002860.shtml

Some deferred technology in specified systems is for managing deferred-time. It is used in memory management and to manage hardware interrupts. It is used in data transfer technology like EDI as deferred data transfer. Edge of network computing is real technology presently researched and used by military.

9
Observations and Exemplar Cases

Introduction

Top-down strategic planning and specification design has not addressed problems of systems integration and coherent design adequately. Ironically, it has resulted in physically and logically isolated stores of data, information and knowledge. Specification design results in specified systems incapable of responding to emergent organization. In practice planned action is abandoned when contingent factors are not represented in design and deferred action is the result to ensure achievement of objectives.

Strategic planning, strategic plans and specification design has not eradicated a contingent approach to systems design necessitated by emergent business requirements – bearing witness to the thesis of deferred action and natural design. Business requirements emerge and are addressed with local systems development problematical for strategic management of IT as it creates incongruence with business strategy. Systems integration is planned but execution of plans is subsidiary to actual solutions implemented. E-Commerce and e-Business requires connection of disparate bespoke systems and components of systems.

gDRASS matrix in practice

Systems type-3 design is characterized as the problem of representing complete SEST. Generalization of deferred action is evident from its use by practitioners and researchers in diverse fields. Systems researchers and developers in Europe have applied DDD principle to legal systems (Elliman and Eatock, 2005), e-Learning systems (Dron, 2005), banking systems (Stamoulis et al., 2003), internet applications (Loverdos et al.,

2002), and citizenship systems. Business systems researchers and consultants have used the theory to inform research and practice. Stamoulis et al. (2001) addresses tailorable IS in business. Systems tailorability has informed work of IS methodology researchers and consultants (Stamoulis et al., 2001) and systems developers.

Deferred action has contributed to interdisciplinary research and practice. Purao et al. (2003) invoke DSD to support development of emergent systems. Management researchers have cited tailorability for life assurance product management (Macmillan, 1997). Probert (1997) cites it for tailorable systems designs reflecting actuality of situations rather than rigid specified design. It is cited in a survey of IS development (Fitzgerald and Philippides, 1999).

Figure 9.1 plots other independently designed systems too numerous to describe here classified according to deferred action design parameters. Full references for some are given in the bibliography. The three-group text structure in each quadrant composes example

Figure 9.1   Populated gDRASS matrix

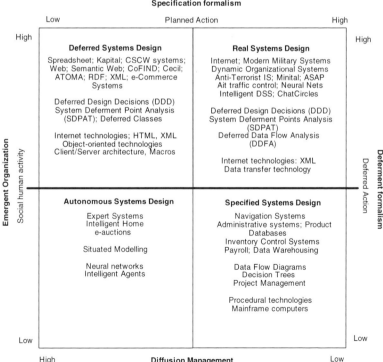

systems, systems analysis and design techniques, and enabling technologies.

To illustrate, air traffic control is plotted as real systems. Its organization is highly emergent contingent on delayed flights, unexpected flights and emergencies. Its management however requires high specification design and planned action. The apparent contradiction works in practice because actual control of air traffic is based on deferred actions of air traffic controllers. They use considerable skills – embodied patterning – to decide operational functionality of the system. This actual work organization is cohered well with supporting systems through deferred action. It is possible to combine highly planned systems with local innovations in real systems. The French Videotext and ASAP are other examples. XML itself is a deferred system based on formal language definition.

The mapping aids strategic and tactical design analysis. It reveals no extant deferred KMS necessary design type for knowledge work because of non-specifiable attributes of knowledge like emergence, tacitness, specificity and social embedment. There are no extant deferred knowledge generation systems. Knowledge work involving innovation is particularly suited for deferred systems design. There are no deferred decision support systems. Executive decision support for mergers or acquisitions is suited for deferred or real systems design. Similar mapping for organizations can reveal gaps in systems provision and raise questions of inappropriateness design types for particular types of organizational work.

Conversations reflecting deferred action

Deferred action design parameters were observed in an ethnomethodological study of knowledge work in a European branch of a marine insurer (Patel, 2005b). It investigated deferred action in organizational knowledge management and knowledge work. Recognizing knowledge as critical resource, the company had commissioned a KMS because management decided it would prevent loss of further clients to competitors and attract new business. The KMS did not produce expected value addition. The study revealed data confirming planned action and deferred action and lack of required synthesis that is 'useful for knowledge management and sustainability design issues in KMS' (Patel, 2005b: 354).

Planned action or specification design parameter was dominant in the design of the KMS. Proprietary specification and diagrammatic formalism of the major management consultancy firm commissioned to develop the system assumed 'mutual intelligibility of formal systems' but did not cater for its absence. Designers tried to determine every aspect of organized activity by specification resulting in detrimental intervention and over specification of work activities. Sales executives were required to make daily contributions to the knowledge base and deploy specific stratagems recommended by the system. Structure and operational functionality were indistinguishable by design and failed to reflect actual work and conditions.

The emergence parameter was evident in the social environment of the system and use of tacit and socially embedded knowledge. Emergence included 'unknown and unfamiliar situations' and 'lack of clarity of knowledge.' This resulted in five forms of deferred action: 'defer to learn continuously', 'defer to learn before taking action', 'defer to gather information before taking action', defer to someone else to objectify and take action' and 'defer to cater for temporal constraints'. The KMS had no mechanisms to cater for emergence and deferred action. Emergent aspects resulted in business workers taking action despite of or contrary to formal KMS.

To sustain successful organized action formalization of knowledge should reflect deferred action as it can account for explicit and tacit knowledge. Deferment was evidenced to support this assumption. Data revealed non-formal context or actuality that should be represented in KMS design. It showed goal-driven business workers deferred at particular points during work to achieve objectives. Deferment varied but essentially arose because of human and formal design limitations. Deferred action arose because of confusion and lack of clarity, unknown situations and unfamiliarity and the need to reflect rather than act. It arose because of limitations of planned action and availability of design knowledge. Limitations of specification design were addressed by deferred action or deferred design as business workers devised non-IT methods to achieve objectives. Confusing, unclear, lacking knowledge or unfamiliar situations are expected to lead to deferred action. The data supported this ontological supposition.

Even assumed explicitness of explicit knowledge is weakened by tentativeness of business workers actions. Data revealed that actual client knowledge and their companies and reports of progress of negotiations is weak, hence action on these matter was mostly deferred. There was confusion and lack of clarity surrounding action in general resulting in various kinds of deferred action relating to different information in records or the utility of available information. In particular deferred action occurred because incorrectness of information and lack of information, doubting its value, need to broaden decision-making and alternative perspectives.

Exemplar systems in next subsections are shown to have inadvertently incorporated deferred action design parameters. There is inadvertent recognition of deferred action. Systems architectures and interrelation mechanisms in these systems are synthesis of specification and deferment formalisms. Commenting on the Web and internet, Tim Berners-Lee states:

> The fact that as we move into the applications we see more and more diverse uses of the Web and the Net does not diminish our reliance on a sound standards in the supporting infrastructure (Personal note by Tim Berners-Lee, W3C).

These systems are successful because they embody complete SEST to enable deferred action formally. They are classed deferred and real design types because they exhibit elements of deferred action design, specified design, TSA, S-SEI, DDD and deferred design. They illustrate advanced synthesis of specification formalism, deferment formalism, emergence, deferred action and diffusion management.

Significantly, eventual state of systems operation results from co-design. Co-design is design of TSA by reflective designers and continuous operational functionality design by action designers. Reflective designers have no knowledge, or seek to gain such knowledge, of operational functionality that action designers will develop in actuality. The systems crystallize duplex design process by separating TSA design and operational functionality design in terms of what reflective designers can expect to know or being and what action designers come to know in actuality or becoming. For each exemplar, system description is given and analysed in terms of emergent behaviour, co-design, systems architecture and Ttools and diffusion management.

IMS learning design specification

IMS Global Leaning Consortium Inc. working in conjunction with the UK government JISC has implemented technically deferred action design parameters independent of knowledge of it for learning and teaching design domain. IMS aim to develop worldwide standards to design interoperable distributed learning on-line and off-line. Its Learning Design Specification (LDS) is an open system specification that incorporates all design types for learning technology and learning design.

System description

LDS features objects, behaviour, and Service Access Points (SAP) achieve functionality similar to deferred systems features of specification design, deferred design and S-SEI. These features distinguish private aspects of the system its TSA from its public aspects the operational functionality. It has specified systems architecture enabling deferred design consisting of interface and services. It is a 'mechanism to define the set of interfaces for which interoperability specification will be needed by some application domain.' (IMS, 2003). This is intradeferment of interoperable specification.

LDS core eight requirements specification are completeness, pedagogical flexibility, personalization, formalization, reproducibility, interoperability, compatibility and reusability (IMS, 2003). This is the structure SEST property. The consequent LDS formalism reflects synthesis of deferred action design parameters. It caters for emergence in learning and the design of learning systems by reflecting emergence and enabling deferred action in systemic terms.

LDS is an example of intradeferment and deferred action among developer community action designers. It is deferred e-Learning system specification based on definition of learning object metadata (LOM). Though IMS do not define it as architecture it is TSA in terms of deferred action design. It is used to model, design and implement any proprietary and individual pedagogy as e-Learning systems. This is the emergence, space and time SEST property. It enables individuals and organizations to design interoperable distributed e-Learning systems operationally. They design operational functionality.

Specified system element of TSA is IMS Abstract Framework (IAS). IAS is described as 'living document which is likely to evolve and be extended' and IMS Learning Resources Meta-data Specification. IAS is specification formalism used in LDS to design structure. It is the specification design composing formal specification of LDS. Specified systems element is modelled with IMS Learning Resource metadata specification formalism. It is to be replaced with IEEE 1484.12.3 Extensible Markup Language (XML) Schema Definition Language Binding for LOM.

Deferred system element of TSA is composed of LDS and 'domain profiles' to design operational functionality, similar to SDP in deferred action. LDS is not planned action. It is deferred action because it provides 'generic and flexible language' capable of allowing expression of various pedagogies. It reflects educators' deferred actions on unique pedagogies they create, adapt and use in context that can be designed as e-Learning systems with LDS for interoperable use. It thus embodies DDD principle and enables deferred design of embodied patterns.

LDS recognizes and caters for emergence and deferred action. Action designers, here as professional systems developers in intradeferment, construct e-Learning systems with IMS implementation elements. Deferred design is implemented by 'application profiling' of the IAS to create a reference model. This requires defining services composed of objects and behaviours and SAP. A complete deferred system design is interoperable and can be made available over electronic networks as a 'package' to others.

LDS has a S-SEI. It is SAP at different planes of the information model and in componentized services. SAP serves two functions. It is an interface between action designers and the service, the true meaning of the deferred action term S-SEI. In IAS it is also an interface between two joining planes. 'The SAP is an abstract representation of the service available through the interface and as such its physical implementation could be referred to as an API.' (IMS, 2005).

LDS Information Model contains deferred action design parameters and incorporates all its design types. It is composed of three levels. The conceptual UML model for Level A is synthesis of deferred action design parameters. It synthesizes planned action, emergence and deferred action. This synthesis enables deferred design. In Level B reflective designers' design decisions enable deferred design. It is specification design using specification formalism to enable deferred design. Reflective designers design extensibility to allow action designers' deferred actions to be implemented as DDD in e-Learning systems. Learning (action) designers can design how they want learners to encounter taught material in a Unit of Learning.

Level C design reflects all deferred action design parameters and models learning and teaching activity as real systems. This is achieved through the event-driven notification mechanism supporting run-time functionality design – operational functionality. Notifications may be directed to humans or systems. Notification is a meso-Ttool in deferred action terms because it results in extending systems functionality.

Emergent behaviour

The field of action requires much interrelation design. Learning and teaching design domain is emergent intrinsically in terms of learning itself and organization of learning and teaching. A single specified system is unable to 'capture' myriads of e-Learning functionalities arising from diversity, variance and emergence in teaching and learning. Organization of e-Learning is diverse varying among individual teachers and between teaching organizations including commercial corporations and varies between educational levels. Variation is complicated by varieties of and developments in general and personal pedagogical knowledge.

Learning is arguably more varied and emergent requiring much deferred action. Learning is not an instant event. An individual's learnt knowledge is accumulated through physically and cognitively disparate events. Learning itself has planned and emergent aspects. Planned learning is execution of planned syllabi. Emergent learning leads learners to develop personal cognitive paths to understanding. It occurs through deferred actions. Such deferred actions in learning design can be translated into deferred design with LDS.

Duplex design process

Duplex design process or co-design is composed of what we know and what we come to know. An LDS e-Learning system combines reflective designers' explicit knowledge of requirements – what we know as declarative knowledge – and action designers' embodied patterning – what we come to know as procedural knowledge.

LDS is based on explicit knowledge of requirements available to reflective designers when designing TSA (what we know) and deferred design based on embodied patterning, socially embedded knowledge and tacit knowledge of teaching and learning, available to action designers only (what we come to know). The argument is recursively applied to reflective designers' own design work, since they too come to know things through work. An instance of this is the specification of the IAS described as a 'living document'.

In terms of SEST properties IMS reflective designers have created structure or systems architecture from explicit knowledge of requirements – the LDS eight core requirements. XML in LDS is used as a 'system' to enable deferred design. As IMS state: 'a system that has to interpret this language does not need to know the pedagogical approach underlying the design: it only needs to be able to instantiate the design, allocate activities and their associated resources to participants playing various roles, and coordinate the runtime flow.' (IMS, 2003). LDS contains intra-deferment of structural and emergent design.

Remaining SEST properties are enabled as intradeferment deferred design. Deferred design requires drawing UML activity models and authoring XML scripts for LOM design. It is operational functionality design by local reflective designers (action designers). An example of deferred action is teachers' aim to develop critical skills and criticality in learners. This local requirement can be met by deferred design.

System architecture and Ttools

Reflective designers have determined TSA, interrelation design and tools for interrelation design. Figure 9.2 is UML representation of IAS specification architecture. The package is composed of model elements applications, application services, common services and infrastructure. LDS is not a software product with operational functionality. It makes use of separation of form and content or duplex design process principle to enable deferred design. It is implemented in XML separating form and content definitions between reflective and action designers respectively.

LDS caters for organizational and societal systems. For organization it has no micro-Ttools, a major weakness in terms of deferred action in the domain of learning. Brain Alger's notion of 'experience designer' learner makes the learner an action designer, a designer of learning tools. Deferred design mechanism in LDS is domain profiling or meso-Ttool for professional action designers. Reflective designers have made use of XML (a macro-Ttool in deferred action terms) to enable professional action designers to do intradeferment-deferred design.

Figure 9.2   UML representation of LDS architecture

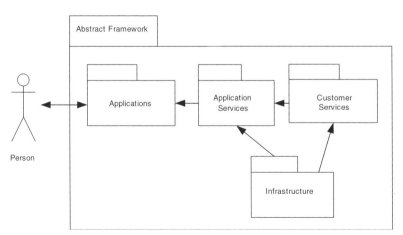

Source: IMS Abstract Framework: White Paper *Revision*: 01 July 2003

For societal purposes LDS has implications for transnational societal macro-design and macro-tailoring of learning systems. It aims to be de facto standard for learning design as the Web is for networked communication. It has set itself societal standards affecting global societies through their representative bodies participating in the project. It is able to do this with the XML macro-Ttool and other standards.

Diffusion management

Diffusion management is evident in LDS. Central direction on specification formalism, design and TSA is distinguished from local policy decisions. Central body is IMS Learning Consortium Inc. Specification management is centralized to it. It manages various specifications for distributed, interoperable e-Learning systems and promotes learning technology and supports adopters.

Management of domain systems development and management are diffused to particular learning design domains within countries and within levels of education within countries. Granularity of particular learning design increases with the actuality of the design domain in terms of 'domain profiling'.

World Wide Web

Tim Berners-Lee inventor of the Web views it as subscribing to the 'minimalist design' principle. It concurs well with SEST. This may be described as creating architectural design that enables policy to be determined locally. He states:

> The W3C Consortium's broadly stated mission is to lead the Web to its 'full potential', whatever that means. My definition of the Web is a universe of network-accessible information, and I break the 'full potential' into two by looking at it first as a means of human-to-human communication, and then as a space in which software agents can, through access to a vast amount of everything which is society, science and its problems, become tools to work with us. (Personal note by Tim Berners-Lee, W3C).

Web is sustainable, deferred systems design type. It inadvertently implements technically deferred action design parameters. Tim Berners-Lee's original Web technology intuitively caters to deferred action and its ethos is continued in further Web technology development by W3C. The stress on connections or links in the Web's architecture reflects actual organized work or interrelation design in fields of action, as it did for Tim Berners-Lee's work with colleagues driving him to invent it. Regarding innovation he notes that:

> The Web arose as the answer to an open challenge, through the swirling together of influences, ideas, and realizations from many sides until, by the wondrous offices of the human mind, a new concept jelled. It was a process of accretion, not the linear solving of one well-defined problem after another. (Tim Berners-Lee, 1999: 3)

Regarding emergence, space and time SEST properties for ways of working, emergent ways of interrelating at work are evident in the following:

> ...I found myself answering the same questions asked frequently of me by different people. It would be so much easier if everyone could just read my database. (ibid.,: 15).

Web enables deferment and deferred action to cater for SEST properties for two groups. It caters to emergence by enabling deferred action. It is intradeferment among developer community as reflective designers of the Web who produce technology for use by other reflective designers in context (action designers). It is extradeferment between developer community and individuals and organizations as reflective designers who produce technology for use by non-professional action designers or business workers.

System description

Web formalism reflects synthesis of deferred action design parameters. Structure SEST property is setup by specification design. Specified system element of TSA is composed of communication protocols and 'recommendations' by W3C. Hypertext Transfer Protocol (HTTP) is specified to locate documents on the internet. Recommendations are specification of Web technologies for designing operational functionality. The browser is of non-W3C origin that has integrated well with the Web. It makes locating and viewing documents on the internet seamless and caters well for multimedia potential of the Web.

Specified systems element is modelled with SGML specification formalism and other context-free formalisms. It is core specification formalism of the Web and the basis of Web markup languages design. Principle of context-free design concurs well with duplex design process.

Emergence, space and time SEST properties are enabled by deferment design. Deferred system element of the Web's TSA is composed of XHTML, CSS, Dynamic HTML, XML, DTD and Schemas. Intradeferment action designers do deferred design by implementing W3C recommendations in unique contexts to design operational functionality. Action designers here may be other professional systems developers and business workers or other kinds of organization workers. Action designers construct Web-based IS from recommendations. The DDD aspect consists of action designers operational design decisions on emergent structure and informational and knowledge content of documents.

Since the S-SEI is the interface to enable interrelation operational DDD recommendations also compose the S-SEI of the Web. W3C recommendations do not specify operational functionality which are not software products. They are universal and open in the sense that action designers determine their operational functionality. The physical manifestation of the Web's S-SEI is any text editor. A subsidiary element of the S-SEI is the DNS interface element to enter domain names that enables location of documents through HTTP mechanism.

Emergent behaviour

The field of action can have much interrelation design. Limitation of control possible by design is well expressed by Tim Berners-Lee and it applies to organization design too, to design in general. He gives 'social difficulties' as reason for the 'centralized model' of networked protocols breakdown:

> As we move on to later protocols, the protocols themselves become more diverse. This is partly because they are at a higher application level. The centralized model starts to break down, as witness some of the social difficulties of getting an IANA allocation for a MIME type an embryonic W3C specification. So new protocols allow new applications to be defined using URIs, allowing anyone who has access to a bit of domain space to allocate them. (Personal note by Tim Berners-Lee, W3C).

In terms of deferred action this is not 'break down' rather it signifies emergence SEST property requiring deferred action. Since emergence results from two or more interrelating entities design cannot predict all such events. It necessitates enablement of deferred action. Web facilitates such emergence well. XML enables custom elements, namespaces and DTD definitions, which is context-free grammar. Custom elements and namespaces features make it deferred markup language. Markup of data is deferred to action designers in actual situations. So terms unique to an organization can be defined for processing like 'author' tagged between <author> and </author>. XML vocabularies give it wider general applicability. Action designers create vocabularies as domain-specific markup languages to define structured data for specific domains or standards. Since DTD definitions cannot be processed, XML allows schemas to be defined that can be processed and manipulated.

Creativity has emergent aspects. The Web was originally meant to be a 'creative space' and even enable 'intercreative' work where collaborative work could be represented. This has not happened. Lack of trust among people is a major issue. Sociological and human factors analysis of this problem could generate workable design principles for intercreative work.

Duplex design process

Deferred action co-design framework applied to LDS system applies to co-design of Web-based systems. In terms of knowledge of what to design the Web is co-designed based on explicit knowledge of requirements (what we know) available to reflective designers and embodied patterned knowledge, socially embedded knowledge and tacit knowledge of particular design domains (what we come to know), available to action designers only. Infinite variety of applications of the Web attest to relevance of such co-design for individual, organizational and societal needs fulfilment.

Reflective design is necessary for Web success. It creates the structure SEST property. It is done by W3C who set standards termed recommendations and upgrade Web architecture and technologies. The term for deferment in the Web is 'decentralization'. Decentralization is the Web design principle that recognizes and separates reflective designers and action designers. This distinction is crucial to sustain the Web and any attempt to make reflective designers more important makes the Web vulnerable. As Tim Berners-Lees argues:

> The Web is by design and philosophy a decentralized system,
> and its vulnerabilities lie wherever a central facility exists. The
> URI specification raises one such general vulnerability, in that
> the introduction of new URI scheme is a potential disaster,
> immediately breaking interoperability. (Personal note by Tim
> Berners-Lee, W3C).

Co-design is further evidenced in the 'separation of form and
content' design principle for Web system architecture. It is the design
principle on which SGML formalism is based, making it deferred
system to organize and tag elements of documents in fields of action.
This deliberate design decision ensures that form (TSA) does not constraint content (operational functionality) – making it duplex design
process. It is synthesis of planned action and deferred action respectively in the Web's design. (This principle of separation of form
and content is implicit in systems architecture design of LDS and
internet.)

The 'content' aspect of the design principle is deferred design or
operational functionality design, catering for the emergence, space and
time SEST properties. Action designers provide sufficiency for global
success of the Web by doing deferred design. They design content as
local policy or operational functionality in actuality. It is this kind of
design for actuality that defines deferred systems and makes it operationally relevant. Reflective designers are unaware of this operational
functionality (content) when determining specified design decisions
concerning form (structure), just as action designers are unaware
of and do not need to know the form when making deferred design
decisions.

System architecture and Ttools

Reflective designers design systems architecture and Ttools to enable
intradeferment and extradeferment. Systems architecture or TSA is composed of the network on which the Web is mounted and recommendations by W3C. Recommendations are not software products with
operational functionality themselves not systems type-3. These technologies enable interoperational deferred design of distinct domain
specific systems.

The Web enables organizational and societal systems design. For
organizational systems it provides micro- and meso-Ttools. Micro-
Ttools include HTML, XHTML; meso-Ttools include XML, RDF and

DTD. These Ttools enable deferred action to be converted into operational design to be implemented as systems type-3, such as permitting customers to place online orders, tracking orders and specifying bespoke products or services. For minimally technically skilled action designer the HTTP hyperlink tag is a significant micro-Ttool, but now it is superseded by meso-Ttools like XHTML and XML and professional action designers do much of the designing of systems type-3 for the Web. For societal systems the Web provides macro-Ttools. Since macro-tailoring is design with societal objectives the Web is by design social. It provides macro-Ttools like XML, DTD and schemas concerned with societal systems.

Diffusion management

W3C is the central body managing the Web which is a standardization organization releasing 'recommendations' standards. Three hosts primarily finance W3C: Massachusetts Institute of Technology (MIT), the European Research Consortium for Informatics and Mathematics (ERCIM) and Keio University in Japan. These host members determine Web strategy. Present priority is Web accessibility and the Web technology and society. It seeks to enable societal macro-tailoring of Web-based systems.

Management of 'the Web' is diffused. It is a deliberate design decision of the Web that local policy design decisions or applications should not be constrained by central design decisions. So 'the Web' takes shape through myriads of actual operational implementations depending on local policy determined by individuals and organizations. These cannot be managed by W3C

Internet

Internet illustrates deferred system design and potential for real system design. Its design is operationally sustainable. ARPANET its precursor laid the critical design principle of sustainability as systems strategy and systems design. It resonates well with the organization's interest in sustainability. If attacked by an enemy ARPANET's purpose was to sustain administrative capability of the US government. It consisted of decentralized digital network that connected defence, research and academic mainframe computers. ARPANET was privatized in 1990. As it was gradually released to the public domain it began to be transformed into the pervasive internet.

System description

Internet formalism reflects deferred action design parameters. It synthesizes specification and deferment formalisms that cater for planned action, emergence and deferred action. Decentralization, interoperability and tolerance design principles make the internet successful. They enable its deferred design and promote its sustainability.

Specified system and deferred system elements of TSA is simultaneously TCP/IP protocols which is also the S-SEI. It reflects structure SEST property. This simple set of mechanisms enables the internet structure to be created. Specified systems network element had no initial modelling notation as specification formalism. Deployment of TCP/IP also reflects emergence, space and time SEST properties but managed by authorized organizations. It recognizes and caters for emergence and deferred action. Deferred design is implemented with these protocol implementation elements. Action designers mount local systems through intradeferment onto the internet with implementation elements TCP/IP.

Emergent behaviour

The field of action has much interrelation design. Internet is the first technology with boundless growth potential. Only the Web matches its emergent potential. Just as the Web become global within six months the internet is growing by the intrinsic nature of networking connections. Emergence is internet connections or interrelation design in fields of action.

Internet is successful because it enables social and organized interrelations. It is not the technology itself that emerges. The basic networking protocol remains the same. Social and organized interrelations emerge. This is true of LDS and Web technologies too. Technological emergence is of course a consequence of emergent social and organized networking. It is organized interrelations or interrelations in fields of action that results in technological networking.

Of the two internal interrelations and external interrelations aspects of interrelation design the latter is deferred in the internet. It defers interrelation design of naturally and socially occurring connections, enabling emergent organized interrelation design. Internet enables this deferred element of interrelation design. It does not specify what the interrelations should be for its domain of application, the emergent behaviour of the domain is not constrained by the technology. Actual connections made are determined by appropriate deferred action.

Duplex design process

In terms of design knowledge the internet is the co-design of explicit knowledge of the need for interrelation design available to reflective designers and embodied patterned knowledge, embedded knowledge and tacit knowledge of actual interrelation design in the design domain available to intradeferment designers only. Interrelation design is intrinsic to organized action which was the reason for creating ARPANET. It succeeded because the designer of TCP protocol understood the structural SEST property of interrelations well and deferred other properties.

Co-design is the design of interrelation design. Reflective designers determine specification for organized interrelation design and design mechanisms. They design protocol systems and identifier assignments, gTLD and ccTLD name system, and root server system. This specification design is for subsequent deferred interrelation design. Action designers determine actual connections made. An organization has the choice to connect to the internet as do individuals. Contexts of such deferred connections are unique to each connecting entity and unknown to reflective designers and not part of specification design.

System architecture and Ttools

System architecture of the internet is composed of proprietary local area networks connected to the internet via ISPs. Decision to connect to the internet is not dictated by ICANN the intranet governing body. In deferred action terms it does not dictate operational functionality. This decision is deferred to organizations and individuals. ICANN enables deferred design. Reflective designers in organization by locally determined policy design LANs and decide whether these are connected to the internet. Internet consists of IP addresses, protocol identifiers, gTLD and ccTLD name system, and root server system.

Internet has meso- and macro-Ttools but it does not have micro-Ttools. TCP and IP originated in ARPANET and internet respectively. IP was designed to enable 'network of networks'. In the internet these are combined and referred to as TCP/IP communications protocols which enables interoperation of otherwise distinct systems. They are meso- and macro-Ttools. Tailoring is by intradeferment by professional action designers.

Internet value to organization is expansion of boundary of organized action. The internet's most valuable Ttool is the macro-Ttools concerned with societal structures. Global organizational structure can be design using this facility. Organizations have exploited this facility to pursue new purposes and objectives enabled by the internet.

Diffusion management

ICANN is a private-public partnership responsible for internet governance. Its governance structure is consistent with the 'the principle of maximum self-regulation in the high-tech economy' or diffusion management. ARPANET was designed for diffusion management it did not have centralized control. This design decision was to ensure its continued operation when one or more nodes failed. Communications would be enabled over alternative paths with diffused management. This design principle is continued by ICANN.

Figure 9.3 depicts ICANN multi-stakeholder organization with equal participation rights designed to enable centralized invention of mechanisms but diffused or local policy decisions. Its Board of Directors devise strategy with current focus on stability, security, competition, choice, bottom up consensus and stakeholder representation.

Figure 9.3   ICANN organization structure

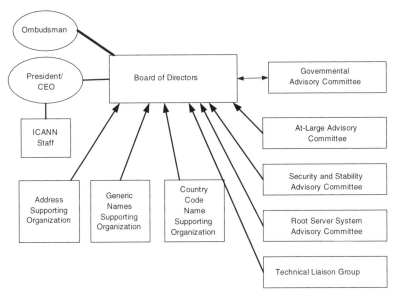

Source: http://www.icann.org/general/org-chart-12jan04.gif

ICANN is responsible for coordinating the internet's unique identifier system. It ensures stable and secure operation of unique identifier systems domain names, IP addresses, protocol and parameters, root server system and policies related to the unique identifiers. It seeks bottom up consensus of global participants. ICANN is dedicated to preserving operational stability of the internet; promoting competition; achieving broad representation of global internet communities; and developing policy appropriate to its mission through bottom-up, consensus-based processes, as reflected by upward arrows in the figure.

The potential of internet macro-tailoring is great. Therefore participants and observers favour the ICANN model of private-public partnership covering civil society, non governmental organizations, commercial and individual users, suppliers, and governments. This attests to the powerful influence of the internet on societies globally.

Rational, technological and natural organization design

Organizations that promote the Web and internet make exemplar deferred action organization design because they embody complete SEST. Strategic direction and operational processes reflect deferred action design parameters. They contain cohered deferred organization by suprapositioning and systems as sub-systems of specified organization and systems by subordinate positioning. Open source and development of Linux exemplifies SEST organization design too. It creates structure that recognizes EPS by letting coders frame and solve problems that concern them.

Organization design depends on ICT progress. Business process re-engineering, networked organization and knowledge management propositions are enhanced by technological capability to enable new organization design. Capability and capacity of organized activity can be improved by applying ICT but with the risk of succumbing to technological determinism. Tendency is for systems design to have primary importance and natural design or human and social elements of organized activity to be secondary. Actuality of human organized activity is more valuable than temporary facility of technology. Technology eventually succumbs to human intention – underdeveloped railway transport system in the USA, demise of VHS and demise of closed software packages in favour of open, interconnected and interoperable systems design.

The extent to which ICT and particularly systems design is permitted to dictate actual organizational behaviour has philosophical and material implications. Value of technology in work design, organization, systems and purpose organizations set for themselves, for technology enables new purposes and requires careful assessment. Graham (1999) asserts two criteria to assess transformative power of the internet: 'ability to serve recurrent needs better (qualitatively as well as quantitatively) and having a major impact upon the form of social and political life.' (p. 37). Generalizing to systems and by adding criterion of facilitating emergent needs consistent with natural design we can ensure that our designs are informed critically.

10
Conclusion

Organization and systems design practice is radically contrary to natural design or actuality. It is design by complete specification akin to 'social engineering'. It is design of some kind of logically prefect entity more so in systems design than organization design. Such plans eventually have to succumb to actuality. Specification design ignores emergence, space and time so it becomes incongruent with actuality or action by natural design. Organization and systems in which emergence, space and time effects are absent becomes obsolete.

Emergence is merely a label to describe being human, social and engaged in organized action. It encompasses myriad aspects of being social that cannot be elaborated and delimited in any natural language text or formal design notations. It cannot be contained by specification formalism. It is off-design. Deferred action thesis applies to this space of natural design beyond text and symbols but paradoxically can be represented in design, enabled by design and be designed as organization design with commensurate systems design.

Civilizations have created myriad designs all succumbing to the end property of the life cycle. They have become obsolete as they have come and gone. The 'design' of civilization itself has succumbed. Reason for failure of artefactual design is sought in shortcomings of specification formalism, strengthened to prevent failure. In general rational design succumbs to the end property of the ubiquitous life cycle whereas natural design persists. It persists because it is the design of structure, emergence, space and time and simultaneously discrete and continuous and therefore capable of better encompassing actuality. For rational design to persist it has to find ways of representing complete SEST in organization and systems design.

Design embodying SEST properties of natural design persists. Invention of writing is an illustration. It is a deliberate structure created to express and communicate thought but the symbols used have continuously changed primarily because of emergent writing technologies. Invention of habitation is similar. Its shape, size and volume continuously changing. These are rational designs responding well to actuality. The reason for success of these designs is deferment formalism. Since no single reflective designer or body of designers can experience actuality, that is they have no prior knowledge of all experiential requirements, deferring design to others who experience actuality is logical.

The deferred action research programme deals with several issues. The aim is to develop a theory of natural design on which to base a theory of rational design. It investigates kinds of specification formalism suitable for deferred action. It seeks to enable deferred and real systems design.

Develop better knowledge of deferred action design parameters and space of organization design itself. Even as the challenge of managing information with ICT has not been adequately met the new challenge of managing organizational knowledge has arisen. Case studies of KMS reveal culture, reflection and attitude cannot be accounted for by specification formalism. Next generation of systems designs for organizational information and knowledge should be based on better knowledge of work and organized action encompassing formal and actual entities.

Space of organization design can be extended by formally acknowledging deferred action. It requires research and development of deferment formalism distinct from specification formalism. This research programme constitutes pragmatic methods necessary to design complete SEST to cater for the space of natural design with its immense richness, variety and capability compared with rational design.

Investigate relationship between emergent organization and diffusion management. Detailed understanding and knowledge of emergent organization can provide strategists and systems designers with prerequisite understanding necessary to determine design types necessary for success and extent of diffusion management required to successfully deploy systems for human and organized purposes.

There is presently no adequate perspective on structure to reflect the space of organization design. No adequate specification and verbal formalisms to model such structure. Research can contribute to understanding the scope of rational design of structure. It can contribute to developing knowledge of managing organization conducive to deferred action and management of systems type-3. Closely related to structural research for organization and systems is the extension of the UML for deferment formalism. Since the UML enables deferred action its stereotypes facility can be deployed to invent deferment notation and its suitability assessed for developing deferred action models.

A crucial theme for organization and systems researchers and designers is the development of deferment formalism suitable for space of natural design. We do not yet have a philosophy of specification or clear understanding of its nature. It should be compared with the philosophy of deferment and its nature. SEST is one perspective by the thesis of deferred action. Formalism should be concerned with sociality. Tim Berners-Lee's comments on decentralization are pertinent. He states that decentralization is:

> a principle of the design of distributed systems, including societies. It points out that any single common point which is involved in any operation tends to limit the way the system scales, and produce a single point of complete failure.... Centralization in social systems can apply to concepts, too. For example, if we make a knowledge representation system which requires anyone who uses the concept of 'automobile' to use the term 'http://www.kr.org/stds/industry/ automobile' then we restrict the set of uses of the system to those for whom this particular formulation of what an automobile is works. The Semantic Web must avoid such conceptual bottlenecks just as the Internet avoids such network bottlenecks. (Personal note by Tim Berners-Lee, W3C)

Researchers of formalism for organization and systems design and designers of organization and systems especially must avoid such restrictive designs and 'single point of complete failure', the philosophical aim of deferred action research.

Bibliography

Ackroyd S and Fleetwood S (2000) Realism in contemporary organization and management studies. In Ackroyd S and Fleetwood S (2000) (eds) *Realist Perspective on Management and Organizations*. Routledge, London, pp. 27–44.

Aldrich H (1999) *Organizations Evolving*. Sage, London.

Alexander C (2002) *The nature of order. The phenomenon of life*. The Center for Environmental Structure, Berkeley, California.

Alger B (2002) *The experience designer: learning, networks and the cyberspace*. Wheatmark Inc., Tucson, Arizona.

Berners-Lee T (1999) *Weaving the Web*. Harper, San Franscisco.

Berners-Lee T (2005) personal notes by Tim Berners-Lee. W3C. www.w3c.org. Accessed July 2005.

Bhaskar R (1978) *A Realist Theory of Science*. Harvester Press, Brighton.

Blacker F, Reed M and Whitaker A (1993) Knowledge workers and contemporary organization. *Journal of Management Studies*, 30(6): 851–62.

Boehm B (2002) Agile and Plan-Driven Methodologies: Oil and Water. Presentation at Agile Universe 2002. 5 August 2002. http://www/agilealliance.com/ articles/articles/agileAndPlanDrivenMethods.pdf. Accessed September 2005.

Briggs R (1985) Knowledge representation in Sanskrit. *Artificial Intelligence Magazine*, 6(1).

Briggs R (1986) Shastric Sanskrit as machine translation interlingua. In *Proceedings of the First National Conference on Knowledge Representation and Inference in Sanskrit*. Bangalore, India.

Brown J S and Duiguid P (2002) *The social life of information*. HBS, Boston, MA.

Bush V (1945) *Science the Endless Frontier*. United States Government Printing Office, SI.

Carley K M (1995) Computational and mathematical organization theory: Perspectives and directions. *Computational and Mathematical Organization Theory*, 1(1): 39–56.

Chris Johnson (2005) Visualizing the Relationship between Human Error and Organizational Failure. www.dcs.gla.ac.uk/~johnson/papers/fault_trees/ organizational_error.html. Accessed May 2005.

Churchman C W (1968) *Challenge to reason*. McGraw-Hill, New York.

Churchman C W (1971) *The Design of Inquiring Systems: basic concepts of systems and organization*. Basic Books, New York.

Clarke E M and Wing J M et al. (1996) Formal methods: state of the art and future directions. *ACM Computing Surveys*, 28(4).

Cyert R M and March J G (1963) *A Behavioural Theory of the Firm*. Prentice Hall, Englewood Cliff, NJ.

de Moor A (2002) Language/Action meets organizational semiotics: situating conversations with norms. *Information Systems Frontiers*, 4(3): 257–72.

Dourish P (2001) *Where the Action Is*. MIT Press, Massachusetts.

Dron J (2005) Epimethean information systems: harnessing the power of the collective in e-learning. *International Journal of Information Technology and Management*, 4(4): 392–404.

Elliman T and Eatock J (2005) Online support for arbitration: designing software for a flexible business process. *International Journal of Information Technology and Management*, 4(4): 443–60.

Fitzgerald G and Philippides A et al. (1999) 'Information Systems Development, Maintenance and Enhancement: Findings from a UK Study.' *International Journal of Information Management*, 19: 319–28.

Garlikove R (2004) Formal systems need discretionary mechanism. www.garlikov.com/philosophy/formalsystems.htm. Accessed 13 May 2004.

Graham G (1999) *The internet://. A philosophical inquiry*. Routledge, London.

Groth L (1999) *Future Organization Design*. Chichester, Wiley.

Harris H J and Patel N V (2001) A Narrative Analysis of Information System Development in a Local Government Organization: Conversations Reflecting Deferred System's Design. *ACM Conference on Object-Oriented Programming, Systems, Languages, and Application (OOPSLA 2001)* International Workshop on Semantics of Enterprise Integration, October 14–18, Tampa Bay, Florida.

HEFCE (2004) Strategic Plan 2003–08 (Revised April 2004). http://www.hefce.ac.uk/aboutus/stratplan/

Hope J and Fraser R (2003) Who needs budgets? *Harvard Business Review*. February 2003. http://www.imsglobal.org/learningdesign/ldv1p0/imsld_bestv 1p0.html/ Accessed 5 May 05. http://www.hero.ac.uk/rae/

IMS (2003) IMS Learning Design Best Practice and Implementation Guide. Version 1.0 Final Specification.

IMS (2003) IMS Learning Design Information Model Revision: 20 January 2003 Accessed June 05.

IMS (2005) http://www.imsglobal.org/af/afv1p0/imsafglossaryv1p0.html#1524452 Accessed June 05.

Keller K (1996) Socio-technical systems and self-organization. *SIGIOS Bulletin*, 17(1) April 1996.

Loverdos C, Saidis K, Sotiropoulou A, and Theotokis D (2002) Pluggable Services for Tailorable E-content Delivery. In Bellahsène Z, Patel D and Rolland C *Proceedings of the 8th International Conference on Object-Oriented Information Systems OOIS-2002*, Montpellier, France, pp. 6–18.

Macmillan, H (1997) Information Systems: four good questions for the board. In Macmillan H and Christophers M (eds) *Strategic Issues in the Life Assurance Industry*. Butterworth Heinemann. ISBN: 0750632801.

Markus L M, Majchrzak A and Gasser L (2002) A Design Theory for Systems that Support Emergent Knowledge Processes. *MIS Quarterly*, 26: 179–212.

Mintzberg H (2004) *Managers Not MBA*. Pearson Education Limited, London.

Mintzberg H, Ahlstead B and Lampel J (1998) *Strategic Safari*. Prentice Hall, London.

Moss S (2005) Declarative Modelling of Structural Change. Centre for Policy Modelling, Manchester Metropolitan University. http://cfpm.org/pub/ workshop/ moss.html. Accessed 27 January 2005.

Nardi B A (1996) Studying context: a comparison of activity theory, situated action models, and distributed cognition. In Nardi B A (ed.) *Context and Consciousness*. MIT Cambridge.

Newell A and Simon H (1972) *Human problem solving*. Prentice Hall, Englewood Cliffs, NJ.

Parnas D and Clements P (1986) A Rational Design Process: How and Why to Fake It. *IEEE Transactions on Software Engineering*. 12(2) February 1986.

Patel N V (1999) The Spiral of Change Model for Coping with Changing and Ongoing Requirements. *Requirements Engineering*, 4: 77–84.

Patel N V (2003) Deferred systems design: Countering the Primacy of Reflective IS Development with Action-Based Information Systems. In Patel N V (ed.) *Evolutionary Adaptive Information Systems*. Hershey, PA USA, Idea Group.

Patel N V (2004) Deferred Systems: Deferring the Design Process and Systems. *Journal of Applied Systems Studies*, 5(1).

Patel N V (2005a) *Critical Systems Analysis and Design: A Personal Framework Approach*. Routledge, London.

Patel N V (2005b) Sustainable systems: strengthening knowledge management systems with deferred action. *International Journal of Information Technology and Management*, 4(4): 344–65.

Peirce C S (1931–35) *Collected Papers of Charles Sanders Peirce*, Hartshorne C and Weiss P (eds) vols. 1–6. Harvard UP, Cambridge.

Peirce C S (1958) *Collected Papers of Charles Sanders Peirce*, Burks A (ed.), vols. 7–8. Harvard UP, Cambridge:.

Perrow C (2004) *A Personal Note on Normal Accidents*. Organization and Environment. Thousand Oaks. March 2004. 17(1).

Pinter C C (1971) *Set Theory*. Addison-Wesley. Reading, MA.

Probert S (1997) The Actuality of Information Systems. In Mingers J and Stowell F (eds) *Information Systems: An Emerging Discipline?* Maidenhead, McGrawHill: 21–62.

Purao S, Truex D and Cao L (2003) Now the twain shall meet: Combining social sciences and software engineering to support development of emergent systems. In *Proceedings of the Ninth Americas Conference on Information Systems*.

Rumbaugh J, Jacobson I and Booch G (1999) *The Unified Modelling Language Reference Manual*. Addison Wesley, Boston.

Sayer A (1992) *Method in Social Science: A Realist Approach*. Routledge, London

Sayer A (2000) *Realism and Social Science*. Sage, London.

Shannon C and Weaver W (1949) *The mathematical theory of communication*. University of Illinois Press, Urbana.

Simon H A (1957) *Administrative behaviour: a study of decision-making processes in administrative organisation*. Macmillan, New York.

Simon H A (1977) *Models of Discovery*. D Reidel Publishing Co., Boston.

Simon H A (1996) *The Sciences of the Artificial* (3rd edn) The MIT Press, Cambridge, Massachusetts.

Stamoulis D, Kanellis P and Martakos D (2001) Tailorable Information Systems: Resolving the Deadlock of Changing User Requirements. *Journal of Applied Systems Studies*, 2(2): 294–311.

Stamoulis D, Theotokis D, Markus D and Gyftodimos G (2003) Ateleogical development of design-decision-independent information systems. In Patel N V (ed.) *Evolutionary Adaptive Information Systems*, Idea Group, Hershey, PA USA.

Stemmer W and Holland B (2003) Survival of the Fittest Molecules. *American Scientist*, 91(6).

Suchman L (1987) *Plans and Situated Action: The Problem of Human-Machine Communication*. Cambridge University Press, Cambridge.

Sullivan C H (1985). Systems Planning in the Information Age. *Sloan Management Review* Winter: 3–11.

Sweeney G (1996) Learning efficiency, technological change and economic progress. *International Journal of Technology Management*, 11(1/2): 1–27.

Truex D P and Baskerville R (1998) Deep structure or emergence theory: contrasting theoretical foundations for information systems development. *Information Systems Journal*, 8: 99–118.

Truex D P, Baskerville R and Klein H K (1999) Growing systems in an emergent organization. *Communications of the ACM*, 42(8): 117–23.

Truex D P, Baskerville R and Travis J (2000) A methodological systems development: the deferred meaning of systems development methods. *Accounting Management and Information Systems*, (10): 53–79.

Tsoukas H (2000) What is management? An outline of a metatheory. In Ackroyd S and Fleetwood S (2000) (eds) *Realist Perspective on Management and Organizations*. Routledge, London, pp. 27–44.

Vickers G (1972) *Freedom in a rocking boat: changing values in an unstable society*. Penguin, Harmondsworth.

Wand Y and Weber R (1995) On deep structure of information systems. *Information Systems Journal*. 5(3): 203–23

Weick K E (1995) *Sensemaking in Organizations*. Sage, London.

Whitehead A N (1967) *Science and the modern world*. Free Press, New York.

Wieringa R (1998) A survey of structured and object-oriented software specification methods and techniques. *ACM Computing Surveys*, 30(4): 459–527.

Wittgenstein L (1953) *Philosophical investigations*. Blackwell, Oxford.

Glossary

Terms

Action designer
Action designer is someone engaged in organized action, needs scope to design within bounds of specified design of formal organization or system design. Has knowledge of actual action, determines design in actual space and time. They *come* to know and have procedural knowledge, which is stronger than declarative knowledge.

Actuality
In realism terms the domain of empirical. Present time.

Assignment
Predetermined design imposed on actuality.

Autonomous design
Design capability afforded to intelligent machines by reflective designers that becomes autonomous of humans.

Autonomous design decisions
Design decision made by intelligent agents or systems.

Autonomous designer
Intelligent agents or systems.

Autonomous organization
The notion that some structure can be set up to facilitate self-organizing agents.

Autonomous system
Systems behaving independently of its human reflective designers.

Co-design
Co-design is design of TSA by reflective designers and continuous operational functionality design by action designers.

Deferment formalism
Deferment formalism is concerned with space and time and how they affect action and how designed artefact interrelates with it. It seeks complete SEST representation.

Deferred action
Deferred action is concerned with enabling actual action as interrelation design within formal design. It is the synthesis of planned action and actual (deferred) action.

Deferred design
Deferred design is design by action designers within formal design to cope with unknowable emergence, space and time, 'equivocal reality'.

Deferred design decisions
Design decisions enabled by reflective designers but made by action designers in context.

Deferred organization
Structure designed by reflective designers whose actual operations take shape in context through behaviours determined by action designers.

Deferred system
Systems architecture designed by reflective designers whose actual operational functionality takes shape in context through behaviours determined by action designers.

Design domain
The planned action notion of an actual organizational problem demarcated for systems design by specification.

Design space
Artefacts are generated in design space by applying enabling techniques and tools. In deferred action it is composed of state space, space of organization design and space of natural design, former two can only be designed rationally.

Diffusion management
The joint responsibility of reflective and action designers to manage organization and systems structure and operations.

Duplex design process
The separation of design process into specification design and deferment design. Each occurring at separate times and different locale and undertaken by reflective designers and action designers respectively.

Embodied patterning
Empirical action of action designers that results in patterns for formal design. It focuses on actuality and context and its relation to design.

Emergence
A term to describe unknowable and unpredictable social action in all its multifarious aspects. Philosophically, it is instrumental in determining being.

Emergent organization
Social action that is organized but subject to emergence.

Enacting
Enacting is the act of putting design in social action with interrelations design capable of real-time structural and operational functionality design. Enacting enables action designers to make design decisions in response to Complete SEST.

E-problem solving
Solving operational problems in context as they arise.

Field of action
The being and becoming of design happens in and is determined by the field of action. The interrelated things and physical space, objects and concepts in which a system or any design is active.

Formal methods
System of symbols representative of reality and rules for abstraction of things form reality and their composition to form models.

Formalism
Prescribed methods containing precise symbols and rules for creating structural forms to achieve set objectives.

Individual deferment points
Junctures in purposeful action within existing formal structures where next steps are indeterminate.

Interrelation design
Interrelation design is individual or organized deferred action directed at shaping formal design placed in actuality.

Natural design
The conscious and unconscious determination of objectives and action leading to its achievement by conscious or unconscious determination of structure and responses to emergence in actual space and time.

Notation language
A notation language is a defined finite set of symbols and their logical interrelationships to represent real social and technical human problems and by manipulation of the representative symbols to propose a solution design that guides action.

Off-design
In terms of SEST structure is designable by specification. Off-design is the emergent, spatial, temporal aspects of organized action that cannot be specified for design. Off-design is the universal set of natural design. Some structural properties of action cannot be specified either.

Organization
Determination of goal-directed actions leading to structural forms whose actual form is the result of responses to degrees of emergence.

Organizational deferment points
Junctures in purposeful organized action within existing formal structures where next steps are indeterminate.

Placing
Placing is the act of putting design in social action with interrelations design capable of deferred operational functionality design. Placing enables action designers to make design decisions in response to emergence, space and time SEST properties.

Planned action
Planned action is prescribed action enacted by design regardless of actuality.

Problem space
Metamorphic space where human concern is progressively systematized and formalized to derive a solution. In deferred action it is divided into SPS and EPS.

Rational design
Rational design is conscious event at some point in organized social action to determine the future. It is abstract design because the design objects are some orders removed from actuality.

Real design
Design of structures and operations by rational design for enactment in emergent actuality and responsive to it in real-time.

Real design decisions
Real-time design decisions by action designers in response to emergent events in actuality.

Real organization
Organizational structure and operations designed and enacted in emergent actuality and in real-time.

Real systems
Systems architecture and operations designed and enacted in emergent actuality and in real-time.

Reflective designer
Designers of structural forms containing deferment mechanisms for deferred operational design. Teams of professional organization and systems designers.

SEST
The attributes of rational design conducive to actuality.

Situated action
Action that is rich in phenomenological attribution.

Specification formalism
Prescribed methods for creating structural forms and operational detail to achieve set objectives.

Specified design
Design by reflective designers from specification obtained from users.

Specified design decisions
Design decisions by reflective designers separated spatially and temporally from actuality.

Specified organization
Organizational structure and operations designed by reflective designers for business workers.

Specified system
Systems architecture and operations designed by reflective designers for business workers.

S-problem solving
Solving structural problems separately from detailed operational design.

Systemic deferment points
Junctures within existing formal systems where operational design (and for real systems structural design) are deferred to action designers.

Systemic deferred objects
Representation of real things in systems by deferred design.

Systems deferment point analysis
Technique to determine structural and operational design deferrable to action designers.

Systems type-1
An organizing tool to help solve human problems mostly concerned with organized action.

Systems type-2
Artefact design based on systems theoretic.

Systems type-3
Artefact designed for further interrelation design with humans in organized action.

Technological deferment points
Junctures within technology where operational design (and for real technology structural design) are deferred to action designers.

Verbal formalism
Prescribed methods for creating structure and operations design to achieve set objectives.

Index

245